Prentice-Hall, Inc.
Englewood Cliffs, New Jersey

Thomas M. Vodola

TOWNSHIP OF OCEAN SCHOOL DISTRICT
OAKHURST, NEW JERSEY

INDIVIDUALIZED
PHYSICAL
EDUCATION
PROGRAM
for the
HANDICAPPED
CHILD

Library of Congress Cataloging in Publication Data

VODOLA, THOMAS M
    Individualized physical education program for the
handicapped child.

    Includes bibliographies.
    1. Physical education for handicapped children.
I. Title.
GV445.V6   613.7'042   70-38292
ISBN 0-13-457028-6

**This book is dedicated to my wife Theresa
and to my children Tommy, Anthony, Ria, and Theresa**

10 9 8 7 6 5 4 3 2 1

PRENTICE-HALL INTERNATIONAL, INC., *London*
PRENTICE-HALL OF AUSTRALIA, PTY. LTD., *Sydney*
PRENTICE-HALL OF CANADA LTD., *Toronto*
PRENTICE-HALL OF INDIA PRIVATE LIMITED, *New Delhi*
PRENTICE-HALL OF JAPAN, INC., *Tokyo*

Printed in the United States of America

contents

iii

C   **constructable items**   **291**

D   **analysis of prekindergarten test results**   **294**

E   **U.S. department of education, office of special education program, development and evaluation services,**

      title VI: education of the handicapped, P.L. 91–230   **297**

      index   **301**

FIGURES

TABLES

preface

A review of the literature related to physical education programs for the handicapped reveals that considerable material is devoted to philosophy, theory, and recommendations for providing instructional services for students with specific disabilities, but there is little information regarding precise, definitive procedures for planning and implementing a comprehensive program.

Mindful of the fact that there are many ways of resolving educational problems and that there exist many critics of those who would propose solutions to multifaceted problems, I have attempted to prepare a text that will provide a practical, step-by-step approach to the formulation of a physical activity program for the handicapped.

I make no excuse for the bias that permeates the text; included is a program that has been field-tested and proven successful in the Township of Ocean School District, Oakhurst, New Jersey. One cannot prepare a compendium of specific proposals without injecting personal convictions. However, a sincere effort has been made to base recommendations on the latest research findings. In specific situations wherein alternate proposals have merit, an attempt has been made to include the alternatives.

In the past decade there has been a trend toward the provision of adapted physical education for the handicapped. However, stumbling blocks exist which have tended to slow down this general movement. According to teachers and administrators, the major deterrents to the provision of services for the atypical child are the lack of a knowledgeable staff and the lack of specific program guidelines. Thus, the text is an attempt to achieve the following goals: (1) to provide a basic understanding of the knowledge necessary to teach a comprehensive program; (2) to provide a specific plan for designing and implementing an individualized physical education program for handicapped children; (3) to provide guidelines for, and sources of, funds for programming; and (4) to stimulate those interested in "our forgotten youth" to use this material as a means of developing more comprehensive and meaningful programs.

The text approach is methodological rather than theoretical because I feel there is a professional need for concrete illustrations on how to start and sustain a program. The material is presented in three parts. Part I provides an overview of the organizational and administrative aspects of the program. Chapter 1 presents topics relating to current status, existing problems, comments from noted authorities and agencies, and research findings. The balance of Part I deals with problems most frequently encountered by those who wish to start a program.

Part II deals with program implementation. Materials related to testing, assessment, prescription, and evaluation are included. Also presented are illustrative approaches to individualizing instruction on the basis of low motor ability, perceptual-motor disorders, nutritional abnormalities, postural deficiencies, and other medically oriented problems.

Part III presents materials regarding the availability of local, state, and federal funds, guidelines for submitting a grant request, and excerpts from an approved federal grant. Finally, the practitioner is provided with five appendices replete with forms and other materials that have immediate applicability.

To summarize, an attempt has been made to provide a pragmatic approach to the planning and implementation of a physical education program for the handicapped. How well the book achieves its primary goal can, realistically, be evaluated in terms of the number of readers who formulate new programs. To those so dedicated, I pledge my full cooperation and assistance.

Acknowledgments

This text is a personal tribute to the Township of Ocean School District. Without the cooperation and support of the administration, teachers, students, parents, and board of education, the K–12 Developmental and Adapted Physical Education Program could not have been established (and thus this text would not have been written). Special thanks go to the school physicians, Donald Bowne, M.D., Helen Jones, M.D., and John Malta, D.O. for their unstinting support and leadership. To Helen Liebhardt, R.N., and the other township school nurses, goes my gratitude for the countless hours they devoted to scheduling students.

I wish to express special appreciation to my personal and professional colleagues who gave of their time to critique sections of the manuscript:

Edwina M. Crystal, psychologist, Township of Ocean School District; Jan Dell'Omo, mathematics teacher, Ocean Township High School; Evelyn Ross, chairman, mathematics department, Ocean Township High School; Rebecca C. Moore, Assistant to the Superintendent, Township of Ocean School District; Alfred N. Daniel, Coordinator of Physical Therapy and Developmental Physical Education, Cherry Hill School District; John H. Doolittle, Assistant Professor, College of Health, Physical Education and Recreation, The Pennsylvania State University; and Paul Porado, Director, Bureau of Program Development and Evaluation: Special Education, New Jersey State Department of Education. Their many constructive remarks aided in the development of the final book. The viewpoints expressed are, however, solely those of the writer.

Illustrations were suggested by Athan Anest, a close friend and a talented artist. Editing was undertaken by Miss Dorothy L. Green. And finally, to Ethel Stroin, my personal secretary, goes sincere appreciation for her ability to transform my hieroglyphics into a legible manuscript.

THOMAS M. VODOLA, ED.D.

Oakhurst, New Jersey

I

ORGANIZATION AND ADMINISTRATION

1

introduction

It has been estimated that a minimum of 10 percent of all children in the public schools require permanent special educational services and that 25 percent or more require special services at some time during their developmental years.[1] Faced with a problem of such magnitude, all agencies serving our youth must strive to meet their obligations by providing services commensurate with the needs of the handicapped. Since physical education can make a valuable contribution to the atypical child's physical, mental, and socio-emotional well-being, we must ask, How well is the discipline meeting its obligations?

Current Status of Programs for the Handicapped

Comprehensive physical education programs geared to meet the needs of the handicapped in the United States are presently inadequate. In his article "Physical 'Education': Are Our Children Being Cheated?"[2] Pollack refers to this general inadequacy and further maintains that physically and mentally handicapped children are overprotected and are often excluded from participating in physical education. To remedy the situation Pollack recommends the hiring of more full-time physical educators to teach the handicapped,

---

[1] James W. Moss, "Background Paper on Special Programs for Handicapped Children and Youth for the White House Conference on Children and Youth" (Washington, D.C.: U.S. Department of Health, Education and Welfare, December, 1970), p. 9. Mimeographed.

[2] Jack Harrison Pollack, "Physical 'Education': Are Our Children Being Cheated?" *Family Health*, II (September, 1970), 15–18.

3

for although many school districts do conduct some facets of a program for the handicapped, few provide a total program to meet the needs of all handicapped children.

For example, a survey of the status of programs for the handicapped conducted by the New Jersey Youth Division[3] revealed that less than 2 percent of the responding public and private school districts provided physical activity programs to meet the specific needs of their handicapped. A generally accepted national average indicates that one out of every seven of the population in this country has some sort of physical handicap. Thus, if we assume that this national average is applicable to the school districts of New Jersey, it becomes readily apparent that a severe discrepancy between need and actual programs exists and, one might add, the state of New Jersey is typical. According to Moss,[4] only 40 percent of the children who require special educational services are receiving them at the present time. Yet to the best of the author's knowledge, only the states of California[5] and Pennsylvania[6] have laws which mandate physical education for all children.

What causes the disparity between the number of handicapped pupils and the educational services provided for them? Why are current practices in physical education not consistent with the prevailing educational philosophy of "gearing the curriculum" to meet the needs of each child? It is particularly disconcerting to note that other disciplines such as mathematics, English, and science are actively pursuing such innovative approaches as individually prescribed instruction, "tracking" of students according to ability level, and honors and enrichment programs. School administrators have stated that adapted physical education classes are limited because of a myriad of factors such as inaccessability of facilities, lack of knowledgeable personnel, the "curriculum squeeze," liability problems, ad infinitum. Is this really true?

Analysis of Existing Problem

Such oft-repeated goals as meeting individual needs, the development of sound interpersonal relationships, and the attainment of self-realization can be found in most educational texts and would be accepted by most school personnel. However, further investigation reveals inconsistencies between philosophies espoused and programs implemented.

[3] Thomas M. Vodola and Alfred Daniel, "The Status of Developmental and Adapted Physical Education in New Jersey Public and Private School Systems," ed. Robert McCollum (Trenton, N.J.: New Jersey Youth Commission Sub-committee on Youth Fitness, 1967), 7 pp. Mimeographed. (Free upon request.)

[4] Moss, *op. cit.*, p. 31.

[5] Genevie Dexter, ed., *Instruction of Physically Handicapped Minors in Remedial Physical Education* (Sacramento, Calif.: California State Department of Education, 1969).

[6] Michael E. Flanagan, *Guidelines for Adapted Physical Education* (Harrisburg, Pa.: Department of Instruction, 1966), 67 pp.

Is the discipline of physical education providing specific physical activities to meet the needs of all pupils? Except for a few isolated cases, athletics is geared solely to the physically gifted child. For example, although intramurals is theoretically available to all students, the handicapped seldom participate because of limited physical ability or fear of being ostracized. Thus, even though some educators may contend that the onus for improving the lot of the atypical child must fall on the shoulders of the physical educator, the author maintains the root cause of the problem is unrealistic teacher preparation in our colleges and universities. All too frequently the college curriculum is focused on the development of team and individual skill competencies rather than on the basis of the developmental needs of typical and atypical children. To the uninitiated, it may seem that the writer is "playing with semantics," but experience has revealed that the former method produces technicians who are competent in teaching skills whereas the latter method results in educators who are equipped to cope with the needs of human beings. (The Epilogue at the end of the book provides the reader with guidelines for resolving the problem.)

In theory, a typical physical education class (in schools without a program for the handicapped) consists of students grouped by grade level; occasionally there would be further grouping based on ability. Unfortunately, prevailing practices present a much more dismal picture. Too often we find mixed grade levels due to inflexibility in scheduling; 50 to 100 students in one class due to insufficient teaching stations; and five or ten students who have been medically excused standing idly on the sidelines. Furthermore, three or four students already dressed for class are inactive because the nature of their disabilities precludes vigorous activity.

Even if we assume that the handicapped students were granted permission to take part in the regular class, individualized instruction would be virtually impossible. Therefore, medical practitioners are justified for approving medical excuses when the foregoing conditions prevail.

Although mixed and overloaded classes are serious problems confronting physical educators, let us return to the main issue—the need for special physical education classes for the handicapped. Is there indeed a specific need? Are there enough handicapped students within a school to warrant the establishment of special classes? One approach to determining the enormity of the problem would be to check with the school nurse, who is required to maintain a daily log of all students who submit medical excuses for missing classes. A periodic check by the author revealed that from 25 to 134 students submitted medical excuses for a given day in a total school population of 1,500.

One must remember that the bulk of daily medical excuses are for transitory problems such as colds and menstrual pain. Add to that list students with handicaps of a more permanent nature such as scoliosis, low physical vitality, nutritional abnormalities, perceptual-motor aberrations, orthopedic problems, asthma and other medically oriented illnesses, and you will begin to get some conception of the total numbers involved.

If you still have some doubts, conduct the following survey in your school: (1) request that your school nurse review all medical folders and list the total number of students who have a medical history of such a nature that they would benefit from an individualized program; (2) solicit from the special services team the names of those students who have learning disabilities or emotional problems; and (3) add to that total the number of students the physical education department has found to be physically subpar. Experience has proven the "one out of seven theory" to be a minimal ratio; a more realistic ratio is that one out of every five students is handicapped, if developmentally handicapped students are included. Thus, a school with an enrollment of 1,000 will have 150 to 200 students who are in need of a physical education program which is adapted to their limitations.[7]

Probably the most common rationale given for exempting the handicapped from physical education is that such an approach is in their best interest. Unfortunately this retort is an indictment of the physical education profession, and it indicates that we have not done an adequate job of "selling" the values of physical activity. A medical excuse may placate a parent, may be most expeditious for an administrator, but by no stretch of the imagination is it in the best interest of a student. An analogous situation would be to state that it is in the best interest of a person to avoid facing the problems of daily living because they upset him emotionally. To the contrary, the prescription should be to help a person objectively analyze his problem(s) so that he can effectively cope with similar situations in the future. Similarly, the handicapped child can best be prepared for life if he is provided with an individualized physical activity program commensurate with his needs.

The theoretical basis for the program should be two-fold: to aid the child in maximizing his functions within his limitations and to provide him with a broad experiential background so that he can attain success in activities that are not precluded by his limitations. Thus, he must be provided with those individualized learning experiences that will help him to function optimally within his limitations and develop his capabilities. He must be taught that he can function successfully in life. Only through such an approach can he become self-actuating—or develop a positive self-image. It is not what we are that counts, but rather what we think we are.[8]

[7] Traditionally, the handicapped child has been viewed solely as one who evidences a physical disability. The author views the handicapped child as one who evidences a physical, mental, or socioemotional problem to the extent that he cannot benefit educationally by being placed in an unrestricted physical activity class. In this broader context, many school districts will find that as much as 25 percent of the student population has handicapping conditions.

[8] Earl C. Kelley, "The Fully Functioning Self," in Arthur W. Combs, ed., *Perceiving,*

Individualized learning experiences will help the handicapped child develop his skill potential to the maximum so that he can function more efficiently and effectively. A direct result of increased skill development will be an increased potential for economic efficiency and qualitative use of leisure time—two important goals of education.

Recommendations of Noted Authorities and Agencies

What do noted authorities have to say about the values of adapted physical education? Ten years ago President John F. Kennedy urged all schools to adopt the specific recommendations of his Yough Fitness Council. The first recommendation of that Council was, "Identify the physically under-developed pupil and work to improve his physical capacity."[9]

The American Medical Association stated:

Excuses from physical education which deprive a young person of desirable developmental experiences in this area should not be granted unless there is a clear and overriding health reason wherein the student cannot participate except in a prescribed program of restricted physical activity. Currently, there is general agreement among both physicians and educators that when good programs exist, "blanket" or overall excuses from physical education are unnecessary.[10]

Mathews, Kruse and Shaw maintain that handicapped children

who for some reason cannot take full advantage of the general physical education curriculum, or who need special attention in addition to the regular program . . . need the values inherent in physical education much more than do children without a physical handicap . . . . Indeed the number of youngsters who would greatly benefit from an individualized as well as [an] adapted physical education program is staggering.[11]

The American Academy of Pediatrics received the following report from their Committee on School Health:

Sometimes the physician is under pressure from parents and children to ask the school to excuse a child from the compulsory physical education program. Such

---

Behaving, Becoming (Washington, D.C.: Association for Supervision and Curriculum Development, 1962), p. 10.

9 President's Council on Youth Fitness, *Youth Physical Fitness: Suggested Elements of School-Centered Program, Part One, Concepts and Foundations* (Washington, D.C.: U.S. Government Printing Office, 1961), inside cover page.

10 Committee on Exercise and Physical Fitness, American Medical Association, "Classification of Students for Physical Education," *Journal of American Public Health Association*, CXCIX (January 23, 1967), 265–67.

11 Donald K. Mathews, R. Kruse, and S. Shaw, *The Science of Physical Education for Handicapped Children* (New York: Harper & Row, Publishers, 1962), pp. 1–2.

excuses should be given only when medically indicated and then only for the necessary period of time. Almost every child can participate in some form of physical activity even though this must be modified from the usual program. Thus, whenever possible, the physician should recommend a modified program rather than an excuse from all physical activity.[12]

In the Preface of "Physical Education for the Exceptional Child," Eunice Kennedy Shriver stated:

It is sad that the children who benefit most from sports and games are the children who have the least opportunity to play—the mentally retarded and the physically handicapped.... Teaching handicapped children to play is one of the greatest experiences available to teachers and parents; more gratifying than others because it so often ends in success—the unfolding of a mind and the enlargement of a personality.[13]

A resolution adopted by the Joint Committee on Health Problems in Education of the National Education Association and the American Medical Association on April 23, 1968 reads as follows:

WHEREAS, it is recognized that participation in appropriate physical activities contributes to physical, mental, emotional and social development, and is a vital factor in the promotion of the health of all children including the handicapped child; and

WHEREAS, effective individualized physical education programs are being implemented by some school systems; therefore be it

RESOLVED, that physical education personnel emphasize instruction in a variety of skills for all boys and girls through development of sound programs of adapted physical education as part of a total curriculum and be it further

RESOLVED, that school personnel seek the assistance of the local medical profession in the development of plans for appraisal and classification of students for physical education.[14]

The supportive list could be expanded to include other authoritative sources. However, one has but to refer to any educational or medical text wherein specific reference is made to the handicapped and their need for physical activity for additional justification.

---

[12] Committee on School Health, *Report of the Committee on School Health* (Evanston, Ill.: The American Academy of Pediatrics, 1966), pp. 70–71.

[13] Thomas M. Vodola et al., "Physical Education for the Exceptional Child" (Trenton, N.J.: New Jersey Youth Division Youth Fitness Committee, 1968), p. 1. Mimeographed.

[14] Joint Committee on Health Problems in Education, "Resolutions," *Journal of Health, Physical Education and Recreation*, XXXIX, No. 9 (November-December, 1968), 18.

Review of Related Literature

A study by Francis and Rarick[15] revealed that mentally retarded boys and girls were from two to four years behind normal children of the same chronological age on physical performance tests. Malpass[16] and J. Stein[17] reported that the mentally retarded population as a whole are less proficient in terms of motor skill performance and physical fitness than their normal counterparts. The emotionally handicapped child tends to follow a similar pattern in that he lags behind his peer group on tests of strength, power, agility, coordination, balance, and speed.

T. Stein[18] conducted a two-year study to assess the affective outcomes of camping experiences on physically handicapped adults. A comparison of group scores indicated that there were no significant differences between pre- and post-camping scores in terms of self-acceptance, patterns of interest, and sociability. It has been postulated, however, that a limited two-week camping period, for each of two years, was not sufficient to modify the affective components under study or to overcome the influence of home and environment.

Although there has been a very noticable increase in research involving handicapped students and programs since the 1950s, there is still much to be done. Most of the studies have been devoted to aspects of mental retardation, and virtually no research has been done on the visually impaired, hearing impaired, or physically handicapped; further, those studies relating to the physically impaired have most frequently been conducted in hospitals where because of a lack of experimental controls the results must be viewed as untenable. There is a definite need for (1) developing more valid and reliable testing instruments; (2) determining the effect of participation in individualized, developmental physical activities upon vocational readiness, competency, and productivity of the handicapped; (3) designing longitudinal and interdisciplinary studies; and (4) developing preschool diagnostic instruments which will identify those students who achieve at a very low level.[19]

15 R. J. Francis and G. L. Rarick, "Motor Characteristics of the Mentally Retarded," *American Journal of Mental Deficiency*, LXIII (1959), 16–17.
16 L. F. Malpass, "Motor Proficiency in Institutionalized and Non-Institutionalized Retarded Children and Normal Children," *American Journal of Mental Deficiency*, LXIV, No. 6 (May, 1960), 1012–15.
17 Julian U. Stein, "Motor Functions and Physical Fitness of the Mentally Retarded," *Rehabilitation Literature*, XXIV (July, 1963), 230–42.
18 T. A. Stein, "Some Affective Outcomes Accompanying a Camping Experience of Physically Handicapped Adults," *Rehabilitation Literature*, XXIV (July, 1963), 194–200.
19 AAHPER and NRPA, *Physical Education and Recreation for Handicapped Children* (Washington, D. C.: Bureau of Education for the Handicapped/Department of Health, Education and Welfare, February, 1969), pp. 62–75.

Summary

1. A need exists to provide comprehensive physical education programs commensurate with the limitations and capabilities of all handicapped children in the public schools of the United States.

2. Children who evidence physical, mental, or socioemotional problems that cannot be resolved in an unrestricted physical activity program should be scheduled in a developmental or adapted physical education program for individualized instruction.

3. Physical education personnel and supervisors must conduct public relations campaigns that expound the virtues of programs for the handicapped. Primary efforts should be directed toward physicians, administrators, board members, and the community at large.

4. Physical well-being and intellectual achievement are not dichotomous goals and consequently must be pursued interdependently.

5. Noted educators, medical authorities, and public and private agencies are in accord; they maintain that the need for adapted physical education is unquestionable. Therefore, individualized programs must be provided for the physically and mentally handicapped.

6. Research studies reveal that mentally retarded and emotionally disturbed children generally are less proficient in terms of motor skill performance and physical fitness than normal children of similar chronological ages.

7. Virtually no research has been conducted on the physically handicapped. Of those few studies that have been conducted, most have revealed spurious results because of a lack of experimental controls.

8. Research studies must be greatly increased quantitatively and qualitatively before many unanswered questions related to the handicapped can be resolved.

Annotated Bibliography

"Children Who Are Handicapped," *Report to the President: White House Conference on Children.* Washington, D.C.: U.S. Government Printing Office, 1970, pp. 195–205. An overview of current trends, problems, and major recommendations emanating from Forum 12 Delegates to the White House Conference.

Health of Children: Selected Data from the National Center for Health Statistics. Washington, D.C.: U.S. Government Printing Office, 1970, 47 pp. Easy to read, highly selective data related to the health of children. One section provides growth and development patterns of American children, ages 6–11 years.

Profiles of Children: 1970 White House Conference on Children. Washington, D.C.: U.S. Government Printing Office, 1970, 187 pp. Cross-referenced charts and graphs provide information for each of four stages of child development: the prenatal period, the first year of life, the preschool years between ages one and six, and the school years.

2

basic considerations in
program planning

The procedure we will use to enumerate and elaborate those factors that should be considered prior to preparation of the operational phase of a program for the handicapped is based on questions most frequently asked by educators who are interested in initiating a program.[1]

Identifying and Classifying the Handicapped

The question of identification and classification poses a great problem for the physical educator who wishes to introduce a program for the handicapped. A brief review of the literature related to students with learning disabilities will illustrate the semantics problem. Within the covers of one journal, one may be confronted with such terms as "the slow learner," "the perceptually impaired," "minimal brain damage," "brain dysfunction," "neurologically impaired," and "emotionally disturbed." Since classification presupposes some precise means of identification to aid in solving educational problems, how can the slow learner be distinguished from the perceptually impaired? Similarly, how do the symptoms of minimal brain damage differ from those of brain dysfunction?

Teacher training institutions are now feeling the impact of the problem. For years departments of special services have been attempting to provide qualified, competent teachers, but the result has been a fragmented approach.

---

[1] Thomas M. Vodola, "Physical Education for the Handicapped," in Emil Praksta, ed., *Tides* (Glassboro, N.J.: Educational Improvement Center, Spring, 1970), pp. 14–16.

According to Longnecker,[2] teacher preparation is far less effective than research and legislation. Attempting to prepare teachers on the basis of educational jargon is a poor pedagogical approach which is ineffective as well as inefficient.

Longnecker recommends the "developmental approach"[3]—testing students on the basis of specific criteria, regardless of terminology used for classification purposes. Of primary concern is the behavior manifested in the classroom. Thus, the method of classification recommended utilizes the developmental concept.

One additional advantage of classifying students on a developmental basis is the mimimization of stigmatizing the child. Classifying or grouping students as neurologically impaired or emotionally disturbed may have a negative psychological effect on the child and hold him up to ridicule by other students. However, when a child is classified developmentally, the implication is that he is not performing up to his capacity on certain aspects of the instructional program.

Once one accepts the developmental approach theory, the question of identification resolves itself. The identification process involves the following steps: (1) determining the specific objectives or goals of the discipline involved; (2) designing valid and reliable instruments to measure the stated goals; (3) using the constructed instruments to pretest all subjects; (4) establishing norms and cut-off scores; and (5) identifying those students who score below the established cut-off scores.

Developmental and adapted physical education (hereafter referred to as D&A) affords the physical educator an opportunity to use the developmental approach. Clarke and Clarke[4] use this approach to identify those students who are sub-par physically. The adapted phase of the program includes those students who have medical problems necessitating a referral by a physician. Extensive testing and prescriptions based on individualized needs make this program worthy of consideration.

The approach utilized by the author is basically an outgrowth of the Clarke and Clarke D&A program, although it is strongly influenced by the Buttonwood Farms Project[5] and the efforts of Kephart.[6] Present curriculum

---

[2] Donald Longnecker, "Seminar: Physical Education for the Exceptional Child" (Trenton, N. J.: New Jersey Youth Division, September 26, 1969).

[3] *Ibid.*

[4] H. Harrison Clarke and David M. Clarke, *Developmental and Adapted Physical Education* (Englewood Cliffs, N.J.: Prentice-Hall, Inc., 1963).

[5] Donald R. Hilsendager, Harold K. Jack, and L. Mann, "Basic Motor Fitness Test for Emotionally Disturbed and Mentally Handicapped Children," National Institute of Mental Health, Grant No. 1–T1–MH–8543–1,5 (Philadelphia: Buttonwood Farms, Inc., 3354 Byberry Road, 1968), 16 pp. Mimeographed.

[6] Newell C. Kephart, *The Slow Learner in the Classroom* (Columbus, Ohio: Charles E. Merrill Books, Inc., 1967).

offerings provide individualized physical activities for students with motor problems, perceptual-motor difficulties, low physical vitality, postural deficiencies, nutritional abnormalities, and breathing allergies, Furthermore, activities are provided to enhance the functional capacities of the orthopedically handicapped and students evidencing other physical or medical limitations.

"Selling" the Program to the Students, School Authorities, and Community

The identification and classification of all handicapped children does not guarantee program adoption. To insure program approval, the staff must utilize all public relations media.

The old cliché, "the best means of public relations is via the students," is so true! When a child returns home from school, the average parent will ask him, "What did you do in school today?" He might reply he had to take "some stupid tests," or he might comment favorably about testing he underwent to assess his personal needs. A composite of the replies to similar questions will be the determining factor in the development of parental attitudes toward the staff and the school.

Since the student is the single most important factor in the school, this text will continually reflect the child-centered rather than the subject-centered approach. For example, the development of sound pupil attitudes toward a program for the handicapped is essential; the student must understand the concepts of developmental and adapted physical education in terms of how he, or others so afflicted, will benefit. Within the regular instructional program, we must demonstrate activities to alleviate postural and obesity problems, provide such learning experiences as having students test one another for adipose tissue deposits and cardiorespiratory index, and discuss the physiological effects of activity on body metabolism. Through the active involvement of each student, the most important facet of sound public relations will be firmly established—a group of good-will ambassadors equal to the number of students in the school population.

As a case in point, a parent confided to the writer that she had overheard two senior girls discussing the school D&A program as they were having their hair set in a beauty salon. The students were discussing "the physical fitness index," "adipose tissue measurements," "somatotyping," and other terms common to the program. It was obvious the parent was favorably impressed!

In too many instances, physical educators and physical education are not accorded their rightful status as integral and essential parts of the educational environment. Although it is not the purpose of this text to discuss the status of physical education as a discipline, it is mentioned here because it relates to the topic being considered—improving communications between the department and the school authorities.

Reducing the communication gap is primarily the function of the department chairman/supervisor; however, the physical educator also plays an essential role. Many or all of the following suggestions can be used to develop an awareness by school authorities of the need for a comprehensive program for the developmentally and physically handicapped:

1. An essential prerequisite for a successful program is the total commitment of all physical educators. This can be accomplished via the dissemination of articles, discussions, and workshops. Many potentially exemplary programs have failed because an insufficient effort was made to elicit from the staff the need for program change. If staff members do not hold sincere convictions, a program for the handicapped will be doomed.

2. A committee consisting of administrators and guidance, medical, and special services personnel should be formed to assess the school or school district's need to institute a program, and to determine policy when and if the program is implemented. The committee (referred to as the D&A Council in the author's school) should, minimally, consist of the school principal, the director of guidance, the school physician, the director of special services, the school nurse, and the chairman of the health and physical education department.

3. An annual report should be disseminated to all administrators and to the board of education regarding the physical fitness status of all pupils. The report should be comprehensive and include mean scores (by sex) for each grade level, a final composite average for all grades (see Table 2–1), and an analysis of the findings, conclusions, and recommendations. Particularly important is the inclusion of the number of students achieving below the established cut-off score—those students classified as developmentally sub-par. (Although student scores should be primarily evaluated longitudinally, for public relations purposes it is more advantageous when scores are depicted in relation to norms.)

4. The development and submission of a federal or state request for funds can create a respect for the program, regardless of the outcome of the request. The normal procedure is to submit the proposal to the building principal and superintendent of schools, in that order, for their consideration. If the proposal is approved, it may next be presented at a board of education meeting (see Chapter 10 for proposal guidelines), which can be an excellent opportunity to "sell" the program to an important part of the power structure.

5. The school newspaper can be used to gain school support via articles relating to innovative approaches, success stories, and student comments regarding their achievement in after-school weight and figure control programs.

6. A constant dialogue between departmental personnel and the staff at large can create an atmosphere that is conducive to support and change.

Educators have long discouraged community involvement in educational matters; some still do. They felt the role of the school was to educate, but the role of the community was to passively accept mandates (and to pay taxes). However, a natural outgrowth of ever-increasing school budgets has

TABLE 2–1   Annual Physical Fitness Index Scores (PFI)[a]

SEASON	GRADE 9		GRADE 10		GRADE 11		GRADE 12		GRADES 9–12	
	boys	girls	boys	girls	boys	girls	boys	girls	boys	girls
Fall	98	102	90	98	90	97	90	86	92	96
Spring	103	113	95	108	99	104	98	93	99	105

Analysis of Data
1. The entire student population improved their level of physical fitness.
2. Percentage gains for the girls were slightly superior to those achieved by the boys.
3. Only the 9th-grade girls (113) approached the national norm of 115.
4. The lowest PFI scores attained were: 12th-grade girls, 93; 10th-grade boys, 95.
5. The composite PFI score for girls in grades 9 and 11 was 109 and for boys in grades 10 and 12 was 101.

Conclusions
1. Increasing the number of instructional periods will improve fitness level.
2. Girls tend to attain their fitness peak at grade 9 and decline thereafter.
3. Discounting the differential in days allowed for the boys' program throughout the grade levels, scores tend to remain constant.

Recommendations
1. Provide three days of physical education per week for all grade levels.
2. Modify the curriculum for the girls in grades 10–12 to include such concepts as the development of femininity, poise, body symmetry, and grace.
3. Minimize lecture time and maximize activity time in an effort to raise all scores toward the national level of 115.

Note: Mean scores can be misleading because they give no indication of population variance. Of next year's girls in grades 10–12, 44 have PFI scores below 75. By comparison, the boys fare worse, having 68 with scores below 75. Students with PFI scores below 75 are classified as the bottom 1 percent of the population.

[a] Sample of an Annual Physical Fitness Report the author submits to the Township of Ocean District Board of Education, Oakhurst, N.J.

been the emergence of the community-school concept[7] which posits that education is no longer a process that evolves during the school years but rather a continuum which ranges from birth to death. Further, the community-school approach views the educational institution as the "hub" of the community; consequently, the school should be vitally linked with all other agencies.

Unquestionably, the adoption of this philosophy is of paramount importance in attaining community support. The parents of the handicapped and those who are interested in improving the instructional program for this group must be involved and demonstrations at P.T.A. meetings should be conducted to elicit support. Parents with children who are afflicted with physical, mental, or social problems are invariably dedicated and enthusiastic. For example, the author, a firm believer of parental involvement, not only

[7] National Recreation Workshop, "Guiding Principles," *Recreation for Community Living* (Chicago: The Athletic Institute, 1952), p. 160.

permitted parents to observe his summer D&A program but allowed them to assist in selected activities (under teacher supervision). As a result of this involvement, the parents urged the principals, the superintendent of schools, and the board of education to implement the program on the elementary level (see Appendix B for summer program guidelines). A direct result of parental support was the hiring of two physical educators to introduce the program at the elementary level the following school year. It would have been difficult to accomplish this goal without community involvement.

However, let us not discount dissidents. Many a dissident has become an extremely ardent supporter as a result of sound public relations. Once they are convinced they were wrong, those who had negative attitudes will most frequently continue to be vociferous but in support of the proposed program, not in opposition.

Other means of soliciting community support are: include an article in the school district newsletter; devote a segment of the annual gym show to demonstrate some aspect of a program for the handicapped; and address the local medical society, Kiwanians, and other such influential groups.

Determining Organizational Team Membership and Duties

The design and implementation of a D&A program for all handicapped children requires a close working relationship among the school physician, school nurse, special services team, learning disabilities specialists, physical education personnel, and department chairman/supervisor. This list should be expanded to include other personnel working directly with the handicapped. The primary role of the team is to meet periodically to plan, organize, and synchronize all aspects of the proposed program.

It must be unequivocally understood that the school physician is the titular head of the organizational team. Thus, all materials disseminated should be submitted for his approval. His duties also include the examination, identification, and classification of all students with medically oriented problems. Furthermore, he or the family physician are the only members of the team permitted to prescribe exercises or activities for the aforementioned group. Other duties he will be periodically required to perform are holding conferences with parents and students, admitting students to the program for scheduling, officially releasing students from the program, and conducting in-service programs for other team members.

It has been accurately noted that an intelligent physical educator is one who ingratiates himself with the school nurse, custodial staff, and maintainence personnel. The school nurse is literally the backbone of the organizational team, serving as the major link in program continuity. Her duties include such divergent activities as checking initial and subsequent medical histories of all students before and at the time of referral to the program; scheduling students for medical examinations; conferring with parents and students; and calling upon family physicians for their cooperation. In fact, no aspect of the program escapes the school nurse's scrutiny. Thus, she is not only vital to program continuity but is also an integral part of the public relations program due to her diversified daily contacts.

The special services team usually consists of a coordinator, a school psychologist, a social worker, and other specialized personnel in accordance with the size of the school district. The primary function of the team is to provide a central agency for coordinating all educational efforts for students who evidence physical, mental, or socioemotional problems. By maintaining a record of all referrals made by the classroom teachers, the members of the team provide an indispensable service by making available the names of those students who are in need of diagnostic testing for physical fitness and motor or perceptual-motor ability. In addition, the school psychologist must identify and prescribe activities for children with mental or socioemotional problems. The physical educator's role is to test the children upon request and to follow recommended prescriptions. (It is important that the physical educator recognize his qualifications and limitations so that he can work effectively as a member of the "team.")

Learning disability specialists such as teachers of the perceptually-impaired or students with reading and/or speech impediments can also aid the program by submitting names of students who may benefit from an individualized physical activity program. The learning disability specialist can often aid in the development of a "total picture" of the child by providing some pertinent anecdotal remarks.

The physical education staff's role as a part of the planning team is primarily devoted to testing and assessing the status of all students to ascertain who needs individualized developmental activities. On the basis of the annual fall testing program, the staff assesses the developmental level of students in terms of muscular strength, muscular endurance, cardiorespiratory endurance, general motor ability, general nutritional status, and overall body mechanics. It must be remembered that this testing and assessing are only screening devices; the school physician or psychologist will make the official judgment.

The department chairman/supervisor could be referred to as the generator or catalytic agent who determines the thrust of the total program. He should possess a sound knowledge of all aspects of the program, contagious enthusiasm that will envelop all who come in contact with him, and boundless energy.

As program director, his role is to plan and prepare the following items:

1. The agenda and dates for organizational team meetings
2. Periodic materials that must be disseminated to keep the committee apprised of progress
3. Test forms and norms for assessment of student status
4. Medical excuse, scheduling, and other forms for administration
5. Demonstrations for public and private agencies
6. Reports to the administration and board
7. In-service programs for departmental members

The support of local medical authorities is of paramount importance. We will present a short historical background of the Township of Ocean Developmental and Adapted Physical Education Program (D&A) to stress the need for "bridging the gap" between the family physician and the physical education staff, school personnel, students, and parents.

Prior to the start of the D&A Program, a letter explaining the physical education program for the handicapped was forwarded to every physician in the vicinity of the school district. The results: not one referral was made for program admission during the 1968–1969 school year by a family physician.

Since that time, the following steps have been taken to bridge the existing gap: parental and student conferences; P.T.A. demonstrations of D&A programs; personal contact with family physicians; visits to the physical therapy departments in neighboring hospitals; and in-service meetings for all school personnel. As of June 1970, approximately 65 percent of the students with medical problems had been admitted to the program with activity prescriptions signed and approved by family physicians. In an effort to achieve the ultimate goal of having every handicapped child in the individualized physical education program, a list of all participating and nonparticipating physicians had been kept. Upon receipt of a medical excuse form from a doctor, a second letter was sent to him, regardless of his decision as to the fitness of the particular child for the D&A program. In essence the letter thanked the physician, extended an invitation to view the program "in action," included a packet of program materials, and solicited additional suggestions and materials (see Appendix A).

It is strongly recommended that anyone who plans a complete program for the handicapped utilize every means to make medical authorities, the team, and the entire community aware of the services available. Regardless of the quality and quantity of the services offered, they will be of no value unless they can be implemented.

The validity of prescriptive programs is enhanced when all involved personnel are contacted and thus can make their contributions. Examples of cooperation among the Ocean Township High School guidance department, special services department, physical education department, and the school nurse are provided via the case study approach. The first student studied was having difficulties with several of her subjects and the guidance counselor asked the physical education department to administer the Township of Ocean School District Motor-Perceptual Test Battery. Following a review of the medical history and anecdotal remarks made by other members of the team, the writer tested the student. The report to the guidance counselor was as follows:

TO: Miss Ruth O'Brian
FROM: Dr. Thomas M. Vodola
RE: Jane Doe   January 22, 1970

Test Evaluation

1. Health-habit questionnaire	Satisfactory
2. Handedness/footedness	Right
3. Vision	20/20
4. Monocularity	Satisfactory
5. Binocularity	Satisfactory
6. Motor skills	Satisfactory
7. Motor patterns	Coordination problem

Comment

The student evidences strengths in motor responses and visuomotor responses. Difficulty seems to evolve around the inability to conceptualize or integrate experiences. Problem is not merely motor-physical, but involves cognition. The only problem related to motor activity was one of poor bilaterality (inability to coordinate opposite parts of the body); will have Mrs. Blair prescribe activities commensurate with the problem.

Would also recommend that the academic areas stress learning experiences that place emphasis on the inductive approach, comprehension, application, analysis, synthesis, and evaluation. During our discussion, Jane revealed she can retain factual knowledge but has extreme difficulty developing meaningful "wholes" out of the factual data. Testing material is included for your files.

During the course of the school year, the child study team of the Township of Ocean School District frequently requests the aid of the physical education department so that they can more effectively evaluate children with learning disabilities. The report of an elementary child's motor performance illustrates another concrete example of utilizing the team approach (while undoubtedly raising the esteem of the physical educators).

TO: Edwina M. Crystal, School Psychologist
FROM: Dennis Bender
RE: Basic Motor Skill Test Administered to John Doe
SCHOOL: Oakhurst   February 4, 1971

Results

1. Preferred right hand and right foot.
2. Awkward and mixed patterning with creep.
3. Used the mechanics of skipping correctly but was stiff and jerky.
4. Could not stay with the beat while marching in place. Would on occasion use bizarre and jerky steps.
5. Static and dynamic balance proved grossly inadequate.

6. Fair skill in ball handling.
7. Jerky, bizarre, unsure lateral ocular pursuit. This is very acute.
8. Did well with the fore/aft swinging of whiffleballs.
9. Fair eye-hand and eye-foot accuracy.
10. Laterality problem.

Observation

1. Total motor, jerkiness, and tightness.
2. Appeared unsure of motor movements.
3. Appeared tired.

Recommendation

1. Optical evaluation.
2. Medical and/or neurological examination.
3. Developmental and Adapted Physical Education class with emphasis on ocular pursuits and smooth, rhythmic body movements.

Summary by Dr. Vodola

John has several developmental problems. Throughout the test he evidenced: a vision problem (inability to follow an object laterally); restricted, inflexible movement patterns; gross inadequacies in terms of basic motor skill; and poor self-image.

I would strongly recommend he be provided with a varied movement exploration program in conjunction with a variety of eye coordination activities (monocular and binocular activities).

The mechanics of structuring a procedure whereby all members of the team are involved in providing a physical education program for the handicapped can be cumbersome and time-consuming. However, the establishment of a uniform plan is essential if one is to avoid omissions and duplications, insure the involvement of all necessary personnel and, above all, enhance program success. The D&A policy procedure recommended is thus presented in its entirety. Its evolvement was the result of two D&A council meetings, a pilot study, final revisions, adoption by the council, and final approval by the chief school administrator.

D&A POLICY STATEMENT

The Scheduling and Releasing of Students in Developmental and Adapted Physical Education (adopted by D&A Council on January 19, 1971).

All personnel desirous of referring a student to D&A shall forward the request via the building principal's office. Requests must be submitted on a teacher referral form (available in the nurse's office) [see Appendix A].

If the principal approves the referral, he shall forward the form to the school nurse. (If the request is denied, he shall fill in the disposition part of the form and forward a copy to the teacher making the referral.)

Upon receiving the teacher referral form, the nurse shall route the form according to the following procedure: (1) Low physical vitality, motor coordination, diagnostic testing—to the D&A teacher; and (2) medically oriented problems (nutritional, postural, orthopedic, postoperative/convalescent, asthmatic, etc.—to the school physician for an examination.

Following scheduling by the D&A teacher (#1 above), he or she shall fill in the disposition part of the form and return it to the building principal via the school nurse. Following the medical examination (#2 above), the form shall be signed and dated by the school physician. At the discretion of the physician, the child may be admitted to the program or referred to the family physician.

If the school physician approves the assignment to D&A, he or she must fill out the medical excuse form (prescribing specific exercises or activities, listing program duration, etc.). The nurse shall record all pertinent information on the disposition part of the teacher referral form and forward it to the D&A teacher. (The nurse shall file the medical excuse form in her office.)

If the school physician recommends referral of the child to the family physician, the school nurse shall forward a medical excuse form to the parent. Admittance to the program requires parental approval (signature), physician's approval (signature), a list of prescribed exercises or activities, and program duration. If admission to the program is granted, the nurse shall fill in pertinent data on the disposition part of the teacher referral form and forward it to the D&A teacher. (The nurse shall file the medical excuse form in her office.) If admission to the program is denied, a follow-up phone call shall be made to the family physician by the school nurse. If admission is still denied, the information is recorded on the medical excuse form and teacher referral form (the former is filed in the nurse's office; the latter is forwarded to the building principal).

Upon receiving the teacher referral form from the school nurse, the principal shall route copies to:

1. The teacher making the referral
2. The D&A teacher
3. The school nurse
4. The learning disabilities consultant
5. The supervisor of health, physical education, and driver education
6. The coordinator of special services

The supervisor's office shall prepare the child study team classification form (C.S.T.F.) for those students who would qualify for supplemental services.[8] The form shall then be forwarded to the respective building principal for his signature and the school physician's signature. All C.S.T.F. forms shall be forwarded to the office of special services for filing [see Appendix A for classification approval form].

Cumulative D&A student progress data are filed and available in the office of the supervisor of health, physical education, and driver education.

Requirements and Restrictions of the D&A Instructor

Special certification requirements are not necessary in order to teach developmental and adapted physical education because the D&A program is completely under the jurisdiction of the school physician. As long as the instructor is a competent physical educator with a sound understanding of child growth

---

[8] The Township of Ocean School District is reimbursed for supplementary services provided by the Physical Education Department in the State of New Jersey. Chapters 9 and 10 will provide teachers of other states with guidelines for soliciting remuneration on a similar basis.

and development, physiology of exercise, kinesiology, and other biological sciences and has taken the basic educational foundation courses, he is not subject to liability or certification problems. However, the instructor must abide by the policies established by the D&A council (to be discussed in Chapter 3). Physical educators can recommend exercises or tasks for students assigned to the developmental phase of the program and thus may prescribe activities to improve physical fitness and motor ability to the extent that they possess the necessary expertise.

However, at no time are they to prescribe activities for those students assigned to the adapted phase of the program. It is imperative that a student with a medical problem not be scheduled for class until the student, the parent, and the school or family physician approve (see the medical excuse form in Appendix A). The instructor must remember that parental approval alone does not suffice; test cases have illustrated that a parent cannot waive the rights of a minor. Furthermore, the physician must state specifically the exercises or activities he wishes to prescribe and the date the student can return to unrestricted activity.

It has been advocated by some educators that the physician should describe the nature of the disability and the physical educator should prescribe the program. Although the logic of such a proposal is sound, one mishap could irreparably damage the image of the entire program. Because of the seriousness of the implications, we must reiterate that the school physician is the titular head of the D&A program and thus only he or the family physician may assign students to adapted physical education. In this regard a program conducted under the auspices of the school physician is cloaked in respectability, thus enhancing the possibility of success.

There is another approach to working with the handicapped that has considerable merit—the correction and remediation of disabilities. This approach requires the hiring of physical therapists who, in addition to a physical educator's background, possess specialized training for administering corrective exercises.

The Cherry Hill School District in Cherry Hill, New Jersey exemplifies the success that can be attained via the use of physical therapists.[9] Coordinated by Mr. Alfred Daniel, the Cherry Hill program has for the past decade been one of the outstanding physical education programs for handicapped children in New Jersey.

Philosophically speaking, the D&A and remediation approaches are very similar in that they both stress the need for a sound physical activity program for all atypical children. There are however two basic differences between the programs. Developmental and adapted physical education stresses the

---

[9] Alfred Daniel, Coordinator, Cherry Hill School District Program for the Handicapped, Cherry Hill, N.J.

provision of activities that increase the handicapped person's capacity to function within his limitations, whereas remedial physical education connotes correction of the physical limitations. Furthermore, the D&A approach utilizes the services of physical educators, but the remedial approach makes use of physical therapists. The program recommended in this text, the use of developmental and adapted activities, requires only the services of personnel certified in physical education.

Special Facilities, Equipment, and Personnel

One of the most perplexing problems in program planning concerns what facilities can be used, since most school districts in the country suffer from overcrowding. We will present a solution to the facilities question in two steps: (1) initiating a program with no apparent facilities, and (2) planning facilities for new school construction.

Physical educators have often stated they could not start a program because of a lack of facilities, which is, at best, a rationalization. Furthermore, such a remark is often inaccurate. A similar rationalization is that one cannot teach a class of 80 students. The truth is that one *can* teach a large class, but the degree of effectiveness will be limited. If the facilities or pupil/teacher ratio problem is to be resolved, one must be positive. We contend that a program can be implemented in any school district in the country, regardless of existing facilities. The essential ingredients are desire, tireless efforts, and a positive, detailed approach to the problem.

The author was confronted with such a situation during the 1967–1968 school year in the Township of Ocean School District. Upon enactment of the Elementary and Secondary Education Act of 1965, a planning grant was submitted and approved for funding during the 1966–1967 school year. However, the continuation grant proposal for 1967–1968 was rejected due to a lack of federal funds and a change in governmental priorities. What could be done? Funds had been denied and neither facilities nor staff were available to provide the additional instruction (or so it was thought). After many rationalization "detours," periods of depression, self-pity, and soul searching, it was decided that at the very least an attempt should be made to implement the program.

Once the problem was confronted positively, a plan of action was prepared. First the existing high school facilities were closely scrutinized in an effort to locate potential teaching stations (initally the D&A program was started in grades 9–12). The only areas available consisted of two team rooms approximately 15′ × 15′ each and a 10′ × 15′ weight training room. Adjacent corridors could also be used plus the three-section gymnasium during the fall and spring, weather permitting.

The second step of the plan was to discuss the problem with the physical education staff and elicit their suggestions for effectuating the program. At a special departmental meeting the staff was told about the limited facilities available. The central problem then became the need for staff members to teach the proposed D&A classes. Since no additional personnel were available, staff members were asked to consider the following requests: "If permission is granted by the administration, will you accept D&A teaching assignments in lieu of study hall or cafeteria duties?" "If your answer to the first question is yes, would you cooperate by teaching the handicapped in the facilities that are available?" Following the requests, an appeal was made for program realization by stating that a vitally needed service would be provided for a large segment of high school youth and that the values derived would justify the provision of additional facilities and teachers in the immediate future. After the discussion, the staff unanimously agreed to cooperate in initiating the planned proposal. Thus the major objective in program planning was achieved—the commitment of the staff to full cooperation.

The final task was to convince the principal of the need for a physical education program for our handicapped youth (aided by the fact that the school physician and school nurse were aware of and approved every phase of the planning). After detailed elaboration of the plan, the principal was requested to schedule staff members for D&A classes in lieu of other non-academic assignments whenever possible. Generally a high school teacher is assigned 25 instructional periods per week, plus five periods of cafeteria or study hall supervision. The principal indicated there was a need for the D&A program and that he would do whatever he could to help expedite its operation. Because of the careful planning, a total of 16 D&A classes were added to the 1967–1968 school curriculum (eight classes for boys and eight classes for girls). As a result of careful, resourceful planning, the program was so successful that one of the larger classrooms was specifically designated as the D&A instructional teaching station for the 1968–1969 school year. The moral is clear: regardless of facilities available, a program for the handicapped can be provided if a determined, positive team effort is made.

Admittedly, it is more difficult to use such an approach on the elementary level where physical educators tend to be assigned to seven or eight instructional classes per day. However, occasionally instructors are assigned to playground or lunchroom supervision so that a limited solution to the personnel problem is possible. One must remember that as long as the program is made operable, it doesn't matter how many classes can be initially scheduled. The inherent values of the program will assure quick success and many opportunities for expansion.

Planning facilities for a school to be constructed in the future should be done using the same general criteria for submitting a request for an additional teaching station. Factors that must be considered to determine the overall size of the room would be the maximum number of students that would utilize the station during "peak load" periods and the specific activities that would be included in the program. Most important is that the design be functional.

The following must be explicitly stated when written plans are submitted: the location and orientation to other facilities, the function(s) of the station, the flexibility of the station, and general and specific design features that must be incorporated.[10] In its suggested plans the J. A. Preston Corporation[11] recommends a large adapted exercising room of $24' \times 45\frac{1}{2}'$ and a small additional area of $17\frac{1}{2}' \times 19'$. Copies of the Preston catalogs[12] can be procured, free of charge, by writing to the New York office. The Athletic Institute and the American Association for Health, Physical Education and Recreation,[13] in their manual on planning facilities, presented a detailed section on specifications for making buildings and facilities functional for handicap usage.

The supplies and equipment recommended by Preston are based on the establishment of a comprehensive program. Although such a program should be the ultimate goal, initial planning need not be as sophisticated. A review of the Preston catalogs mentioned above will disclose many items that are available in most physical education departments.

The determination of specific supply and equipment needs must be made on the basis of the program to be implemented. Will the program initially consist of activities for children with perceptual-motor problems? Will it consist of all activities involved in a comprehensive developmental program? The old adage, "crawl before you walk," is applicable. It is suggested that a program be planned that is at first limited in scope, requiring minimal supplies and equipment (unless unlimited funds are available). Further, a limited program should afford the staff time to "grow" as the program expands. Because supply and equipment needs vary with each program, a recommended inventory of items will not be listed here. Rather, as reference is made to each aspect of the program, specific recommendations for supplies and equipment will be itemized.

Before we turn to other matters, however, let us revert to the cliché about

[10] Harold K. Jack, "Lecture: Management and Planning Facilities in Physical Education," Temple University, Philadelphia, Spring, 1967.
[11] J. A. Preston Corporation, *Adapted Physical Education: Suggested Equipment Lists and Layouts*, 71 Fifth Avenue, New York, N.Y. 10003, 1969, pp. 14–17. Free upon request.
[12] J. A. Preston Corporation, *Adapted Physical Education: Suggested Equipment Lists*, 19 pp.; and *Equipment for Physical Medicine and Rehabilitation*, Catalog 1080, 71 Fifth Avenue, New York, N.Y. 10003, 1968, 208 pp. Both free upon request.
[13] National Facilities Conference, *Planning Areas and Facilities for Health, Physical Education and Recreation* (Chicago: The Athletic Institute and the American Association for Health, Physical Education and Recreation, 1965), pp. 245–55.

the intelligent physical educator who ingratiates himself with the school nurse and custodial and maintenance staff. If one teaches in a school district blessed with a cooperative custodial and maintenance crew, many supply and equipment items may be available at nominal cost. For example, an overhead ladder which sells for $200 was constructed by the Township of Ocean maintenance personnel for approximately $25. Money saved is not the only advantage, for frequently devices can be constructed that are not commercially available (see the posture screening grid, tapered balance beam, and modified Howland Alignometer construction specifications in Appendix C).

The concept of developmental and adapted physical education provides for an individualized program of exercises, tasks, and games prescribed for the needs of the handicapped. Facilities must therefore encompass the entire program. Assuming that the program stressed in this text is implemented, an area of not less than $30' \times 60'$ is recommended for a teaching station at the elementary or secondary level.

Scheduling Students for Grades K–12

The scheduling of students requires a close working relationship among the program director, guidance department, special services department, physical education staff, school nurse, and the school administration. Since the departmentalized and self-contained classrooms on the high school and elementary school levels, respectively, create problems that require different approaches, separate scheduling guidelines will be recommended for each level.

Schools that schedule on a departmental basis allow the chairman to resolve the problem via the use of study halls. (The advent of independent study poses a problem to this approach; hopefully, before all schools provide independent study, the states will realize the necessity for mandated physical education programs for the handicapped.) The following procedural steps are sound guidelines for scheduling students on the basis of available study halls.

1. Compile a list of all students eligible for admittance to the program.
2. Forward the list to the school nurse so that the students can be scheduled for a medical examination. It is not necessary to request a medical examination for the physically sub-par child, but, if possible, it is advisable.
3. Obtain the list of those students approved for scheduling.
4. Personally interview those students who have medical problems; explain the nature of their disability and the benefits of the program. Give them a copy of the medical excuse form that must be signed by the parent and family physician. It is not necessary to seek medical approval for students being scheduled for developmental activities.

5. Obtain from the guidance or nurse's office an alphabetical listing of student schedules to determine the available study halls for each student on the approved list; be sure to list all study halls since conflicts will require adjustments. Scheduling can be done by the guidance department, but flexibility is increased if the task is performed by the department chairman. For example, "shuttling" the handicapped child into an unusual program, according to program offerings, is facilitated if all scheduling is performed by the chairman.

6. Prepare a listing of the day and period that each class is offered.

7. Refer to student names and study hall schedules and then assign developmental students to one day per week of the special program in addition to the regular activity class. Students for the adapted program, who are medically excused from unrestricted physical activity, are to be scheduled to a number of periods equal to the regular class which had been waived.

8. Record the names in a master manual (see Appendix A). Try to assign ten students to a class; maximum is fifteen since instructional effectiveness decreases for larger classes.

9. Prepare individual admission/release passes and forward them to the teachers who have been assigned to teach the classes (see Appendix A). D&A teachers then go to the scheduled study halls to have the students they have listed "released" from the study hall rosters. "Releases" require the study hall teacher to initial each pass and record the information on his attendance roster. This procedure provides the central office with the location of all students. (*Note:* Delay scheduling until the second or third week after school starts to permit time for students to adjust scheduling errors.) The pass is retained by the D&A teacher and filed in the student's individual folder. Subsequent admissions to the program may be handled by having a student in the D&A class take the admission/release pass to the proper study hall.

10. Releasing a student from the D&A program requires simply the reversal of the admittance procedure plus the return of the release pass to the department chairman so that he can keep the master scheduling manual up to date.

Self-contained classrooms necessitate a different approach to the scheduling problem. Since students remain with one teacher for most of each school day, the supervisor must work closely with the classroom teacher, subject to the approval of the school principal. The following sequential approach is advisable at the elementary level.

1. Follow procedures for steps 1 to 4 above for scheduling students in a departmentalized program.

2. Forward the approved student list to the principal, who will do the scheduling himself or delegate the work to the supervisor or staff member in conjunction with the classroom teachers.

3. Prepare a master list of all classes scheduled.

4. Follow steps 7 and 8 of the departmentalized plan.

5. Due to the age of elementary students, the instructor should pick up and return all students to their respective classes. However, if the admission/release pass plan can be adopted, it will allow more time to be devoted to instruction.

We must remember that the recommended scheduling procedures are guidelines which have proven successful but may not be feasible in a particular school district. A little thought and experience will, undoubtedly, provide you with more effective and efficient means of resolving the problem.

Scheduling Time Blocks for D&A Classes

The scheduling of all classes is the prime responsibility of the building principal. However, the chairman/supervisor should recommend basic guidelines that will enhance program effectiveness.

Factors that determine the number of classes scheduled at either level are: (1) the availability of a teaching station, (2) the total school population, (3) the number of pupils approved for D&A, (4) the number of physical educators available to teach the course, and (5) the medical reasons for assigning the pupils (the greater the severity of the handicap, the more instructional periods per child needed). At the high school level, an attempt should be made to assign boys and girls on a staggered schedule, alternating both days and periods. This will allow more students to be scheduled via their study halls since the most frequent school pattern of assigning students to study halls appears to be a "block assignment" of the same period five days a week.

Another guideline, although difficult to incorporate, is to schedule D&A class rosters so that student assignments run concurrently with their regular physical education classes. For example, if a senior has physical education and health for a total of four periods during the first-period time slot, it would be advantageous if he were assigned to D&A during the remaining first-period time slot. Such a pattern would permit greater flexibility for returning the student to the regular class for certain activities, a practice that has great merit. However, regardless of the pattern of scheduling classes, the ultimate goal should be to have a D&A class available every period of every day.

The proposed scheduling pattern is based on the premise that boys and girls are taught in integrated physical education classes for grades K–3 and segregated classes for grades 4–12. Many school districts have found it advantageous to utilize coeducational instruction throughout all grade levels. However, it is the contention of the writer that students with certain disabilities tend to feel embarrassed when participating with members of the opposite sex (particularly when they are first introduced to the program). Therefore, it is best to use the eclectic approach whereby classes may participate together when the instructor feels the limitations are not excessive. It is interesting to note that assigning students on a coeducational basis will increase the total number of participants in the high school program by at least 10 percent.

How Often Should the Handicapped Be Assigned to D&A?

The question of how often students should take D&A classes is dependent upon many of the variables stated previously, such as number of students in the program, instructors available, etc. The plan recommended is based on the assumption that there is one teaching station available for every period of the day and every day of the week. This would provide forty potential instructional periods (based on an eight-period day). Thus, a total of twenty boys' and twenty girls' classes, or forty coeducational classes, could be scheduled.

Previous reference was made to the number of days a student should be scheduled, but the proposal must be philosophically clarified, for the handicapped should remain in the regular instructional program in all situations in which it is not detrimental to their personal well-being. Often the child with physical limitations can effectively take part in classes with his "normal" peer group, especially because of the trend toward introducing more recreational units in the curriculum. If we are truly interested in developing the total child and if education is really "preparation for life," we must provide realistic learning experiences that will equip the handicapped child with the necessary tools for coping with the complex problems of daily living. By maximizing participation in the unrestricted activity class, we accentuate the positive capabilities of the individual and minimize the limiting aspects of his disability.

For example, a blind student who was scheduled in the D&A program was assigned to the regular class during a unit on weight training. As the weights were set up at permanent stations, the student had no trouble maneuvering from station to station without assistance. However, since weight training is primarily a developer of muscular strength and muscular endurance, all students were required to run one mile during the pre-instructional phase of the program to develop cardiorespiratory endurance. It would have been "easy" to excuse the blind student from participation in running, but would it have been in his best interest? Would it enhance his self-image? Would it enhance him in the "eyes" of his peer group? Could he participate without fear of injury? Imbued with the aforementioned philosophy, the writer assigned a "buddy" to run the daily mile with the blind student. Two preconditions to this approach were that the handicapped student be receptive to the idea and the "buddy" be empathetic and patient, but not sympathetic. The value of the approach was unquestionable! Subjective observations and remarks by the blind student's classmates indicated he was more respected, admired, and accepted as a result of his total involvement.

His response to the plan was even more enthusiastic! He related to the writer that as a blind student he had always taken short, faltering steps because of a constant fear of colliding with objects. Since running with a "buddy," he has learned to increase his stride and his confidence. One could see the development of a more positive self-concept and a growth of the total being, not just the improvement of cardiorespiratory endurance.

In light of the espoused philosophy, students in need of developmental physical activities should be scheduled for one period per week in addition to the regular physical education classes. Those students with medical excuses should be assigned to the adapted program in lieu of the regular program only when the medical form indicates no unrestricted activity. However, via a close working relationship with the nurse and the physician involved, programs can be designed whereby the child can take part in both programs. As an example, a child with scoliosis (lateral curvature of the spine) can and will benefit from exposure to both programs. A general prescription might be one or two days of D&A plus regular program participation, exclusive of those activities that are contraindicated.

Must All Handicapped Students Participate in D&A?

The proposed program is not mandatory. Essential ingredients for effective teaching are teacher/pupil rapport and intrinsic motivation of the learner. An atmosphere for learning can only be engendered when fear, intimidation, and coercion are minimized or eliminated.

The author has used the term "quasivoluntary" for the procedure used to schedule students. The program is neither completely voluntary, nor completely mandatory. Basically, the procedure is to assign all students in need of developmental activities to one period per week, without parental or student approval. Students are made aware of the fact that test scores below established standards will necessitate inclusion in the developmental phase of the program. To this extent the program is mandated. However, once a student has been scheduled, he has the prerogative of having his parent request his being excused from the program; this is the voluntary aspect of the program. Requests for exemption must be made via a personal conference or telephone call so that the teacher can explain directly to the parent the nature of his child's problem, the program prescribed, the values to be derived from participation and, above all, can eliminate any erroneous misconceptions as to why the child was scheduled. Testimony as to the success of the quasivoluntary method of scheduling lies in the fact that less than 10 percent of the 700 students scheduled for D&A during the 1968–1970 school years have been released as a result of parental requests. To this figure can be added the 200 to 300 students who requested voluntary admission to the weight and figure control programs. Finally, one must consider the positive public relations that was established via these personal contacts. Whereas approximately 15 percent of the parents initially requested student exemption, this figure was reduced to less than 10 percent when the parents were made aware of the comprehensive program provided.

For example, posture screening by the staff and a medical examination by the school physician revealed that a 10th-grade girl had a severe scoliotic condition. The family orthopedic physician fitted the child with a brace and recommended specific corrective exercises which were performed under the supervision of a physical therapist. When the parent was contacted and made aware of the program offered in the school she permitted her daughter to be admitted to the D&A program. It was made quite clear to the parent that her daughter would only be permitted to practice those exercises prescribed by her physician.

Scheduling students for adapted physical education is entirely dependent upon parent and school/family physician approval. It is the contention of the writer that all handicapped students who can attend school should be assigned to some modified activity program. The liability aspect, however, mandates the aforementioned approval. How well one achieves the goal of involving all handicapped students in some phase of the D&A program will be determined by the degree of school and community involvement. The more knowledgeable all parties are of the values to be derived by the students involved, the more the child is actively involved in and totally receptive to the program and the greater the possibility of maximum participation.

Summary

Consideration should be given to an organizational plan which will incorporate the following features:

1. The identification and classification of students on the basis of developmental or functional characteristics.

2. The adoption of a child-centered rather than a subject-centered approach to instruction.

3. The instituting of a public relations campaign that focuses on the youth of the school while at the same time utilizing a variety of media to gain school and community support.

4. A basic planning committee consisting of the school physician, school nurse, administrator, special services team, learning disability specialists, physical education personnel, and the department chairman/supervisor.

5. The acknowledgment of the school physician as the titular head of the D&A program.

6. A careful reconnaisance of existing facilities to identify those areas that can be used for instructional purposes.

7. The complete involvement of the physical education staff and administration in the initial planning.

8. The inclusion of a written report (if additional facilities are requested) in terms of justification, location, function, flexibility, general and specific design features, and orientation to the gymnasium complex.

9. A coordinated scheduling plan designed by the chairman/supervisor, in conjunction with guidance personnel, the physical education staff, school nurse, and school administration.

10. The use of coeducational instruction in grades K–3 and segregated instruction in grades 4–12 unless handicaps are such that boys and girls will not be stigmatized by mixed grouping.

11. The inclusion of the physically handicapped in the regular instruction program as often as possible as long as it is not detrimental to the well-being of any individual.

12. The provision of an instructional program that accentuates the atypical child's positive capabilities and minimizes his limitations.

13. The scheduling of students on a voluntary or quasivoluntary rather than mandated basis since coercion negates motivation and enthusiasm and would thus be detrimental to the learning process and to the ultimate success of the program.

Annotated Bibliography

AMERICAN ASSOCIATION FOR HEALTH, PHYSICAL EDUCATION AND RECREATION, UNIT ON PROGRAMS FOR THE HANDICAPPED. *Helpful Sources for Developing Physical Education and Recreation Programs for the Handicapped.* Washington, D.C.: 1201 Sixteenth Street, N.W. 20036, 5 pp. Mimeographed. Contains a bibliography of books, publications, and personnel carefully selected to provide the reader with basic information necessary for implementing a program for the handicapped. Many of the sources (40) will, upon request, provide specific materials related to organization and administration. Free upon request.

————. *Information Sheet: Camping for the Handicapped.* Washington, D.C.: 1201 Sixteenth Street, N.W. 20036, 5 pp. Mimeographed. Provides a number of agencies and individuals that may be contacted for assistance and information about developing camping programs and facilities for the handicapped. Also includes, in outline form, the many factors that must be considered in planning and implementing camping programs for the handicapped. Free upon request.

————. *Information Sheet: Facilities, Equipment, Supplies for Physical Education, Camping, Outdoor Education and Recreation Programs for the Handicapped.* Washington, D.C.: 1201 Sixteenth Street, N.W. 20036, 7 pp. Mimeographed. Includes individual contacts, organizations and associations, books and periodicals, and audiovisual aids. Free upon request.

————. *Instructional Materials Center Network for Handicapped Children*. Washington, D.C.: 1201 Sixteenth Street, N.W. 20036, 1 p. Mimeographed. Provides a list of Special Education IMC Centers located throughout the United States. Free upon request.

————. *Records for Fun, Fitness, Recreation and Educational Development of Mentally Retarded and Handicapped Children and Adults*. Washington, D.C.: 1201 Sixteenth Street, N.W. 20036, 4 pp. Mimeographed. Provides guidelines for record selections and a list of commerically available records. Free upon request.

AMERICAN STANDARDS ASSOCIATION. *Making Buildings and Facilities Accessible to, and Usable by, the Physically Handicapped*, New York: United Cerebral Palsy Association, Inc., 1961. 11 pp. Presents minimal requirements for the construction of buildings and facilities so that individuals with physical handicaps may be afforded easy access to and use of these areas. Free upon request.

Handicapped Children: The Playscape and the Instructor. Long Island City, N.Y.: Playground Corporation of America, 1969. 17 pp. Describes playground equipment which can be adapted to meet the needs of all handicapped children. Free upon request.

Helping Rehabilitate the Handicapped Through Successful Physical Play. Long Island City, N.Y.: Playground Corporation of America, April 1, 1969. 24 pp. Series of articles describing how the playscape (playground equipment) can be adapted to meet the needs of the mentally retarded, sightless children, the deaf and nonambulatory, orthopedically handicapped. Free upon request.

HUCKLEBRIDGE, Ted H. *Developmental Physical Education Teaching Guide, Project No. 2645*, Title III, P.L. 89–10, A Segmented Demonstration Physical Education Program. Healdsburg, Calif.: Healdsburg High School District, 1968. 99 pp. A guidebook for teachers working with the physically deficient pupil. Includes procedures for initiating a program; some behaviorally written objectives; criteria for student enrollment; and other general program guidelines. Also provides a cumulative fitness record scoring chart for boys and girls in grades 4–12.

————. *Physical Education Teaching Guide for Corrective-Adapted Physical Education Program* (preliminary working copy), Project No. 2645, Title III, P.L. 89–10, A Segmented Demonstration Physical Education Program. Santa Rosa, Calif.: Healdsburg High School District, July, 1968. 30 pp. Provides an overview of corrective-adapted physical education and plans for organizing and administering the program. Includes a series of medical excuse forms used in the federally funded program.

POMEROY, JANET. *Recreation for the Physically Handicapped*. New York: The Macmillan Company, 1964. Provides the reader with suggestions relating to principles, policies, and procedures for initiating and conducting a recreation program for the physically handicapped. Describes procedures that have proved effective in serving the recreation needs of the physically handicapped at the Recreation Center for the Handicapped in San Francisco.

WHEELER, RUTH H., and AGNES M. HOOLEY. *Physical Education for the Handicapped*. Philadelphia: Lea and Febiger, 1969. A "how to do it" book regarding the planning and conducting of physical education/recreation programs for the handicapped.

II

PROGRAM
IMPLEMENTATION

3

identification of students
in need of developmental activities

In Part I we attempted to provide the reader with a general overview of material related to the provision of a physical education program for the handicapped child. Solutions were provided for the most frequent problems regarding organizational and administrative procedures. No priority or sequential order was established, but an attempt was made to give the reader some insight into the thought and planning that must go into the establishment of a comprehensive D&A program.

In Part II, sequentially structured, implementary procedures will be considered, starting with behavioral outcomes and culminating with program evaluation. Materials will be listed prescriptively so that the program can be implemented in its entirety, or modified according to the prevailing situation or philosophy of the reader. References will be made to exemplary features of other programs; the reader is urged to use the references for elaboration. It must be remembered that there are many valid and reliable test items that can be used in a program for the handicapped; there is nothing sacrosanct about the test items and batteries listed. It is most important, however, to preplan carefully and to design the program on a developmental basis.

Behavioral Outcomes

The developmental theory stresses the use of a logical, ordered approach based on program objectives. Thus, the first step in program implementation is the determination of what we are attempting to achieve via our activity program for the developmentally handicapped. Prior to the statement of objectives, let us define the term *developmental physical education*[1]:

Developmental physical education is the phase of the total program that has been designed to modify the physical activity program commensurate with the needs of those students evidencing low physical vitality, motor/perceptual problems, postural abnormalities or nutritional deficiencies.

The outcomes or goals should be stated in specific behavioral terms, including selection of test items, student learning experiences, and evaluative techniques. Mager states that a meaningful objective is one that "succeeds in communicating to the reader the writer's instructional intent."[2] We will now list the behavioral outcomes expected of the learner as a result of developmental activities.[3]

1. The student can attain a minimum average standard score of 40 on the Motor/Perceptual Test Battery (with no single component score of less than 10), or a score that is satisfactory in terms of his somatotype (K–8).

2. The student can attain a minimum score of 70 on the New York Posture-Screening Test (with no single component score of 1) (K–8).

3. The student's predicted body weight is less than 20 percent above or below his actual body weight (K–8).

4. The student can name and/or list his areas of weakness in terms of specific motor/perceptual factors, postural abnormalities, or nutritional deficiencies (K–8).

5. The student can perform his prescribed exercises or motor/perceptual tasks correctly (K–8).

6. The student can name and/or list those activities in which he can achieve reasonable success (K–8).

7. The student can attain a minimum score of 100 on the Rogers PFI Test, or a PFI score that is satisfactory in terms of his somatotype (grades 9–12).

8. The student can attain a minimum score of 85 on the New York State Posture Screening Test (grades 9–12).

9. The student can list his areas of weakness in terms of specific fitness factors or postural abnormalities (grades 9–12).

10. The student can demonstrate the ability to administer the following battery of tests accurately (those items that are part of his program): skinfold calipers; Pryor's width-weight calipers; leg, back, and grip dynamometers; dry spirometer; tape measurements and flexometer (grades 9–12).

11. The student can evaluate his progress and represcribe exercises under the teacher's supervision (grades 9–12).

[1] Thomas M. Vodola, *Course of Study, Grades K–12: Developmental and Adapted Physical Education* (Oakhurst, N.J.: Township of Ocean Board of Education, January, 1970), p. 1. Mimeographed.
[2] Robert F. Mager, *Preparing Educational Objectives* (Palo Alto, Calif.: Fearon Publisher, 1962), p. 10.
[3] Vodola, *loc. cit.*

12. The student can perform the following exercises or tasks correctly (those exercises that are part of his program): modified Harvard Step Test, modified cable jump, posture exercises, rope skipping, shuttle run, motor/perceptual activities (grades 9–12).

13. The student can compute the caloric requirements necessary to maintain his present weight (grades 9–12).

14. The student can design a weight control program so that he can decrease or increase his weight by one pound per week (grades 9–12).

15. The student can list symptoms and causes of postural abnormalities (grades 9–12).

16. The student can list symptoms and causes of nutritional deficiencies (grades 9–12).

17. The student can list those activities in which he can achieve reasonable success (grades 9–12).

18. The student can describe and classify himself in terms of Sheldon's three basic body structure components (grades 9–12).

19. The student can list symptoms and causes of low physical vitality (grades 9–12).

Motor Skills

One of the prime objectives of physical education is the development of fundamental motor patterns. Unfortunately, as physical educators we tend to devote too little time to development of general basic skills and too much time to the development of sports-oriented skills. For example, this neglect is evidenced by the student who has had no motor training and as a result cannot coordinate his opposite extremities (bilaterality) to perform such tasks as lay-up shooting or bowling a ball. The irony of the misdirected methodological approach is that sound instruction in the basic motor skills will provide the necessary tools for more proficiency in complex sports skills because of the logical instructional sequence from the simple to the complex. Furthermore, such experiences will better prepare the child to perform the tasks of adult life.

The child who is motorically handicapped can be identified as one who evidences a "clumsy gait," poor coordination when performing complex tasks, and a tendency to be a social "isolate." Many may question the need for placing the poorly coordinated child in an individualized program, their contention being that as the child matures, he will overcome those awkward tendencies. Radler and Kephart[4] maintain that maturation does not insure the development of skill competence, but provides a readiness for—although not necessarily a competency in—motor skill development. The student must be exposed to a wide variety of tasks that are oriented toward the specific

---

[4] D. H. Radler with Newell C. Kephart, *Success Through Play* (New York: Harper & Row, Publishers, 1960), p. 12.

behavioral outcome expected of him. One has but to reflect on children he knows who are still lacking in motor efficiency to realize that these children need specialized instruction. When we also consider that the mentally retarded, emotionally disturbed, or neurologically impaired child frequently demonstrates motor skill inadequacies, we find sufficient justification for the inclusion of a battery of test items to assess motor skill ability.

The motor skill battery presented is a modification of the Temple University–Buttonwood Farms Project.[5] The material has been clustered in terms of factors the author hypothesizes are being measured, thus providing a meaningful procedure for gathering and analyzing raw data (see Appendix A, Basic Motor Skill Test). The test battery is recommended for use in the lower grades and with those students who have been referred for diagnostic testing for motor skills.

MOTOR SKILL BATTERY

General Test Directions: The tester should observe student performance carefully and record anecdotal remarks for all failures so that an individualized program can be prescribed (see Appendix A for scoring form).

A. Gross Body Coordination

TEST ITEM #1: Walk
  FACTOR: Gross body coordination
    Bilateral coordination of opposite arm and leg is required, i.e., left arm–right foot and right arm–left foot, plus subjective evaluation of gross body coordination.
  ATTEMPTS: 2
  SCORING: Pass or fail

TEST ITEM #2: Creep
  FACTOR: Gross body coordination
    Bilateral coordination of opposite hand and knee is required, i.e., left hand–right knee must come forward at the same time and right hand–left knee must come forward at the same time. Subject must creep (hands and knees) at least ten feet (5×10 mat) to pass.
  ATTEMPTS: 2
  SCORING: Pass or fail

TEST ITEM #3: Climb stairs
  FACTOR: Gross body coordination
    Subject must climb at least four consecutive steps (twelve-inch high) by using alternate footwork. Both feet must not come together on a step, but rather one foot will be on one step and the other foot on the next step; no support may be given. (Corridor stairs may be used.)

[5] Donald Hilsendager, Harold K. Jack, and Lester Mann, *Basic Motor Fitness Test for Emotionally Disturbed Children,* National Institute of Mental Health, Grant 1–T1–MH–8543–1, 5 (Philadelphia: Temple University, n.d.), pp. 7–11.

ATTEMPTS: 2

SCORING: Pass or fail

TEST ITEM #4: Skip

FACTOR: Gross body coordination
Subject must skip at least ten feet in a smooth manner (without extra hops). One practice attempt shall be permitted.

ATTEMPTS: 2

SCORING: Pass or fail

TEST ITEM #5: March in place

FACTOR: Gross body coordination
To pass, the subject must keep in cadence with the tester who claps a cadence of one clap per second (15 seconds) for the first attempt and two claps per second (15 seconds) for the second attempt.

ATTEMPTS: 2

SCORING: Pass or fail
Note: Subject's score on gross body coordination is the number of successful accomplishments in ten attempts. All of the gross body coordination skills should evidence total body coordination for a passing attempt.

B. Balance-Postural Orientation

TEST ITEM #6: Stand on both feet

FACTOR: Balance–postural orientation
Subject must stand with feet together, arms extended forward from shoulders at a 90° angle, and eyes closed for fifteen seconds. An unsuccessful attempt is recorded if the subject shifts his feet, or moves arms 15° from the 90° position (see Fig. 3–1).

ATTEMPTS: 3

SCORING: Pass or fail

FIGURE 3–1 Test Item #6: Standing on both feet. Courtesy of the Township of Ocean School District.

FIGURE 3–2 Test Item #9: Jumping with one foot leading. Courtesy of the Township of Ocean School District.

TEST ITEM #7: Standing on the right foot

FACTOR: Balance–postural orientation

Subject must stand on the right foot with the left foot off the floor and not touch any stable object for fifteen seconds (eyes open). Unsuccessful attempt if subject shifts right foot or touches left foot to right leg, foot, floor, or any other supporting structure before the elapse of fifteen seconds.

ATTEMPTS: 3

SCORING: Pass or fail

TEST ITEM #8: Standing on the left foot

FACTOR: Balance–postural orientation

Same directions as for test item #7 except feet are reversed.

ATTEMPTS: 3

SCORING: Pass or fail

TEST ITEM #9: Jumping with one foot leading

FACTOR: Balance–postural orientation

Subject must jump off eighteen-inch high step or bench with one foot in front of the other. No support is allowed and balance must be maintained on landing (no shift of feet). The tester should have the subject jump and land in an area immediately adjacent to the bench (see Fig. 3–2).

ATTEMPTS: 3

SCORING: Pass or fail

TEST ITEM #10: Jumping on both feet simultaneously

FACTOR: Balance–postural orientation

Same procedure as test item #9 except feet are side by side.

ATTEMPTS: 3

SCORING: Pass or fail

TEST ITEM #11: Stationary jump on both feet

FACTOR: Balance–postural orientation
Subject must jump on both feet for at least three jumps without stopping, losing balance, using a support, or stepping on or out of an 18-inch square.

ATTEMPTS: 3

SCORING: Pass or fail

TEST ITEM #12: Stationary hop on right foot

FACTOR: Balance–postural orientation
Subject must hop on the right foot for at least three hops without stopping, losing balance, using a support, or stepping on or out of an 18-inch square.

ATTEMPTS: 3

SCORING: Pass or fail

TEST ITEM #13: Stationary hop on left foot

FACTOR: Balance–postural orientation
Same procedure as test item #12 except the subject hops on left foot.

ATTEMPTS: 3

SCORING: Pass or fail
Note: Subject's composite score on balance–postural orientation is the number of successful accomplishments in twenty-four attempts.

C. Eye-Hand Coordination

TEST ITEM #14: Catch

FACTOR: Eye/hand coordination
To pass, the subject must catch a whiffle ball (the circumference of a softball) using only his hands. Juggling the ball, having it strike any part of the body other than the hands, or a drop constitutes a failure. The toss must be from a distance of eight feet and thrown in a soft underhand manner. The trajectory should be such that it does not rise higher than the subject's head and reaches the receiver at chest level.

ATTEMPTS: 3

SCORING: Pass or fail

TEST ITEM #15: Ball bounce and catch

FACTOR: Eye/hand coordination
The student must drop or push an eight-inch diameter utility ball to the ground and catch it on the rebound immediately with no intervening bounces. Juggling the ball, having it strike any part of the body (other than the hands), or a drop constitutes a failure.

ATTEMPTS: 3

SCORING: Pass or fail

TEST ITEM #16: Touching a ball swinging laterally

FACTOR: Eye/hand coordination
With dominant hand on shoulder (palm down, index finger extended, and hand motionless), the subject on command "touch" must touch laterally a

swinging whiffle ball (softball circumference) with the index finger on the side of the ball. The instructor holds the whiffle ball suspended on an eighteen-inch cord at mid-chest level and proceeds to swing the ball laterally. Commands are issued: (1) when the ball is at full arm extension across the midline; (2) when the ball is at the midline; and (3) when the ball is at full arm extension on the dominant side of the midline. An unsuccessful attempt is recorded if the subject delays response, touches the ball with other than the index finger, misses, or moves his head (see Fig. 3–3).

ATTEMPTS: 3

SCORING: Pass or fail

TEST ITEM #17:   Touching a ball swinging fore and aft

FACTOR: Eye/hand coordination

With dominant hand on hip (palm up, index finger extended, and head motionless), the subject on command "touch" must touch fore and aft a swinging whiffle ball (softball circumference) with index finger on the under surface of the ball. The instructor holds the whiffle ball suspended on an eighteen-inch cord at mid-chest level and issues commands: (1) when the ball is at full arm extension; (2) when the ball is at midpoint; and (3) when the ball is closest to the subject. An unsuccessful attempt is recorded if the subject delays response, touches the ball with other than the index finger, misses, or moves his head (see Fig. 3–4).

ATTEMPTS: 3

SCORING: Pass or fail

FIGURE 3–3 Test Item #16: Touching a ball swinging laterally. Courtesy of the Township of Ocean School District.

FIGURE 3–4 Test Item #17: Touching a ball swinging fore and aft. Courtesy of the Township of Ocean School District.

FIGURE 3–5   Test Item #20: Throwing with the right hand. Courtesy of the Township of Ocean School District.

TEST ITEM #18:   Bat a ball with one hand

FACTOR: Eye/hand coordination
Same procedure as test item #17 except that subject bats the ball with an open hand held in readiness between the waist and shoulder. An unsuccessful attempt is recorded if some part of the hand does not touch some part of the ball.

ATTEMPTS: 3

SCORING: Pass or fail

TEST ITEM #19:   Bat a ball with a bat

FACTOR: Eye/hand coordination
Same procedure as test item #17 except the subject bats the ball with a plastic whiffle ball bat which is held in readiness between the waist and the shoulder. An unsuccessful attempt is recorded if some part of the bat does not touch some part of the ball.

ATTEMPTS: 3

SCORING: Pass or fail

TEST ITEM #20:   Throwing with the right hand

FACTOR: Eye/hand accuracy
The subject throws a whiffle ball (softball circumference) at a target as designed by Johnson[6] (see Fig. 3–5). The subject may use either an overhand or underhand throwing motion; minimum throwing distance is ten feet. The ball must hit the target without previously touching the floor for a correct attempt.

SCORING: 3 points inner rectangle and lines; 2 points, middle rectangle and line; 1 point, outer rectangle and line (see Fig. 3–6).

ATTEMPTS: 3

SCORING: Total points for three attempts

[6] L. William Johnson, "Objective Test in Basketball for High School Boys," unpublished master's thesis, State University of Iowa, 1934.

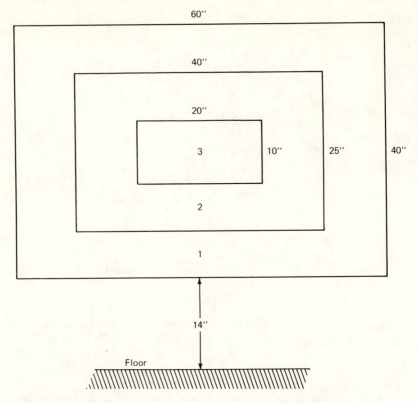

FIGURE 3–6 Johnson basketball accuracy target. Reproduced from L. William Johnson, "Objective Test in Basketball for High School Boys," unpublished master's thesis, State University of Iowa, 1934, by permission of the State University of Iowa.

TEST ITEM #21;   Throwing with the left hand

FACTOR: Eye/hand accuracy
Same procedure as test item #20 except that subject throws with the left hand.

ATTEMPTS: 3

SCORING: Total points for three attempts
Note: Subject's composite score on eye/hand accuracy is the total number of points in six attempts.

E. Eye-Foot Accuracy

TEST ITEM #22:   Kicking with the right foot

FACTOR: Eye/foot accuracy
Same procedure as test item #20 except the subject kicks a stationary volleyball at the target with his right foot. The ball must strike the target without previously touching the floor for a valid attempt.

ATTEMPTS: 3

SCORING: Total points for three attempts

TEST ITEM #23:   Kicking with the left foot

FACTOR: Eye/foot accuracy
Same procedure as test item #20 except the subject kicks a stationary volley-ball with his left foot.

ATTEMPTS: 3

SCORING: Total points for three attempts
Note: Subject's composite score on eye/foot accuracy is the total number of points scored in six attempts.

The procedure for compiling and analyzing the data will be presented in Chapter 5.

Physical Fitness

The advent of an era of affluence with all of its debilitating concomitants has seen the fitness level of our youth retrogress so much that our leaders in Washington have been openly concerned for the past decade. The President's Council on Youth Fitness[7] has urged the identification of the underdeveloped pupil; fifteen minutes of vigorous physical activity daily; and valid periodical testing to assess progress. The state of New Jersey[8] subsidizes and requires all local public school districts to identify, classify, and provide individualized instructional programs for children with handicaps or learning disabilities. Of the eleven classifiable handicaps, the child with lowered vitality is listed under "chronically ill."

Many experimental and case studies have been conducted using students classified as sub-par physically. Indications are that a majority of the students so classified made significant improvement when provided with intensified physical activity programs. In the remaining cases (in which students did not improve), it was found that a variety of other factors were causing the lowered physical vitality; medical referrals, in many instances, ameliorated the problem.

The proposed developmental program includes a category for those students who evidence low physical vitality, or are sub-par in terms of physical fitness. Clarke[9] defines physical fitness as encompassing muscular strength, muscular endurance, and circulo-endurance. Based on a factor analysis study, Fleishman[10] identified six components of fitness: explosive strength;

---

[7] President's Council on Youth Fitness, *Youth Physical Fitness; Suggested Elements of a School-Centered Program, Parts One and Two* (Washington, D.C.: U.S. Government Printing Office, 1961), inside cover page.

[8] New Jersey Department of Education, *Tentative Rules and Regulations Pertaining to Chapter 29 Laws of 1966* (Trenton, N.J.: Division of Curriculum and Instruction, 1966), pp. 74–76g.

[9] H. Harrison Clarke, *Application of Measurement to Health and Physical Education*, 4th ed. (Englewood Cliffs, N.J.: Prentice-Hall, Inc., 1967), p. 202.

[10] Edwin A. Fleishman, *The Structure and Measurement of Physical Fitness* (Englewood Cliffs, N.J.: Prentice-Hall, Inc., 1964), pp. 99–100.

extent flexibility; dynamic flexibility; gross body equilibrium; balance with visual cues; and speed of limb movement (his text should be in every physical educator's professional library since it gives a clear analysis of the major physical fitness test items and factors measured). The proposed program recommends the identification of students with low physical vitality on the basis of muscular strength, muscular endurance, and cardiorespiratory endurance (and gross body balance at the elementary level).

It is a truism that the test items included in a test battery will be determined by one's definition of physical fitness. However, two criteria are recommended when selecting valid, reliable, objective test items: the test item must be selected in terms of the specific fitness component to be measured and the norms that are derived from the data must be structured so that the assessments for all body types are valid. Both criteria pose problems because at present there are no clear-cut solutions.

In the Fleishman text,[11] a solution to test item selection is offered. The term *factor loading* is used to refer to how highly a test item correlates with a specific factor. For example, if one wanted to select a test item to measure the students' explosive strength (agility), should the "shuttle run" or the "standing broad jump" be included in the test battery? The factor analytic study reveals that the shuttle run has a factor loading of .77 as compared to the standing broad jump loading of .66. Thus, if one wanted a test item as a part of a test battery to measure explosive strength, the shuttle run should be selected, because the raw score derived from that test contributes most to the measurement of that factor. In other words, the shuttle run is more valid than the standing broad jump when measuring agility (according to the Fleishman study).

The second criteria to be considered poses a problem of greater magnitude. For years, physical educators have been plagued with the problem of designing test battery norms that can validly assess student performance in terms of a student's body structure. Is it fair to state that all boys must perform sixteen pull-ups at age 17 to score 100 percent? What about requiring all 17-year-old boys to run the 50-yard dash in 5.4 seconds in order to attain a score of 100 percent? These two norms are taken from the AAHPER Fitness Test,[12] the most widely used fitness test in the United States. I do not mean to condemn the AAHPER Fitness Test, but rather to focus attention on an existing problem. The AAHPER Fitness Test was an expedient solution to a pressing national problem, the design of a test that would establish functional, standardized norms for any school district in the country, but is it fair to expect all students of the same age to achieve the same fitness level?

[11] *Ibid.*, p. 66.
[12] Harold M. Barrow and Rosemary McGee, *A Practical Approach to Measurement in Physical Education* (Philadelphia: Lea & Febiger, 1964), pp. 193, 197.

What happens, psychologically, to the obese child who cannot perform at the expected level? Are there any solutions to the problem? At the present time, there are no practical, clear-cut solutions; however, the inclusion of the following suggestions will make the test battery norms more valid for determining individual student achievement levels:

1. Establish norms on the basis of the school population you are working with. Although national norms may be used for comparative purposes, they may well not be valid instruments in your situation and should not be relied on. For example, how many days of physical education per week are the national norms based on? How many days of physical education do your students have? What about the difference in the social and economic background of the two populations?

2. Establish norms by age rather than grade level. Most assuredly, the task involves more work, but the norms derived are more valid instruments of measurement since some grade levels have a "chronological age spread" of three to four years.

3. Develop norms based on standardized scores rather than on percentiles (see Chapter 5 for further discussion).

4. Reflect on and make adjustments for body structure when assessing performance on the basis of a student's composite standard score.

5. Select norms, when possible, that have been constructed in light of an individual's somatotype.

6. Construct a test battery that includes those components of fitness you want to measure.

7. Select test items with the highest factorial validity.

You must also consider practical problems before designing a test battery to identify those students who are sub-par physically. The test battery should be such that it can be administered in a reasonable amount of time and consist of test items selected in terms of available supplies, equipment and facilities.

Physical Fitness Test Battery, Grades K–8

The physical fitness test battery recommended for grades K–8 is a modification of the Buttonwood Farms Test[13] (see Appendix A, Physical Fitness Test Form, K–8). Individual scores are to be analyzed in conjunction with a student's somatotype; see Chapter 5 for detailed scoring procedures.

TEST ITEM #1: Walking on the tapered beam
  FACTOR: Gross body balance static/dynamic
      Subject walks the tapered balance beam (in shoes or sneakers), unassisted, by placing the heel of the forward foot against the toe of the rear foot. An attempt is terminated if the subject touches the floor or any other supporting

---

[13] Hilsendager, Jack, and Mann, *op. cit.*, pp. 11–15.

FIGURE 3–7 Test Item #1: Walking on the tapered beam. Courtesy of the Township of Ocean School District.

structure, does not touch heel to toe, or turns either foot at an angle to the direction of the beam. The student may be assisted to mount the beam (see Fig. 3-7).

ATTEMPTS: 2

SCORING: Average distance (in inches) covered in two attempts.

TEST ITEM #2: Push-dynamometer

FACTOR: Arm strength

The dynamometer is positioned at chest height with the dial face pointing away from the body of the subject. The subject grasps the handles, palms facing inward, and pushes as forcefully as possible; arms must be kept horizontal and no contact with the body is permitted.

ATTEMPTS: 2

SCORING: Record (in pounds) the higher score from two trials.

TEST ITEM #3: Pull-dynamometer

FACTOR: Arm strength

Same procedure as for test item #2 except the subject pulls on the handles of the push/pull attachment.

ATTEMPTS: 2

SCORING: Record (in pounds) the higher score from two trials.

TEST ITEM #4: Sit-ups (maximum 100)

FACTOR: Abdominal strength

The subject executes sit-ups from a supine position, with hands behind his head. The tester holds the ankles of the subject so that the soles of the feet are flat on the floor. The attempt is terminated when the subject removes his hands from behind his head or rests momentarily.

ATTEMPTS: 1

SCORING: Record number of sit-ups performed by rising to vertical position.

TEST ITEM #5: Standing broad jump
FACTOR: Explosive leg strength
Subject stands with toes up to but not touching the starting line and jumps forward simultaneously on both feet. Crouching and swinging of arms are to be encouraged as correct jumping technique, but any form is acceptable. Measurement is taken from the back of the starting line to the point nearest the starting line which is contacted by some part of the jumper's body.
ATTEMPTS: 2
SCORING: Record (in inches) the better of the two jumps.

TEST ITEM #6: Modified Harvard Step Test
FACTOR: Cardiorespiratory endurance
Take subject's resting pulse rate for sixty seconds (after he has been seated and resting for ten minutes). Check pulse rate by placing index and/or fore-finger on wrist artery or carotid artery (below jawbone). Student must perform a four-count step test thirty times in one minute. Stepping procedure: using a twelve-inch bench or step, have the student place left foot up on the count of one; right foot up on the count of two (standing straight); left foot down on the count of three; and right foot down on the count of four. Repeat for one minute. To establish correct rhythm, the tester should verbally count cadence, clap hands and strive to have the subject achieve eight cycles in 15 seconds, 15 cycles in 30 seconds, 23 cycles in 45 seconds, and 30 cycles in one minute.

Immediately after the test, have the subject rest for one minute; then take his pulse rate again. Endurance index equals resting pulse rate minus pulse rate after exercise. If the subject fails to complete thirty cycles or cannot keep in cadence record "did not complete."

Note: The above directions are for grades K–3. For grades 4–8, use the same testing procedure but increase step height to sixteen inches, perform the step test for two minutes, and take the pulse rate after the exercise after a two-minute rest period.
ATTEMPTS: 1
SCORING: Record (1) pulse rate before and after and (2) endurance index.

Physical Fitness Test Battery, Grades 9–12

The physical fitness test battery recommended for use at the high school level consists of four modifications of the Rogers' Physical Fitness Index Test.[14] The concept of the original PFI Test was accepted primarily because it provided a valid means of comparing a student's physical fitness status (total strength) with norms based on his sex, age, and weight. Thus, the student's score is compared to a norm which represents what he should achieve. Rogers[15] patterned his formula after Terman's I.Q. formula by

[14] Frederick Rand Rogers, *Physical Capacity Tests in the Administration of Physical Education* (New York: Bureau of Publications, Teachers College, Columbia University, 1926).
[15] Frederick Rand Rogers, "The Strength Index, the Physical Fitness Index and Their Uses," Presentation to a Symposium on Fitness at Springfield College, Massachusetts, July 21, 1961.

reasoning that just as a person's intelligence quotient could be attained by dividing his mental age by his chronological age, a person's physical quotient could be attained by dividing his total strength by the norm for his age and weight. Clarke[16] gives a detailed account of the original test battery.

However, as originally stated, four modifications of the PFI Test were proposed because they reduced administration time with a minimal loss of validity. Clarke and Carter[17] and Widness[18] computed regression equations for each of the test batteries. The multiple correlations between Rogers' original strength index and the strength index batteries of the four modifications ranged between .977 and .998.

The administration of the PFI Test procedure requires leg and back dynamometers which are expensive, if purchased commercially. However, Clarke has adapted the tensiometer, a device designed to measure the tension of aircraft control cables, for use in testing the strength of individual muscle groups. This same principle can be used to adapt tensiometers for use in measuring leg and back strength; however, these instruments are also expensive. The Physical Education Department at Temple University[19] has constructed relatively inexpensive leg and back dynamometers by adapting tensiometers purchased from government surplus supplies at a very nominal price.

The formulae and procedures for administering the modified PFI tests are provided as guidelines. Refer to Clarke's text for complete details.

REGRESSION EQUATIONS

Junior high school boys[20]

$$\text{Strength Index } (SI) = 1.12 \text{ (leg lift)} + .99 \text{ (arm strength)} + 5.19 \text{ (right grip)} + 129$$

Junior high school girls[21]

$$\text{Strength Index } (SI) = 1.04 \text{ (leg lift)} + 1.03 \text{ (arm strength)} + 1.37 \text{ (back lift)} + 175$$

Senior high school boys[22]

$$\text{Strength Index } (SI) = 1.07 \text{ (leg lift)} + 1.06 \text{ (arm strength)} + 1.42 \text{ (back lift)} + 194$$

[16] Clarke, *op. cit.*, pp. 145–60.

[17] H. Harison Clarke and Gavin H. Carter, "Oregon Simplification of the Strength and Physical Fitness Indices for Upper Elementary, Junior High and Senior High School Boys," *Research Quarterly*, XXIX, No. 4 (March, 1959), 3.

[18] Joanne Widness, "Simplification of the Rogers Strength and Physical Fitness Indices for Junior and Senior High School Girls," unpublished master's thesis, University of Oregon, August, 1964.

[19] Joseph Oxendine, "Modified Leg and Back Dynamometer," Biokinetics Laboratory Department of Health and Physical Education, Temple University, Philadelphia.

[20] Clarke and Carter, *loc. cit.*

[21] Widness, *op. cit.*

[22] Clarke and Carter, *loc. cit.*

Senior high school girls[23]

$$\text{Strength Index } (SI) = 1.04 \text{ (leg lift)} + 1.08 \text{ (arm strength)} + 1.46 \text{ (back lift)} + 125$$

Arm strength formula[24]

$$A.S. = (\text{pull-ups} + \text{push-ups}) \left(\frac{\text{Weight}}{10} + \text{Height} - 60'' \right)^{25}$$

Achieved strength index

Score attained by use of the proper regression formula.

Normal strength index

Score indicated by referring to proper norm chart according to sex, age, and weight (norm charts based on belt usage).

Physical fitness index[26]

$$PFI = \frac{\text{Achieved } SI}{\text{Normal } SI} \times 100$$

Factors measured

Leg lift: static leg strength
Back lift: static back strength
Pull-ups and push-ups: dynamic arm strength
Right grip: static grip strength

Computational procedure

For illustrative purposes, the *PFI* scores of two hypothetical senior boys will be computed.

John Jones is 17 years old, weighs 140 pounds and is 68″ tall.   Fred Smith is 18 years old, weighs 220 pounds and is 74″ tall.

	JOHN		FRED	
	raw scores	*weighted scores*	*raw scores*	*weighted scores*
Pull-ups	10		8	
Dips	8		7	
Arm strength	396	419	540	572
Leg strength	1000	1070	1450	1552
Back strength	300	426	400	568
Constant		194		194
Norm *SI*	2256		3986	

[23] Widness, *op. cit.*
[24] Clarke, *op. cit.*, p. 156.
[25] Girls perform modified push-ups and pull-ups; boys perform dips in lieu of push-ups.
[26] Clarke, *op. cit.*, p. 157.

$$\text{Arm strength} = (\text{pull-ups} + \text{push-ups})\left(\frac{\text{Weight}}{10} + \text{Height} - 60''\right)$$

John's: *Fred's:*

$$A.S. = (10 + 8)\left(\frac{140}{10} + 68'' - 60''\right) \quad A.S. = (8 + 7)\left(\frac{220}{10} + 74'' - 60''\right)$$

$A.S. = (18)(22)$ $A.S. = (15)(36)$

Arm strength $= 396$ Arm strength $= 540$

Note: In spite of the fact that John achieved a greater total number of pull-ups and dips, Fred attained a higher arm strength score. The higher arm strength score is attributable to that portion of the formula which acts as a correction factor in terms of height and weight. Thus, the scores attained are reasonably valid for assessing the arm strength of students of different body structures. Furthermore, the scores are comparable and it is reasonably safe to assume that Fred possesses greater arm strength for his height and weight than John does for his height and weight.

$$\text{Achieved } SI = 1.07 \text{ (leg lift)} + 1.06 \text{ (arm strength)} + 1.42 \text{ (back lift)} + 194$$

John's:

Achieved $SI = 1.07(1000) + 1.06(396) + 1.42(300) + 194$

Achieved $SI = 1070 + 418 + 426 + 194$

Achieved $SI = 2108$

Fred's:

Achieved $SI = 1.07(1450) + 1.06(540) + 1.42(400) + 194$

Achieved $SI = 1552 + 572 + 568 + 194$

Achieved $SI = 2886$

$$PFI = \frac{\text{Achieved } SI}{\text{Normal } SI} \times 100$$

John's: *Fred's:*

$$PFI = \frac{2108}{2256} \times 100 \qquad\qquad PFI = \frac{2886}{3986} \times 100$$

$PFI = 93$ $PFI = 72$

Note: In the 1920s, the average *PFI* score was 100; today the average *PFI* score is approximately 115. Thus, although Fred has a greater total strength, he has a lower physical fitness index for his age, height, and weight than John. In fact, Fred's *PFI* score places him in approximately the bottom

1 percent when compared to national norms, and makes him a prime candidate for the developmental program.

Since the *PFI* test measures only muscular strength and muscular endurance, it is recommended that the modification of the Harvard Step Test, included in the K–8 fitness battery, be used at this level also to assess cardiorespiratory endurance. The original version developed by Brouha[27] was designed for college men; the test performance time was five minutes. The modified version, developed by the author, is practical for grades K–12 and takes only two minutes to administer.[28] The latter has been found to be extremely practical in regular physical education classes at the high school level since existing gymnasium bleachers can be used to administer the test to the entire class at one time. Moreover, whereas the five-minute test was found to be too demanding physiologically, the two-minute test can be completed by almost every student.

TEST ITEM: Modified step test

FACTOR: Cardiorespiratory endurance

FORMULA: Endurance, or recovery index = resting pulse rate — pulse rate after exercise.

$$\text{EXAMPLE: } R.I. = 80 - 110$$
$$= -30$$

In the example listed, the student had a resting rate of 80 and a pulse rate of 110 two minutes after the exercise; thus his recovery index was −30. The rationale for the test is that a pulse rate taken after a two-minute rest period (following a two-minute exercising regimen) should return to the initial resting pulse rate; a score of "zero" would be indicative of an optimum level of physiological fitness. Conversely, the greater the discrepancy between the two pulse rates, the poorer the level of physiological fitness.

Another test item practical for use as a measure of endurance is the *endurance ratio.*[29] Basically, the test involves having a student run a short distance and then, a longer distance; the ratio derived between the two times is, theoretically, a measure of the student's endurance. For example, a student's time for the 50-yard dash is 6 seconds and for the 600-yard run is 80 seconds.

Endurance ratio formula

$$E.R. = \frac{(\text{time for 60 yards})(10)}{\text{time for 600 yards}} \times 100$$

---

[27] Lucien Brouha, "The Step Test: A Simple Method of Measuring Physical Fitness for Muscular Work in Young Men," *Research Quarterly*, XIV, No. 1 (March, 1943), 31.

[28] Recommended bench heights are as follows: K–3, 12″; 4–8, 16″; and 9–12, 18″. Administration times: K–8, one minute; 9–12, two minutes.

[29] Clarke, *op. cit.*, p. 200.

$$E.R. = \frac{(6)(10)}{80} \times 100$$

$$E.R. = 75$$

The rationale for the endurance index implies that if one can run 60 yards in 6 seconds (and possesses perfect "staying power") he should be able to traverse 600 yards in 10×6, or 60 seconds; thus, the utopian score would be an endurance ratio of 100.

Nutritional Status

There is sufficient documentary evidence to ascertain that obesity not only shortens life but also contributes to cardiovascular disease, diabetes mellitus, and other degenerative diseases.[30] Estimates have indicated that obesity, depending upon the degree, increases the risk of mortality by 40 to 70 percent. In addition, empirical studies refute the misconception about a child losing his "baby fat" as he gets older. On the contrary, in most cases the obese child tends to grow up to become the obese adult. Wyden gives some indication of the significance of the obesity problem in his book *The Overweight Society*.[31]

There is a strong justification for including a weight control program in the developmental phase of physical education based on the generally accepted premise that increased physical activity deters the onset of obesity. How can this be better accomplished than via a diversified physical education program? Naturally the elimination of obesity requires in addition to physical activity a complete change in one's pattern of living in terms of practices, habits, and attitudes (assuming the problem is based on improper eating habits rather than a medical or emotional origin). Thus, instruction should involve student learning experiences related to proper nutrition, proper daily habits, and physical activity. There is no discipline in the school curriculum wherein such services can be provided other than via an individualized developmental physical education program.

To objectify the program one must also identify each child who evidences nutritional deficiencies. The recommended proposal is that those students who are a minimum of 20 percent above or below their predicted body weight be identified as nutritionally deficient and admitted to the D&A program. The obese usually evidence a deficiency in protein intake; the underweight, a deficiency in carbohydrate and protein intake. However, at this point a distinction must be made between "obesity" and "overweight." A child may

---

[30] Fred V. Hein and Allan J. Ryan, "The Contributions of Physical Activity to Physical Health," *Research Quarterly*, XXXI, No. 2 (May, 1960), 263–85.

[31] Peter Wyden, *The Overweight Society* (New York: Pocket Books, Inc., 1966).

be overweight and not be obese. The term "overweight" implies weight in excess of the requirement of one's body structure but not necessarily an excess of adipose tissue. Many athletes tend to be overweight due to the emphasis on weight training programs which accelerate muscle tissue development. Thus, one's identification of the obese individual involves the use of the aforementioned definition, plus an evaluation of the adipose tissue deposits.

The determination of the nutritional status on the basis of age-height-weight tables is totally inadequate because body structure and body composition, two major factors, are not considered. The use of these tables is, at the very best, a poor estimation of nutritional status. Furthermore, as with the use of the Snellen Eye Chart, proper diagnostic procedures can be deterred or eliminated on the basis of an erroneous diagnosis. The malnourished child cannot be identified on the basis of his age, height, and weight, nor necessarily can the obese, as one needs to assess body composition in light of body structure.

The Wetzel Grid[32] provides consideration for the child's physique as well as for age, height, and weight. Periodic assessments afford a means of detecting growth and developmental patterns on any of nine body structure channels. However, the grid does not provide an objective method of evaluating body composition.

The proposed means of identifying those students who should be admitted to the developmental program for nutritional deficiencies is based on the use of the Pryor Width–Weight Technique[33] and skinfold measurements. The Pryor method predicts body weight according to bone structure by height, straight-arm caliper measurements of chest and hip width, and referral to the proper chart. Tables are available for both sexes for ages 1 to 41, and each age category is further subdivided into three charts based on narrow, medium, or broad chest. Predicted body weight is ascertained by referring to the proper body structure chart based on sex, age, and chest measurement and noting the weight that is indicated at the point where height and hip measurements intersect. Pryor's tables present a detailed procedure for predicting nutritional status on the basis of sex, age, height, weight, and hip and chest widths.

Whereas the use of width-weight measurements provides a means of assessing nutritional status on the basis of bone structure, the Lange Skinfold Caliper[34] provides for an assessment on the basis of adipose tissue. Brozek[35]

[32] Barrow and McGee, *op. cit.*, pp. 345–50.
[33] Helen Pryor, *Width-Weight Tables*, 2nd rev. ed. (Stanford, Calif.: Stanford University Press, 1936), 15 pp.
[34] Manufactured by Cambridge Scientific Instruments, Inc., 18 Poplar Street, Cambridge, Maryland.
[35] Josep Brozek, ed., *Body Measurements and Human Physique* (Detroit: Wayne State University Press, 1956), p. 10.

recommends measuring fatty deposits at three sites: the upper arm, the tip of the inner border of the scapula (shoulder blade), and the side of the waist at the umbilical level (see Clarke's text for the procedures[36]).

The determination of whether or not a student should be scheduled on a nutritional basis involves:

1. Weighing the student in a gym suit to determine his actual body weight.

2. Ascertaining the student's predicted body weight on the basis of width–weight measurements.

3. Dividing the student's weight in excess or deficient pounds by his predicted weight.

4. Recording the result of the division as a percentage.

5. Determining skinfold measurements for upper arm, scapula area, and side of waist.

6. Making a final decision regarding classification as a result of nutritional index, plus skinfold measurements.

Example: student's actual weight = 240
student's predicted weight = 200
weight above predicted weight = 40.

$$\text{Nutritional Index} = \frac{40}{200} = 20\%.$$

On the basis of the example, the decision of whether or not to classify the student would be borderline. Final disposition would be based on skinfold measurements.

Regardless of one's preference for assessing the nutritional status of students, the important point is that a weight control program for boys and a figure control program for girls be implemented. Past experience has indicated that both sexes, particularly at the high school level, are extremely conscious of their physical self-image. Intrinsic motivation has been so intense and results so gratifying that the weight/figure control program at Ocean Township High School has undoubtedly been the most successful phase of the total D&A program. As a result it has provided the program with its best means of sound public relations. One senior girl stated to the writer that of all her physical education experiences, the figure control program "made the most sense" and was most meaningful. Another member of the distaff sex related that she lost 40 pounds and as a consequence made a positive psychological adjustment; formerly a "social wallflower," she converted to a "social butterfly." Similar responses came from boys who improved their physiques. To give some further indication of the value of a

---

[36] Clarke, *op. cit.*, pp. 95–96.

nutritionally oriented program, a case history of a former student will be presented.

Mary has had an obesity problem since early childhood. She attended the public elementary grades until the school required all students to wear gym suits during physical activity; at that point, her parents transferred her to a private school that did not require elementary students to dress for physical education. Upon graduation, Mary was informed she would be required to wear a gym suit when she entered high school. (During the intervening years her problem became more severe. Greater depression led to compulsive eating and a constant weight increase.)

She became emotionally upset and adamantly informed her parents she would not go to school. Via a discussion with a guidance counselor on the Ocean Township High School staff, the father was made aware of the individualized figure control classes for girls. Upon further discussion with Mary, she agreed to enter the high school if she could take developmental physical education in lieu of the regular program. She further agreed to wear a gym suit for all classes. The Guidance Department first scheduled Mary for D&A and then filled in the rest of her program. During the first year, Mary lost approximately 30 pounds and it was quite evident, both physically and psychologically. Her parents stated she made a complete metamorphosis! She became "clothes conscious" and seldom stayed home to watch television (her former passion).

I wish the sequel to the story could reflect a further decrease in weight, but it was not so. Mary regained most of the weight during the subsequent summer. It was obvious she had learned correct habits and practices, but she apparently suffered a relapse in terms of her attitude toward physical activity and eating habits.

Although all attempts to improve the eating habits of malnourished and obese children are not successful, it is quite obvious that the weight-control program has considerable merit and should be given a trial. This could well be the proper starting point for the initiation of a complete D&A program.

Body Mechanics

Sound body mechanics, often described as "efficiency of movement" or "posture training," implies the need for the proper segmental alignment of all body parts so that the tasks of daily living can be performed without undue stress or fatigue. Because the parts of the skeletal structure are interdependent and are adversely affected by gravitational forces, physical education programs should include learning experiences that focus on the development of proper practice, habits, and attitudes regarding body carriage. In addition, specific exercises that develop the antigravity muscles should be included in every preactivity warm-up period.

The term *body mechanics* is used here because it is specific in that it relates to efficient use of the body and is also general in that it infers dynamic as well as static action. (When the term *posture* is used, it is to be understood that it implies dynamic as well as static posture.) In other words, a unit on the development of proper body mechanics should include the proper use of the body in performing a variety of tasks that have carryover value for daily living. For example, girls must be made aware of the effect of wearing high heels (shifting the center of gravity forward) on lower back pain potential, or the improper lifting of an object from the floor while keeping the knees locked.

The need for incorporating a unit on body mechanics in the developmental program is justifiable. Experience has proven that poor body mechanics, lowered physical vitality, and nutritional deficiencies go hand in hand, necessitating an individualized program prescribed to ameliorate all of these problems. Moreover, a commonplace ailment today is the "lower back syndrome" which afflicts a good many people in all walks of life and which is indicative of the need to inculcate our youth with good body mechanics practices and attitudes. The alleviation of this problem for the next generation of adults necessitates the inclusion of a unit on proper body mechanics in developmental physical education.

According to Clarke,[37] tests for identification of those with body mechanics problems may be divided into two categories: subjective posture appraisals and objective posture appraisals. Of the two techniques, objective evaluations involve the use of specialized apparatus, photography, and sometimes both. Cureton's Posture Measurement Test[38] involves the use of the conformateur, the spinograph, and the silhouetteograph (later reduced to the first and third instruments). Other objective posture evaluation instruments were designed by MacEwan and Howe[39] and Wickens and Kiphuth.[40]

The Iowa Posture Test provides a means of subjectively assessing dynamic posture on the basis of an ordinal scale and thus easily screening students for functional problems. The appraisal technique provides a means of assessing foot mechanics, standing position, walking, sitting, and stooping to pick up an object[41]:

A three-point scale could be used; 3, good; 2, fair; and 1, poor. Standing and walking posture would doubtless be included. Use of the feet in walking is more easily rated separately from the general rating of walking. The additional items to be included in the test would probably be chosen from activities such as running, stair climbing, sitting, stooping, reaching overhead, carrying a load, pushing, or pulling.

In preparing for the test ten chairs are placed in line, one in front of the other,

37 *Ibid.*, pp. 118–136.

38 Thomas K. Cureton, "The Validity of Antero-Posterior Spinal Measurements," *Research Quarterly*, II, No. 3 (October, 1931), 101.

39 C. G. MacEwan and E. C. Howe, "An Objective Method of Grading Posture," *Research Quarterly*, III, No. 3 (October, 1932), 144.

40 Stuart Wickens and Oscar W. Kiphuth, "Body Mechanics Analysis of Yale University Freshmen," *Research Quarterly*, VIII, No. 4 (December, 1937), p. 38.

41 Reprinted from M. Gladys Scott and Esther French, *Measurement and Evaluation in Physical Education* (Dubuque, Iowa: William C. Brown Company, Publishers, 1959), pp. 418, 420–21, by permission of the authors.

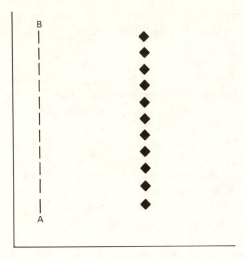

FIGURE 3–8   Arrangement of a class for body mechanics test. The area between A and B = the area in which the examiner moves while he observes each student. The space between the dotted lines and the chairs is for the students' use in performing activities for the rating. Reproduced from M. Gladys Scott and Esther French, *Measurement and Evaluation in Physical Education* (Dubuque, Iowa: William C. Brown Company, Publishers, 1959), p. 418, by permission of the authors.

with a little space between. There should be some open floor space beside them. Names of squad members are entered on the score sheet; when the test is given, students are seated in the same order as on the list and they remain in the same order throughout the test. Adequate rating can be given only if the students are dressed in swimming suits or dance leotards, and are barefooted. The examiner stands to one side of the row of chairs [see Fig. 3–8].

Procedure in Rating Posture

1. Each student in turn walks a few steps toward the examiner, turns and walks away again. This gives opportunity for judging the foot alignment and pronation.

2. Each student in turn walks a few steps forward (with side to the examiner). This gives opportunity to examine for heel contact, weight transfer, and toe drive.

3. Each student stands in line while the examiner moves down the line rating standing posture.

4. The students walk two or three at a time back and forth beside the line of chairs. The examiner rates the walking posture. Having more than one walk at a time helps to avoid self-consciousness and unnatural gait.

5. Students sit in the chair in a natural sitting position for rating. Each rises and then sits again to be judged on balance and movements.

6. Movement on stairs should be both up and down. The test may be given on real stairs, preferably wide ones for a better view and to accommodate two persons at a time; or it may be given on stairs constructed for this use in the gymnasium.

Other items in the test can be set up in a similar manner, preferably with some properties or a setting to make movements seem natural. Whereas the Iowa Test screens on the basis of dynamic posture, the New York Posture

Rating Test,[42] among others, focuses appraisal on the static aspects of proper body mechanics. The New York Posture Rating Chart and test directions are reproduced in Fig. 3–9.

The recommended procedure for identifying students with postural abnormalities is a hybrid version of the New York Screening Test and the Iowa Test. The proposed test thus incorporates the assessment of both static and dynamic body mechanics. Although the appraisal is actually classified as a subjective screening device, objectivity is attained via use of an ordinal scale. Empirical studies conducted for the past eleven years at Wall High School[43] and Ocean Township High School[44] have revealed objectivity coefficients among staff members and between staff members and school physicians of .80 to .90. These coefficients were based on the results of several experienced physical educators who screened the same subjects and comparisons between staff referrals, made on the basis of screening, and the school physician's subsequent decisions.

The values of the recommended identification procedure are:

1. An overall appraisal or cut-off score can be determined for static posture.

2. Individual aspects of static body alignment can be appraised.

3. Dynamic as well as static factors can be considered.

4. Test administration time is practical for school use (approximately 20 to 25 students can be screened in a 50-minute period).

5. The need for specialized testing instruments is minimal.

Obviously, the procedure has limitations. Shall precious activity time be used to screen subjects? Is it not true that the subject's different body positions will affect test reliability and objectivity, making subjective judgments questionable? Although both questions must be answered "yes," the problems can be resolved. Students need not be screened every year but only in grades 3, 6, and 9. Students transferring from other school districts should be examined as part of the admission procedure. The combining of classes or the temporary excusing of teachers from extra-duty assignments are means of freeing staff members for the time needed.

Although studies indicate techniques used for appraising sound body mechanics are questionable in terms of reliability and objectivity, it is contended that stringent appraisal guidelines and experienced staff members will minimize these problems. Further, the appraisal instrument recommended is only a screening device for detecting possible abnormalities; final identification is based on the follow-up examination by the school physician.

[42] *New York State Physical Fitness Test: For Boys and Girls, Grades 4–12* (Albany, N.Y.: New York State Education Department, 1958).

[43] Wall High School, *Posture Screening Program, 1960–1964*, Wall Township, New Jersey.

[44] Ocean Township High School, *Posture Screening Program, 1965–1971*, Oakhurst, New Jersey.

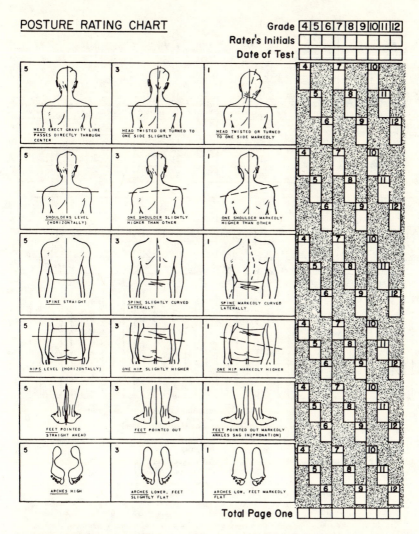

POSTURE RATING CHART

Grade 4 5 6 7 8 9 10 11 12

Rater's Initials

Date of Test

Total Page One

FIGURE 3–9 New York Posture Rating Chart and test directions. Courtesy of New York State Education Department.

Recommended screening procedures for identifying students with potential body mechanics problems involves the following series of steps:

1. Procure New York Posture Rating Charts from Bardeen's, Inc.[45] and record students' names on individual sheets prior to class.

2. Use constructed posture grid or Symmetrigraf[46] to screen students. Also have

---

[45] "New York Posture Rating Charts," Form H–27, Bardeen's, Inc., Syracuse, N.Y.
[46] "Symmetrigraf," Reedco, Inc., 5 Easterly Avenue, Auburn, N.Y.

Mo ___ 19___	Mo ___ 19___	Mo ___ 19___	Mo ___ 19___	Mo ___ 19___
Yrs___ Mos___	Yrs___ Mos___	Yrs___ Mos___	Yrs___ Mos___	Yrs___ Mos___
Ft ___ In___	Ft ___ In___	Ft ___ In___	Ft ___ In___	Ft ___ In___
lbs ___	lbs ___	lbs ___	lbs ___	lbs ___

raw score	achievem't level	raw score	achievem't level	raw score	achievem't level	raw score	achievem't level	raw score	achievem't level
P		P		P		P		P	
Ac		Ac		Ac		Ac		Ac	
St		St		St		St		St	
Ag		Ag		Ag		Ag		Ag	
Sp		Sp		Sp		Sp		Sp	
B		B		B		B		B	
E		E		E		E		E	
SUM=		SUM=		SUM=		SUM=		SUM=	

PROFILE   PROFILE   PROFILE   PROFILE   PROFILE

P Ac St Ag Sp B E

CUMULATIVE RECORD CHART

For Use with the

New York State Physical Fitness Test (1958 Edition)

of the

New York State Education Department

INSTRUCTIONS

The *Cumulative Record Chart* provides a convenient grade by grade record of pupil status and progress with respect to total physical fitness as measured by the New York State Physical Fitness Test.

The pupil's *total physical fitness level* in each grade is indicated by a solid horizontal line drawn across the profile at the appropriate place on the achievement level scale.

A pattern of the pupil's relative strengths and weaknesses is indicated by a solid heavy line connecting the series of points on the seven vertical lines, showing the achievement level for each of the seven components.

The shaded area on the profile chart represents the levels attained by the middle 50 percent or average group of New York State pupils. The white portion below and above the shaded area represents the physical fitness levels of pupils in the upper and lower quarters of the grade.

FIGURE 3–9 (cont.)

available a tray with a foam-rubber insert filled with a foot disinfectant solution; a chair; a stadiometer; and a reasonably bulky object. See Fig. 3–10 for the procedural set-up for equipment.

3. Students to be tested (maximum of five at a time) should line up alphabetically; as one finishes, he returns to class and sends in the next student. While they wait, boys remove gym shoes, stockings, and shirts and don shorts, and girls remove shoes and stockings and don bathing suits.

4. The testing sequence involves: height and weight check by an assistant, posture

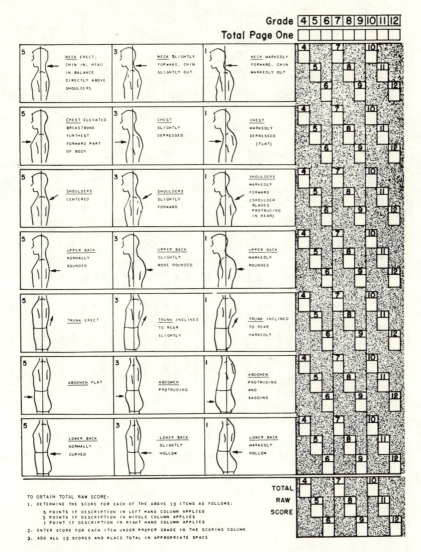

FIGURE 3–9 (cont.)

screening to detect static posture (use foot bath solution to provide imprint for detecting flat feet and as a disinfectant); and walking to a chair, sitting, and rising, and lifting and placing an object on the floor as a means of assessing dynamic posture.

5. The student's total score is a composite of the 13-item New York Posture Rating Test plus anecdotal comments regarding the Iowa Test items.

Note: Although the 13-item test is scored on a 5–3–1 basis, the recommended

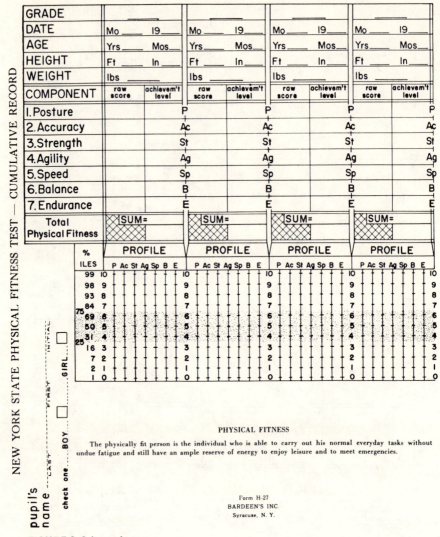

FIGURE 3–9 (cont.)

procedure is to score on a basis of 7–4–1. A perfect score on the New York Test is 65; a maximum score under the proposed procedure would be 91 (the addition of 9 points to all raw scores gives a potential maximum score of 100). This adjustment tends to make the scores more meaningful to the students since they like to view scores in terms of the arbitrary 100 standard.

6. Students with scores of 70 or below, a single-item score of 1, or a composite of a borderline score on the New York Posture Screening Test and poor functional performance in walking, sitting and rising, and raising and lowering an object are to be recommended for a posture examination by the school physician.

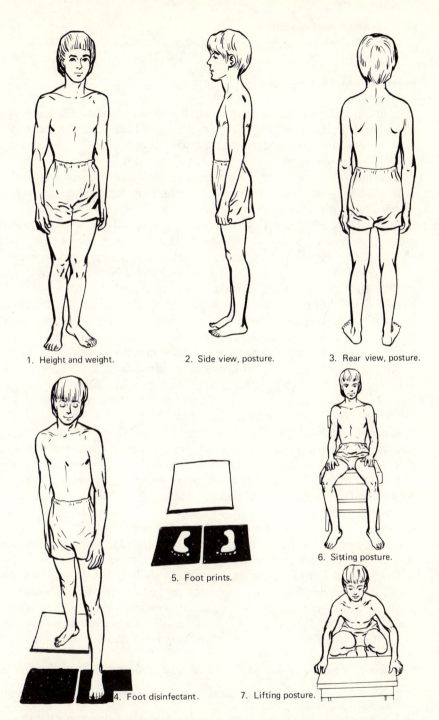

1. Height and weight.

2. Side view, posture.

3. Rear view, posture.

5. Foot prints.

6. Sitting posture.

4. Foot disinfectant.

7. Lifting posture.

FIGURE 3–10 Body mechanics screening procedure. Courtesy of the Township of Ocean School District.

Perceptual-Motor Development

During the 1960s a series of research studies were conducted relating to the child with learning disabilities. Studies investigated the characteristics of the slow learner and the content and methodological approaches to learning.

During this period more and more attention had been directed toward the relationship of motor activity to intellectual achievement. Some maintain that proper motor development is a necessary prerequisite for intelligence and that learning takes place via a continuum: motor development, perceptualization, conceptualization.[47] Others contend that a "prescribed diet" of motor activities will eliminate perceptual disorders. Finally, some theorists claim that visuoauditory training is a panacea for problems afflicting the slow learner.

Many educators are incorporating comprehensive perceptual-motor programs into the curriculum and making rash statements regarding values to be derived. At the present time, the evidence about the value of such programs is inconclusive. One study cannot substantiate or negate an entire theory. Rather, repeated replications of a study which reveal consistent findings must be conducted before a valid generalization can be made.

Another problem is the lack of a uniform definition of the term *perceptual-motor*. If a select group of educators is polled, a variety of responses will be given. In fact, some educators may not even accept the term perceptual-motor, but may offer such alternatives as "motor-perceptual," "psychomotor," "cognitively oriented," or "perceptual-movement." Getman[48] clarifies the problem by defining perceptual-movement in operational terms. He maintains that the total involvement of the child requires two or more information systems functioning at the same time, one of which is movement, the others being visual, auditory, tactile, gustatory, olfactory, or kinesthetic; and the process of making a decision. If we apply this definition to many of the existing studies, we will find that they fail to meet one or both criteria. Of critical importance is the fact that the child be required to make his own decision as a result of his experience.

Some well-designed experiments, empirical studies, and general observations indicate perceptual-motor programs can benefit the child with learning disabilities. It is generally agreed that as the handicapped child improves his fitness level and motor ability he is more readily accepted by his peer group. In addition, a study by Ishmail and Gruber[49] revealed a significant increase

---

[47] Newell C. Kephart, *Learning Disability: An Educational Adventure* (West Lafayette, Ind.: Kappa Delta Pi Press, 1968), pp. 19–32.

[48] G. N. Getman, "Lecture: Perceptual-Movement Programming," E.D.A.–AAHPER workshop, Philadelphia, Pa., April, 1971.

[49] A. H. Ishmail and J. J. Gruber, *Motor Aptitude and Intellectual Performance* (Columbus, Ohio: Charles E. Merrill Books, Inc., 1967), p. 190.

in academic achievement scores when motor activities were designed so that the child was also cognitively involved. Even though, as previously stated, one study does not justify the acceptance of a generalization, it does seem logical that increased involvement will result in increased benefits. Thus, a skill taught in a rote fashion will result in rote learning, whereas perceptual–motor–cognitive involvement will result in the total development of the child. Kephart worded it succinctly when he stated, "what is involved here is not movement for the sake of movement but rather purposeful movement."[50]

Behavioral scientists, psychologists, and special educators have furnished the impetus for the psychomotor movement. Physical educators have not generally grasped the significance and implications of a physical education program based on perceptual–motor–cognitive involvement, yet for years they have been trying to eliminate the misconception that man consists of a dichotomy, physical and mental. Physical educators probably have the best opportunity of all educators to plan programs that integrate physical and mental activities and thus involve each child. Furthermore, physical educators should diligently research the problem, implement innovative programs on the basis of valid generalizations, develop valid and reliable instruments for identifying slow learners, and determine the longitudinal effects of psychomotor activities on these handicapped children.

A developmental program for children with learning disabilities, as well as for other students, should include the sequential structuring of units based on the perceptual–motor–cognitive approach (especially at the elementary level). Careful analysis indicates that such a program would be founded on logical skill development from the simple to the complex. Furthermore, as a participant in such a program the child would be involved in the "why" of the learning process (present program emphasis is focused on the "how" of the activity).

The proposed Perceptual-Motor Achievement Test is a modification of Roach and Kephart's "Visual Achievement Forms."[51] Vodola and Bender[52] modified the battery so that it would be adaptable to the developmental approach by listing the factor that each item measured, constructing a rating scale for each test item so that norms could be established, and developing transparent overlays to objectify the scoring technique.

Verbal instructions and rating procedures are listed below. Figure 3–11 provides a sample test form (see Appendix A for Perceptual-Motor Achievement Test Overlay Forms).

[50] *Ibid.*, "Foreword" by Newell C. Kephart, p. vi.
[51] Eugene G. Roach and Newell C. Kephart, *The Purdue Perceptual-Motor Survey* (Columbus, Ohio: Charles E. Merrill Books, Inc., 1966), pp. 64–65.
[52] Thomas M. Vodola and Dennis Bender, "Perceptual–Motor Achievement Test," Township of Ocean School District, Oakhurst, N.J., 1971.

Student Name _____,_____,_____,_____,_____

Last   First   Age   Grade   School

Directions: Have the students reproduce each form on the blank side of the paper.
Stress illustrations should be an exact replica of the original.

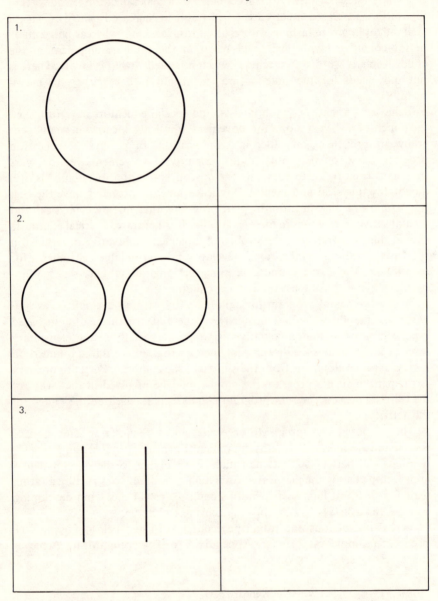

FIGURE 3–11 Perceptual-motor achievement test. Visual forms have been reduced in size. Sheets for student testing should have the first four forms

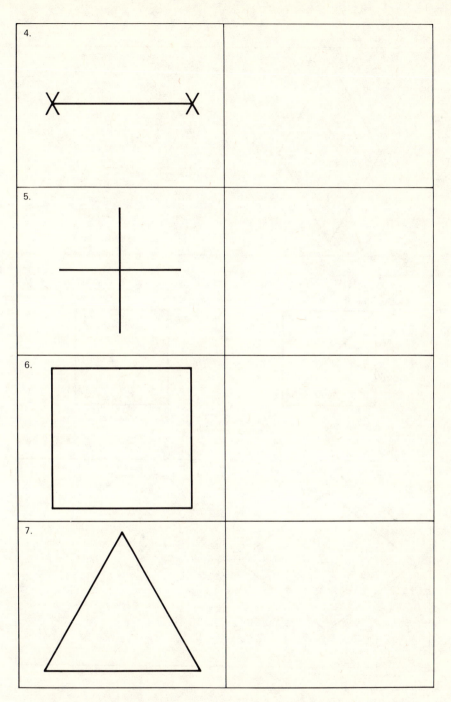

on page 1, the next three forms on page 2, and the remaining three forms on page 3.

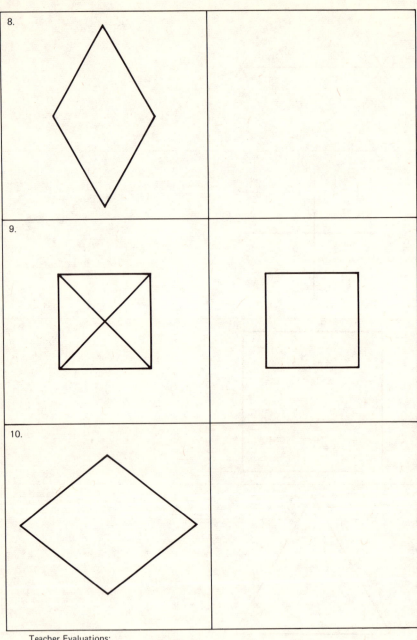

8.

9.

10.

Teacher Evaluations:
Raw Score Total ————————
Anecdotal Remarks: ————————

FIGURE 3–11 (cont.)

PERCEPTUAL-MOTOR SKILLS

General test directions: The subject is to draw the required form on the right side of the paper provided. The tester informs subject that he should attempt to replicate the illustration as closely as possible. The tester will use a transparent template to assess position, size, and conformation of each form. (*Note:* reproduction can have conformation without fitting template size.) *Important:* The tester should observe student performance carefully and record anecdotal remarks for all incorrect perceptual-motor responses such as smooth or restricted motor pattern and left-to-right and top-to-bottom direction, so that individualized programs can be prescribed.

TEST ITEM #1: Draw a circle.

  FACTOR: Directionality
  Award: 1 point for position; 1 point for size; 1 point for conformation; 1 point for closure; 1 point for smooth uninterrupted motion; and 1 point for direction (right-handed, counterclockwise; left-handed, clockwise).

  ATTEMPTS: 1

  SCORING: Possible total of 6 points.

TEST ITEM #2: Draw two circles simultaneously.

  FACTOR: Laterality/directionality
  Same procedure as for test item #1 except that the subject draws both circles simultaneously (starting and completing circles at the same time). Award points as for test item #1 with 1 additional point for simultaneous hand movements.

  ATTEMPTS: 1

  SCORING: Possible total of 7 points.

TEST ITEM #3: Draw two vertical lines simultaneously.

  FACTOR: Laterality
  Award: 1 point for position; 1 point for size; 1 point for conformation (parallel, straight lines); 1 point for smooth uninterrupted motion; 1 point for proper direction (top to bottom); and 1 point for simultaneous hand movements.

  ATTEMPTS: 1

  SCORING: Possible total of 6 points.

TEST ITEM #4: Connect two X's.

  FACTOR: Laterality
  Instruct the subject to draw two X's on the paper (duplicating the ones shown on the left) and then connect them with a straight line.

  Award: 1 point for position; 1 point for size; 1 point for conformation (straight line); 1 point for smooth crossing of the mid-line; 1 point for direction, left to right; and 1 point for starting and stopping on X's.

  ATTEMPTS: 1

  SCORING: Possible total of 6 points.

TEST ITEM #5: Draw a cross.

    FACTOR: Directionality

        Award: 1 point for position of intersection; 1 point for size of horizontal and vertical lines; 1 point for conformation (90° angle); 1 point for smooth, uninterrupted motion; 1 point for proper direction (top-to-bottom and left-to-right); 1 point for straight lines; and 1 point for equal line bisection.

    ATTEMPTS: 1

    SCORING: Possible total of 7 points.

TEST ITEM #6: Draw a square.

    FACTOR: Directionality

        Award: 1 point for position; 1 point for size; 1 point for conformation (straight lines, 90° angles); 1 point for closure.

    ATTEMPTS: 1

    SCORING: Possible total of 4 points.

TEST ITEM #7: Draw a triangle.

    FACTOR: Directionality

        Award: 1 point for position; 1 point for size; 1 point for conformation (60° angles); 1 point for closure.

    ATTEMPTS: 1

    SCORING: Possible total of 4 points.

TEST ITEM #8: Draw a diamond.

    FACTOR: Directionality

        Award: 1 point for position; 1 point for size; 1 point for conformation (straight lines and proper angles); 1 point for closure.

    ATTEMPTS: 1

    SCORING: Possible total of 4 points.

TEST ITEM #9: Draw a segmented square.

    FACTOR: Directionality

        Award: 1 point for starting and stopping on line; 1 point for conformation of top left to bottom right diagonal line; 1 point for conformation of bottom left to top right diagonal line; 1 point for drawing top left to bottom right line from left to right; 1 point for drawing bottom left to top right line from left to right.

    ATTEMPTS: 1

    SCORING: Possible total of 5 points.

TEST ITEM #10: Draw a horizontal diamond.

    FACTOR: Directionality

    Same procedure and scoring as for test item #8.

    ATTEMPTS: 1

    SCORING: Possible total of 4 points.

    Note: Subject's composite score on perceptual-motor test items is the total points scored of a potential 53 points (see sample test items in Fig. 3–11).

To aid in the identification of perceptual-motor problems the instructor should observe each student throughout the testing. For example, when asked to do so, does the child use both hands simultaneously or does he "drag" one behind? Does the child have a mid-line problem (the inability to move from left to right or vice versa without faltering or changing hands)? Does the child exhibit difficulty in rounding corners? These types of problems can only be discerned via careful observation. Anecdotal comments should be recorded on the test paper to aid in later assessment and individual prescription. Finally, the use of different colored test papers for pre- and post-testing will permit comparisons with a minimum of confusion.

When the instructor administers the Motor Skill Test Battery, he should use similar observational procedures to identify developmental problems. Objective scoring plus careful subjective evaluation will often enable one to note abnormal performance patterns and thus prescribe for individualized programming.

Prekindergarten Testing

In the near future, most schools and private institutions will be providing instruction for children of 3 to 5 years of age. A very important aspect of the educational program for the preschool child should be the provision of a variety of gross and fine motor experiences. Thus, the physical educator should be prepared to identify problems and provide activity programs for these children.

Further justification for prekindergarten testing is based on the fact that the school admission requirements of most states are inadequate in that they are limited to a specific chronological age group and require the approval of the family physician. The elementary principals of the Township of Ocean School District, feeling there was a need for more information regarding readiness for school, recommended that the writer design a prekindergarten screening test.[53] As a result of an interdisciplinary meeting, the screening test was adopted and administered during "Prekindergarten Round-Up Days." The purposes of the test were to provide parents with information regarding developmental activities that would benefit their children prior to admission to school and to provide the kindergarten teachers with some insight as to the capabilities of their incoming students. It was made quite clear that the test was not designed to delay admission but rather to furnish essential student data. Furthermore, the test was administered as a screening device, with no stigma attached. Students with suspected medical/psychological problems were referred to the school physician/school psychologist (see Appendix D for an analysis of the prekindergarten test results).

[53] Township of Ocean School District, "Pre-Kindergarten Screening Test," Oakhurst, N. J., March, 1971.

PREKINDERGARTEN SCREENING TEST

TEST ITEM #1: Hop 2L, 3R, 2L

FACTOR(S) MEASURED: Balance/postural orientation, coordination, serial order, laterality, and cognition

Test description: Teacher demonstrates hopping and changing feet without identifying left or right. Instruct the child to hop twice on left foot, and then perform the entire test.

Note: If the student cannot distinguish his right foot from left foot, the instructor is to place his hand on the leg he wants the child to hop with.

ASSESSMENT:

Balance on one foot	_____
Shifting weight smoothly	_____
Gross coordination	_____
Serial order (1, r, 1, or r, 1, r)	_____
Laterality	_____
Concept of numbers	_____

TEST ITEM #2: Bouncing and catching a ball

FACTOR(S) MEASURED: Eye/hand coordination

Test description: Have the child bounce a six-inch playground ball to waist height and attempt to catch the ball with two hands (without the aid of any part of the body). Three attempts.

ASSESSMENT:

Eye/hand coordination	_____
Color discrimination	_____

TEST ITEM #3: Ocular pursuit

FACTOR(S) MEASURED: Monocularity, binocularity, convergence

Test Description: Holding a pencil twenty to twenty-four inches from the subject's eyes, the instructor moves the pencil horizontally, vertically, diagonally (both directions), and in a circle. The subject is asked to follow the movements with both eyes, without moving his head (move the pencil in an eighteen-inch arc with the head as the center of the circle).

ASSESSMENT:

Tracking horizontally	_____
Tracking vertically	_____
Tracking diagonally	_____
Tracking circle	_____
Jerky pattern	_____
Midline problem	_____
Loses object	_____
Lazy eye	_____

TEST ITEM #4: Speech

The reader is referred to *Physical Education and Recreation for Handicapped Children*[54] for an overview of research findings related to the child with

[54] AAHPER and NRPA, *Physical Education and Recreation for Handicapped Children* (Washington, D. C.: Bureau of Education for the Handicapped/Department of Health,

learning disabilities. Other pertinent materials that should be read to gain insight into the perceptual–motor–cognitive approach have been authored by Cruickshank,[55] Delacato,[56] Frostig and Hornee,[57] Getman and Lane,[58] and Cratty.[59]

Summary

A comprehensive developmental physical education program should provide a means of identifying those students who are sub-par physically, mentally, and socioemotionally. The adoption of the following steps will aid in the achievement of that goal:

1. Define developmental physical education so that direction is given to the entire program.
2. State expected program objectives in terms of student behavior and design to measure psychomotor, affective, and cognitive outcomes.
3. Identify the motorically handicapped via an instrument that provides a means of assessing gross body coordination, balance-postural orientation, eye-hand coordination, eye-hand accuracy, and eye-foot accuracy.
4. Determine specific factors to be included before constructing a test battery.
5. Consider the individual's body structure when assessing a student's performance on physical tasks.
6. Establish norms on the basis of the population being tested.
7. Utilize the Rogers Physical Fitness Index Test, a modification thereof, or any other battery with norms which have been constructed in light of different body structures.
8. Determine which children are nutritionally deficient by using an instrument or instruments that predict normal weight on the basis of bone structure and adipose and muscle tissue measurement.
9. Appraise body mechanics via an instrument that provides for the identification of static and dynamic postural problems.
10. Design instructional units for the slow learner on the basis of the perceptual–motor–cognitive approach.
11. Develop a prekindergarten screening test to assess the performance of all incoming students.

Education and Welfare, February, 1969), 81 pp.
[55] William M. Cruickshank et al., *A Teaching Method for Brain-injured and Hyperactive Children* (Syracuse, N.Y.: Syracuse University Press, 1961).
[56] Carl H. Delacato, *The Diagnosis and Treatment of Speech and Reading Problems* (Springfield, Ill.: Charles C Thomas, Publisher, 1963).
[57] Marian Frostig and David Hornee, *The Frostig Program for the Development of Visual Perception* (Chicago: Follett Publishing Company, 1964).
[58] G. N. Getman and Elmer K. Lane, *The Physiology of Readiness* (Minneapolis: Programs for Accelerating School Success, P.O. Box 1004, 1964).
[59] Bryant J. Cratty, *Active Learning: Games to Enhance Academic Abilities* (Englewood Cliffs, N.J.: Prentice-Hall, Inc., 1971).

Annotated Bibliography

AMERICAN ASSOCIATION FOR HEALTH, PHYSICAL EDUCATION AND RECREATION, UNIT ON PROGRAMS FOR THE HANDICAPPED. *Information Sheet: Resources on Perceptual Motor Programs for the Handicapped.* Washington, D.C.: 1201 Sixteenth Street, N.W. 20036, 10 pp. Mimeographed. Provides the teacher interested in working with children who have learning disabilities with an extensive list of references. Free upon request.

BRALEY, WILLIAM T., GERALDINE KONICKI, and CATHERINE LEEDY. *Daily Sensorimotor Training: A Handbook for Teachers and Parents of Pre-School Children.* Freeport, N.Y.: Educational Activities, Inc., 1968. Provides a comprehensive variety of sensorimotor activities which may be taught in schools or at home. The manual provides daily lesson plans for a 34-week training program with weekly evaluation of student progress.

KAPFER, PHILLIP G. "Behavioral Objectives and the Curriculum Processor," *Educational Technology*, X, No. 5 (1970), 14–17. Focuses on behavioral objectives and the new role of the teacher as a curriculum processor, with emphasis on the development of objectives that will not restrict human behavior, but will foster individual effectiveness.

KENDALL, HENRY O., and DOROTHY A. BOYNTON. *Posture and Pain.* Baltimore: The Williams & Wilkins Company, 1952. Provides a detailed explanation of proper body mechanics, mobility, and treatment and prevention of postural faults. A variety of pictures and figures lend clarity to the text. Includes a comprehensive procedure for postural examinations.

KRATHWOHL, DAVID R., BENJAMIN S. BLOOM, and BERTRAM B. MASIA. *Taxonomy of Educational Objectives: The Classification of Educational Goals, Handbook II: Affective Domain.* New York: David McKay Company, Inc., 1956. Patterned after the approach used to design Handbook I which dealt with the cognitive domain. Provides examples of how to construct objectives which emphasize feeling tone, an emotion, or a degree of acceptance or rejection.

MCASHAN, H. H. *Writing Behavioral Objectives: A New Approach.* New York: Harper & Row, Publishers, 1970. Assists the teacher in developing behavioral objectives based on special goals for instructional programs. Strong emphasis on the development of evaluative statements to measure desired outcomes.

Perceptual-Motor Foundations: A Multidisciplinary Concern. Washington, D.C.: AAHPER, 1201 Sixteenth Street, N.W. 20035, 1969. Provides a comprehensive analysis of perceptual–motor development and learning. Includes sections related to the evolution of perceptual–motor behavior, implications for the teaching/learning process, interdisciplinary implications for child development, and areas in need of further study and research.

VANNIER, MARYHELEN. *Figure and Weight Control.* New York: Association Press, 1965. Instructor's manual for teachers or leaders of a course in figure and weight control for women and girls. Suggests ways to help students gain a concept of total fitness and concrete learning experiences for helping improve health and fitness.

4

identification of students
in need of adapted activities

The identification of those students in need of adapted physical activity programs is not the responsibility of the untrained classroom teacher. Since adapted physical education deals with that phase of the D&A program for students with medical and/or psychological problems, identification and classification of such students is dependent upon a thorough medical examination by the school or family physician and/or the school psychologist. More specifically, adapted physical education may be defined as that phase of the total program which has been designed to modify physical activity commensurate with the needs of the physically handicapped, mentally handicapped, socioemotionally handicapped, or some combination thereof.

This simple means of classification is consistent with the developmental approach to education as espoused in this text. If one were to attempt to classify all medically oriented problems, the list would be extensive and often confusing. For example, structuring separate programs for students with infantile paralysis, cerebral palsy, etc., would result in unnecessary repetition of certain practices, curriculum fragmentation, and consequent attenuation of instructional effectiveness.

Mindful of the fact that the medical inspector will identify students for the adapted program on the basis of existing medical problems, the physical educator must plan the identification process so that it will be efficient and effective. In other words, one must begin with the assumption that physical activity can contribute to the well-being of the individual and then program the student's activities in light of his needs. Thus, the first step in identifying those in need of adapted physical education activities would be a thorough medical examination, followed by subclassifications based on the individual developmental needs of the child.

Ury utilizes the developmental approach when he states that the physically handicapped child may be divided into four groups:

those whose handicap involves one or more special senses, including the blind, the partially-sighted, the deaf, the hard of hearing, and the deaf and blind; those whose handicap results in motor disability or limitations, including orthopedic cases (infantile paralysis, spastic conditions, osteomyelitis, bone tuberculosis and congenital deformities, cardiac problems); those suffering from respiratory diseases in certain stages and malnutrition cases; and those with various types of speech of whatever origin.[1]

Use of this subgrouping procedure aids the teacher in the identification process by determining the degree of limitation involved. In Chapter 4 we will list the recommended major classifications, subclassifications, and suggested teacher testing techniques.

Behavioral Outcomes

The behavioral outcomes of students who have taken D&A classes must be student-oriented, i.e., expressed in terms of student behavior[2] which should be identifiable at the end of the unit or after a period of years. Included after each such outcome listed below are suggested grades for appearance of such behavior.

1. The student can explain the physical limitations caused by his handicap (grades K–12).
2. The student manifests a positive attitude toward his handicap by constantly striving to achieve maximally within the limitations imposed (K–12).
3. The student evidences a positive attitude toward members of his peer group and adults (K–12).
4. The student demonstrates the ability to utilize the following testing equipment (those items that are part of his program) (K–12).
   a. Flexometer or goniometer
   b. Tensiometer
   c. Wet or dry spirometer
   d. Skinfold calipers
   e. Measuring tape
   f. Stadiometer
   g. Pryor's Width-Weight Calipers
   h. Leg dynamometer
   i. Back dynamometer

[1] Claude M. Ury, "Introduction: Education of the Handicapped and Educational Technology," *Educational Technology*, X, No. 8 (August, 1970), 11.
[2] Thomas M. Vodola, *Course of Study, Grades K–12: Developmental and Adapted Physical Education* (Oakhurst, N.J.: Township of Ocean Board of Education, January, 1970), p. 9.

5. The student can perform a variety of modified exercises to maintain and improve his level of fitness (K–12).

6. The student demonstrates proficiency in a variety of leisure-time skills that will serve him advantageously in his adult years (9–12).

7. The student evidences an awarenes of his tolerance limits regarding his exercising and recreational activities (K–12).

8. The student demonstrates the proper knowledge, practices, and attitudes toward avoidable safety hazards (K–12).

9. The student demonstrates followship and leadership qualities by accepting responsibilities commensurate with his ability level (K–12).

10. The student demonstrates a basic proficiency in motor skills, perceptual tasks, and perceptual-motor activities (K–8).

11. The student demonstrates the ability to relax the various muscle groups of the body (K–8).

Note: An effort should be made to structure outcomes that can be measured objectively at the end of each unit. Try to include specific goals that focus on affective behavior (i.e., how the student "feels" toward his peer group, changes in attitude, etc.). The attainment of all outcomes should be evaluated in light of grade level and intellectual and physical ability of the student.

Physically Handicapped

Students identified as physically handicapped will be subcategorized in terms of communication disorders, motor disability limitations, and circulatory-respiratory restrictions.

Communication Disorders

Communication disorders may be defined as physical handicaps which impede the functioning of one or more of the special senses. Examples of those who would be so categorized would be the deaf, the hard of hearing, the blind, the partially sighted, the autistic, and those with various speech impediments. Except for medical procedures for identifying those with communication disorders, there are no known testing instruments to aid in determining student limitations, certainly none designed by physical educators.

The lack of testing equipment should not deter the physical educator but should motivate him to design valid, reliable instruments for assessing the status of children with sensory impairments. In the meantime, he should devise activities to maximize achievements within the prescribed limitations. For example, instruments could be developed for assessing the partially blind student's peripheral and discriminatory ability; the blind student's depth perception and general kinesthetic ability; or the autistic child's ability to relax.

Extensive testing instruments involving all senses (auditory, visual, tactile, gustatory, and kinesthetic) should be developed and administered to these children. Contrary to popular belief, a blind child does not possess supernatural hearing but must develop the ability to discriminate among voices and sounds to minimize the limtations imposed upon him by his disability. The deaf, the hard of hearing, and the autistic child must be provided with those experiences that will help them improve the use of their eyes. Through the identification of the developmental level of all of the child's sensory capabilities and prescriptive programming to enhance such development, the instructor can provide a practical means of compensatory adjustment.

Motor Disability or Limitations

This category includes but is not limited to children who have cerebral palsy, poliomyelitis, orthopedic problems, congenital deformities, multiple sclerosis, and muscular dystrophy—physical handicaps which result in a motor disability or limitation thereof. Conditions such as mononucleosis and diabetes mellitus do not create a permanent motor disability but do limit one's motor ability and as a consequence are included in this category. In addition students who are postoperative or convalescent fall under this subcategory.

It has been said that necessity is the mother of invention. This adage was certainly proven valid during World War II when army convalescent hospitals were extremely overcrowded due to the many war injuries. Formerly it had been thought that complete recovery from operations and orthopedic mishaps necessitated an inordinate convalescent period, but because of the shortage of beds, G.I.'s were forced to ambulate almost immediately after surgery. Contrary to the beliefs held at that time, not only did recovery rates not retrogress, they actually improved. At that time, DeLorme and Watkins[3] developed their "progressive resistance exercise" technique, a procedure which hastened the rehabilitation of armed forces members who suffered from orthopedic disabilities.

Since that time Clarke and Clarke[4] have designed a series of cable-tension strength tests to measure various muscle groups of the body (see their text for a detailed description and illustrations of all procedures and construction specifications). To determine the effect of muscular exercise upon strength decrement and strength recovery rate, Clarke and his associates[5] devised a Strength Decrement Index Formula which is computed as follows:

---

[3] Thomas L. DeLorme and Arthur L. Watkins, *Progressive Resistance Exercise: Technique and Medical Application* (New York: Appleton-Century-Crofts, 1951), pp. 23–28.

[4] H. Harrison Clarke and David H. Clarke, *Developmental and Adapted Physical Education* (Englewood Cliffs, N.J.: Prentice-Hall, Inc., 1963), pp. 73–96.

[5] H. Harrison Clarke, Clayton T. Shay, and Donald K. Mathews, "Strength Decrement Index: A New Test of Muscular Fatigue," *Archives of Physical Medicine and Rehabilitation*, XXXVI, No. 6 (June, 1955), 376.

$$SDI = \frac{S_b - S_a}{S_b} \times 100,$$

where: SDI = Strength Decrement Index,
        S_b = strength before exercise, and
        S_a = strength after exercise.

The formula determines the percentage loss in strength following a series of exercises.

Use of this formula is recommended for students who have motor disabilities or limitations, for the atrophied muscle groups of the body can be tested for initial strength by the formula. In addition, the SDI can be used to determine a student's fatigue tolerance limits. For example, if a student had a bicep strength of 100 lbs. both before and after a series of "curls," his SDI would be 0 percent. In other words, the exercising regimen would not have been fatiguing and additional repetitions could be prescribed. Thus, the use of the strength decrement index procedure aids the instructor by providing him with a means of assessing muscle strength and prescribing tolerance limits for isolated muscle groups.

Quite frequently, students identified as possessing motor disabilities or limitations experience difficulty in executing a complete range of motion of all joints; the spastic child would be a good example. The use of instruments to measure flexibility will aid the instructor in assessing these limitations. The Orthopedic Equipment Company[6] has designed an *international standard goniometer* for this purpose which consists of two plastic arms hinged together. It is used by placing the axis of the instrument as close as possible to the functional axis of the body; placing the "fixed arm" in line with the stabilized part of the body; and following the motion of the body part that is to be measured by the movable arm. The indicator for reading the degrees displaced is located on the fixed arm (see Fig. 4–1). Detailed procedures and illustrations are provided by the manufacturer for measuring and recording the range of motion for the three basic planes and rotations of the body.

The *arthrodial protractor* manufactured by the Reedco Company[7] is another instrument, similar to the flexometer, for measuring joint flexibility. This measuring device is a one-piece plexiglass instrument which is placed in varied positions, depending upon the joint to be measured. Instructions, including the range of motion norms established by the American Academy of Orthopedic Surgeons, are provided by the company.

The Leighton flexometer[8] is another instrument for measuring range of

[6] The international standard goniometer is manufactured by the Orthopedic Equipment Company, Bourbon, Ind.

[7] The arthrodial protractor is manufactured by the Reedco Company, Inc., 5 Easterly Avenue, Audubon, N.Y. 13021.

[8] Jack R. Leighton, "A Simple Objective and Reliable Measure of Flexibility," *Research Quarterly*, XIII, No. 2 (May, 1942), 205.

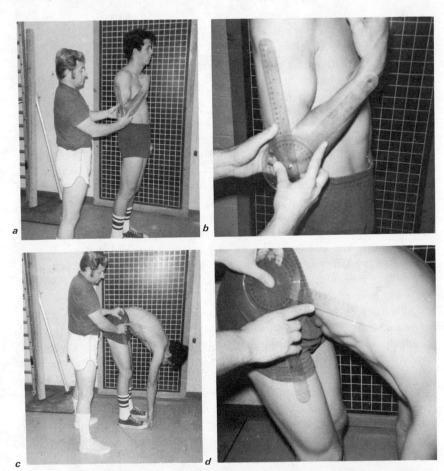

FIGURE 4–1 Measuring trunk flexion (*a, b*) and forearm flexion (*c, d*) using a goniometer. Courtesy of the Township of Ocean School District.

motion. The device is used by strapping it to the moving part being tested, locking a circular disc in place at that point, and then locking a pointer in place after the range of motion has been completed. Thus, the pointer will indicate the amount of joint flexibility (see Fig. 4–2). The flexometer provides a more accurate means of assessing flexibility than the goniometer and arthrodial protractor because the testing procedure minimizes the use of subjective landmarks. A modified version of the Leighton flexometer is available from the Preston Corporation.[9] Preston[10] also has made a "Univer-

---

[9] The flexometer is manufactured by the J. A. Preston Corporation, 71 Fifth Avenue, New York, N.Y. 10003.

[10] The universal goniometer is manufactured by the J. A. Preston Corporation, 71 Fifth Avenue, New York, N.Y. 10003.

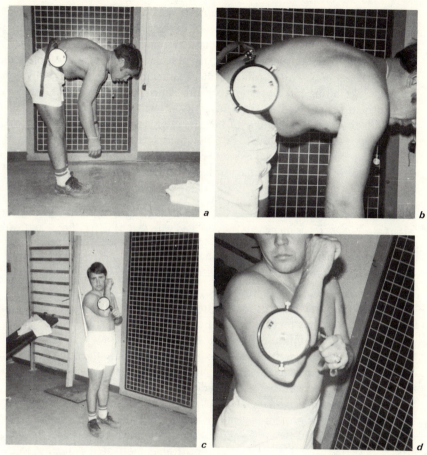

FIGURE 4–2   Measuring trunk flexion (*a, b*) and forearm flexion (*c, d*) using a flexometer. Courtesy of the Township of Ocean School District.

sal Goniometer" available which involves a combination of the goniometer/flexometer principles and is more moderately priced than the flexometer.

The strength and flexibility testing provided by these instruments will aid the physical educator in identifying the limitations of the child with a motor disability. In addition, testing can be conducted to assess basic locomotor and recreational skills so that individualized physical activity programs can be prescribed.

Circulorespiratory Restrictions

Many educators, including the writer, maintain that true fitness is dependent upon efficient cardiorespiratory endurance. This subclassification would include those students who evidence medical problems related to the circulatory system, including those with cardiac problems and respiratory abnormalities such as heart murmurs and asthma.

For many years physicians have disapproved of any form of physical activity for patients with chronic medical ailments; this was especially true for those exhibiting circulorespiratory problems. However, studies such as the one being conducted at the University of San Francisco[11] are causing physicians to question the logic of the "inactivity prescription." The activity program was designed to investigate the incidence and severity of coronary disease for those patients who exercise regularly and the effects of exercise on the incidence of repeated coronary attacks for the same individuals. Although the results of the program are still inconclusive, the physicians involved have noted the following changes in patients:

Stress and apprehension generally associated with fear of heart disease and with reduced cardiac capacity have been lowered; exercise tolerance has increased markedly; some patients exhibit less anginal pain; virtually all patients exhibit greater physical awareness; patients say they enjoy and look forward to exercise; patients generally feel and eat better.[12]

Similarly, programs are being developed to aid the student with breathing allergies. (It is interesting to note that a recent United States Health Survey revealed that breathing allergies such as asthma and hay fever cause one-third of the chronic conditions afflicting those under seventeen years of age.)

A major difficulty encountered by an individual with asthma or emphesema is the inability to expel air. This difficulty may be observed particularly with the person suffering from a severe case of emphesema who will literally "double over," thus providing a means of compressing the abdominal cavity and forcing air out of the lungs. An awareness of the need for a series of exercises designed to aid diaphragmatic breathing motivated Adams[13] to develop "A Physical Conditioning Exercise Program for the Asthmatic Patient."

Adams recommends that "the exercises be performed on a self-competitive basis, emphasizing diaphragmatic, costal and asymmetrical breathing, and be carried out daily upon onset of an attack of asthma."[14]

After two years of experimentation with the asthmatic exercise program, two phases have been modified in the Township of Ocean program. The origi-

[11] George J. McGynn, "Exercise Gets to the Heart of the Matter," *Outlook*, I, No. 3 (December, 1969). Unit on Programs for the Handicapped, AAHPER, 1201 Sixteenth St., N.W., Washington, D.C. 20036.

[12] *Ibid*. (McGynn), p. 3.

[13] Ron Adams, Director, "A Physical Conditioning Exercise Program for the Asthmatic Patient," Therapeutic Recreation and Adapted Physical Education, Children's Rehabilitation Center, University of Virginia Hospital, Charlottesville, Va. 22901.

[14] Personal communication with Ron Adams, Director, Therapeutic Recreation and Adapted Physical Education, Children's Rehabilitation Center, University of Virginia Hospital, Charlottesville, Va., May 11, 1971.

nal version suggested the use of a stop watch to record the time required to expel all air from the lungs; the modification recommends the replacement of the stop watch with a dry spirometer to reliably measure the student's vital capacity (volume of expelled air). The second modification involved slight changes in the chart for recording student progress so that it is adaptable for use with the dry spirometer. Figure 4–3 illustrates the procedure for keeping a record of student progress.

The modified version of Adams' asthmatic exercising program is presented here for consideration. Experience has proven it to be easy to administer, valid and reliable for identifying and assessing student progress, and very successful in aiding the student with a breathing allergy.

PHYSICAL CONDITIONING EXERCISE PROGRAM FOR THE ASTHMATIC PATIENT

Name _____ Instructor _____ Grade ____

Exercise program
1. Standing breathing with arm swing (20 times)
2. Bicycle exercise (moderate speed, 30 seconds)
3. Toe stand inhale–exhale (20 times)
4. Chest breathing, supine position (20 times)
5. Running in place (50 cadences on the right foot)
6. Sitting toe touch (20 times)

Objectives
1. To increase expiration and therefore lessen bronchial spasm
2. To prevent postural defects such as narrowed chest and kyphosis
3. To strengthen auxiliary breathing muscles (scaleni, pectorals, abdominals)
4. To help relax
5. To condition as well as evaluate
6. To provide additional steps for monitoring the convalescence of a patient by measuring overall expiration efficiency
7. To provide an exercising regimen which can be performed at home
8. To increase forced expiration volume, which will indicate a positive step toward lessening the severity of the pulmonary condition (asthma)
9. To increase tolerance and allow a child to take part in normal play activities
10. To restore the patient's confidence and lessen his fear during an attack

Precautions
1. Avoid fatigue.
2. Make sure the child does not take part in any vigorous activities immediately prior to exercising.

Chart tabulation
1. Each curve test chart should include the vital capacity (V.C.) score.
2. The date of each pre-exercise V.C. count should be recorded below the chart; the final pretest score for each week should be recorded on the chart.

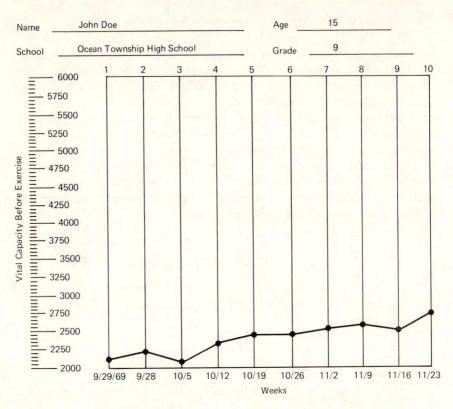

| | Name | John Doe | | Age | 15 |
| | School | Ocean Township High School | | Grade | 9 |

Note: The forced expiration volume is achieved by having the standing patient take a deep breath and then exhale as slowly as possible into the mouthpiece of the wet spirometer. *Be sure the subject keeps both nostrils closed and does not let any air escape around the outer edges of the mouthpiece.*

	Test Date	Pre-Test V.C.	Post-Test V.C.	Exercise Circuits
1.	9/21/69	2200	2150	1
2.	9/28/69	2250	2250	1
3.	10/5/69	2200	2200	2
4.	10/12/69	2300	2500	2
5.	10/19/69	2400	2300	3
6.	10/26/69	2400	2500	3
7.	11/2/70	2500	2300	4
8.	11/9/70	2550	2500	4
9.	11/16/70	2500	2700	4
10.	11/23/70	2700	2600	5

FIGURE 4–3 Expiration test for asthma patient with forced expiration volume chart.

Scoring the expiration test
1. The test is scored satisfactory if the patient's V.C. is increased daily.
2. Gradual daily increase in V.C. proves that the exercise program is a positive step toward lessening the severity of the pulmonary condition.

Equipment
1. Ruler
2. Book (minimum twelve inches thick for toe stand, inhale-exhale exercise)
3. Wet or dry spirometer

Exercise procedures
1. Patient must assume standing position, flexed at waist.
2. Resting vital capacity is taken. Patient is allowed three trials and the best score is tabulated on V.C. curve chart.
3. Execution of six listed exercises. No rest period allowed between exercises (see Figs. 4-4 and 4-5).
4. Patient returns to the standing position.
5. Vital capacity is recorded from the wet or dry spirometer reading. Patient is allowed three trials and the best score is tabulated on the V.C. curve chart.
6. Curve chart line is drawn for V.C. progress by connecting weekly dots. A ruler is used to plot the V.C. curve line.
7. The date of the expiration test should be recorded below each respective week.

Note: If the subject receives the same or a higher vital capacity score after exercise than before exercise, it is permissable to repeat the exercise.

As mentioned previously, the asthmatic program has been very successful in the writer's school district. As an example, the case history of Barbara is presented:

An annual task of the high school nurse is to review the medical history of each incoming 9th-grade student; one of the purposes is to refer students to developmental and adapted physical education. Barbara's history indicated that periodically she was subject to severe asthmatic attacks for which her physician had prescribed daily medication to minimize the bronchial spasms. The history further revealed that she had been excused from all physical education activities except for those involving minimal movement. After consultation with the school physician, the nurse, and the child, Barbara was scheduled in the D&A program in lieu of physical education. (The nurse had discussed the schedule adjustment with the parent via the phone.) It must be added at this point that although Barbara was very cooperative, she was also very apprehensive. Experience has indicated that the asthmatic child frequently suffers psychologically due to the traumatic effect of an attack—the feeling of suffocation or strangulation.

Periodic review of Barbara's folder revealed that her daily pretest vital capacity scores were gradually increasing, indicating an increased ability to expel air. As part of her program, she was required to visit the school nurse once a week. The nurse related to the writer that medication has been reduced drastically and even eliminated on some days. Of greater significance was Barbara's psychological adjustment; she no longer evidenced fear of participation in physical activity. As a consequence another adjustment was made in Barbara's schedule, a flexible arrangement whereby she remained in D&A for a portion of the time for testing purposes and during very strenuous activities, but the balance of the time she participated in the regular

90

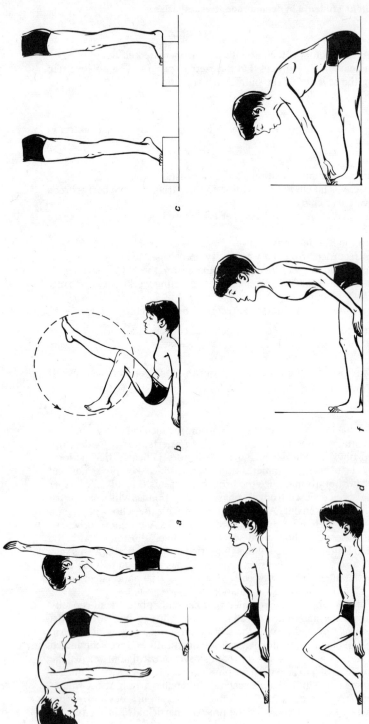

FIGURE 4–4 A physical conditioning exercise program for the asthmatic patient. (a) Standing breathing with arm swing. Child is standing, leans forward, arms dangling. He stretches arms overhead, rising to erect position on the toes, breathing in. Then he drops forward, breathing out through his mouth, making a hissing sound. Relax. Repeat twenty times. (b) Bicycle exercise. The child lies on his back and makes a circular motion with his legs as if peddling a bicycle. Continue for thirty seconds. (c) Toe stand inhale-exhale. (left) The child stands on his toes, using a book for foot support, and inhales. (right) The child exhales and relaxes by placing the heels of his feet on the floor. Repeat twenty times. (d) Chest breathing, supine position. (top) The child breathes in through his nose, expanding his abdomen, then his chest. (bottom) He breathes out through his mouth, making a hissing sound as he lowers the abdomen, then the chest. Repeat twenty times. (e) Running in place exercise (not shown). The child raises and lowers his feet far enough to clear the floor. He then counts to fifty, the number of right contacts only. (f) Sitting toe touch. (left) The child sits on the floor, feet against the wall, knees stiff; he inhales. (right) He touches his toes with his fingertips. Exhale. Repeat fifteen times.

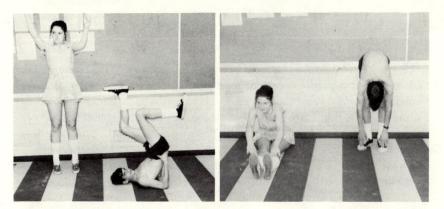

FIGURE 4–5 Students performing asthmatic breathing exercises. Courtesy of the Township of Ocean School District.

program. This helped reinforce her self-image. As a result, Barbara could and did successfully participate with her peer group.

Another example of how physical activity can help the asthmatic individual is revealed in Dwight's case history. Interestingly, this experience occurred prior to the advent of the D&A program:

Dwight, a student in the writer's 12th-grade class, revealed that he had never been permitted to run since childhood due to the severity of his asthmatic attacks. Armed with the philosophy that organs which are not used will atrophy, the writer scheduled a parent/student conference at which it was agreed that an individualized running program could be devised for Dwight during which he would be permitted to walk or stop completely if he developed undue breathlessness. At the start of the program, he could not jog around the 440-foot track even one time without stopping, but by the conclusion of the unit, Dwight actually "covered" the required mile distance (without walking) in a respectable time. Although there is no question of the physiological value involved, it is the author's opinion that in this case the greatest gain was actually psychological.

Hayden[15] refers to a similar program which was sponsored and coordinated by the Wayne County, Michigan, Tuberculosis and Health Society. The program consists of a series of postural and breathing exercises and other physical activities modified to meet the needs of children with breathing problems. Although no tangible evidence of physiological progress appeared, some children learned to allay their apprehensiveness of an asthmatic attack by resorting to the diaphragmatic breathing exercises they had been taught.

[15] Herbert Hayden, "B is for Breathing," *Outlook*, I, No. 3 (December, 1969), 1, 5.

Mentally Handicapped

In Chapter 3 a section was devoted to the identification of the slower learner and to his subsequent placement in the developmental program. We mentioned the student who manifested a learning disability conceivably due to cultural deprivation or the lack of an experiential background necessary to furnish a foundation for the three R's. The *slow learner*, thus, evidences developmental needs but is not to be construed as *mentally handicapped*.

Those identified as mentally handicapped are usually extremely deficient in intellectual potential due to limited intellectual capacity or brain damage caused by disease or injury (hereafter referred to as *brain-injured*). In previous explanations we emphasized that terminology for classification was not of paramount importance; rather, primary consideration was to be given to the needs of the individual in light of the discipline involved. If that is true, there seems to be a conflict because the slow learner and the mentally retarded child manifest similar needs. However, although there is indeed a commonality of problems requiring a similar instructional approach, mentally handicapped children usually exhibit other special characteristics that should be identified to aid in programming. Even though these characteristics are not exhibited by all mentally handicapped children, a significantly greater number of the traits, to some degree, are manifested by the mentally handicapped than the nonhandicapped.

Stein maintains that the physical educator must be particularly concerned about the following characteristics:

Physical—poor body mechanics, low vitality, poor motor coordination but with less deviation from the nonhandicapped than in social and educational efficiency, and poor functioning of the sense receptors and preceptors.

Mental—lack of ability to concentrate and to retain, difficulty in following directions, tendency to lose interest in remote goals, greater response to the concrete and practical than to the abstract and theoretical, varying interest span, lack of initiative, and inability to experiment and innovate with activities. . . .[16]

Children identified as mentally handicapped due to brain injury or disease will evidence the physical and mental anomalies as listed by Stein, but more frequently, and more severely than the retarded. In addition, they may be identified as possessing one or more of the psychological characteristics referred to by Cruickshank et al.[17]: hyperactivity, dissociation, figure-background disturbances, and perseveration.[18]

---

[16] Julian U. Stein, "A Practical Guide to Adapted Physical Education for the Educable Mentally Retarded," XXXIII, No. 9 (December, 1962), 30–31.

[17] William M. Cruickshank et al., *A Teaching Method for Brain-injured and Hyperactive Children* (Syracuse, N.Y.: Syracuse University Press, 1961), pp. 4–7.

[18] The author has subsumed Cruickshank's terms *distractibility* and *motor disinhibition* under *hyperactivity*.

The hyperactive child manifests an inordinate sensitivity to visual, auditory, or tactile sensations. He may be identified as the student who cannot concentrate on the skill being taught, the child who counts the ceiling tiles or is distracted by the ticking of the clock.

Dissociation means that the child does not possess the ability to conceptualize a totality. Evidence of this type of behavior may be detected by having the student take the Geometric Form Completion Test (see Appendix A). This inability to integrate experiences is theorized by psychologists and psychiatrists to be caused by an abnormal fear of the unknown. The child may become very adept at performing one skill but extremely apprehensive or completely unwilling to attempt the same skill with only slight modifications. As a case in point, a brain-injured child in the writer's summer program would repeatedly climb the twenty-two-foot rope in gym class but refused to perform pull-ups on the chinning bar which was suspended nine feet above the floor. The fear evidenced in this case was not a fear of height, but rather the fear of failure as a result of performing a different task.

The normal child has no difficulty reading a textbook with a variety of nontextual elements such as cartoons, graphs, and pictures. On the other hand, the brain-injured child may not be able to distinguish the text from the other materials. Since it may be difficult for the reader to understand the concept of figure-ground relationship, Rubin's Figure: The Peter and Paul Goblet is illustrated in Fig. 4–6. Try this simple experiment. Concentrate on the image for sixty seconds. Do you note the tendency to vacillate between the visual image of an urn and two people facing one another? This is the problem that confronts many children who are brain-injured during the

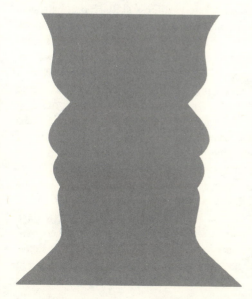

FIGURE 4–6 Figure-ground relationship: Rubin's Figure: The Peter and Paul Goblet. Do you see an urn or two people facing one another?

FIGURE 4–7   Figure-ground relationship: test illustration. Can the sailboat be discerned from the background of wavy lines?

performance of daily schoolwork. Figure 4–7 presents an illustration of a test that can be used to discern these types of problems. The task for the child is the identification of the sailboat (the figure) from the background (the wavy lines).

Simple tests of this sort can be constructed by drawing a solitary figure, with a distracting background, on 9 × 12″ manila sheets; a marking pen should be used to make the graphic illustrations more identifiable. An example might be a figure of a ball, bat, or some other item currently being used during the activity unit; a series of twelve cards is recommended. Test procedure would be to "flash" the card momentarily and have the child attempt to identify the dominant figure in the foreground.

Another testing procedure that might be devised for use with the brain-injured requires the use of a pegboard and pegs, or a sheet of paper. If possible, it is recommended pegboards be purchased or constructed since they may be used to teach a veriety of academic readiness skills. To construct a pegboard have the industrial arts department cut a 4 × 8′ sheet of $\frac{1}{4}$″ masonite into thirty-two 12 × 12″ pieces and paint them with one coat of non-gloss black paint to provide a background for multicolored pegs as well as enhance the appearance of the pegboard. Golf tees, which may be purchased in large quantities for a nominal sum, may be used as pegs. Insert and glue golf tees in all corners of the individual pegboards (if the background is painted black, use black tees). Cut off the sharp edges of the remaining tees so that they do not touch the table when inserted in the holes; snipping off sharp edges is also a safety factor. Glue the pegs in the boards according to predetermined geometric patterns or figures. Figure 4–8 presents two patterns that could be used. For testing purposes, set up at least twelve figures; use one color for each pattern to minimize distractibility.

The procedure for their use is similar to that for manila arithmetic flash cards. If pegboards are not available, a stencil may be mimeographed with superimposed pegboards. Figures can then be placed on individual sheets and used for testing purposes. The use of pegboards, or reproduced simulated

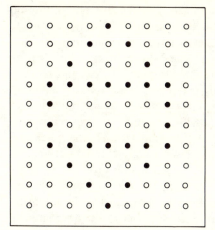 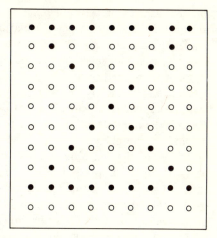

FIGURE 4–8   Sample figure-background pegboard test patterns.

sheets, can provide a variety of meaningful learning experiences for the slow learner or mentally retarded child who displays visuomotor problems.

Perseveration is another psychological characteristic that is manifested by the brain-injured child. It is evidenced by the seeming inability to cease performing an act. Examples of perseveration exhibited by normal individuals might be the repeated swinging of a leg, or repetitively humming or whistling of a tune. When a normal person develops an awareness of what he is doing, he may volitionally stop the act. However, the brain-injured child may continue performing the act again and again.

The student referred to previously who repeatedly climbed a rope day after day was perseverating. Another brain-injured, autistic child carried keys in his hand for three weeks; regardless of his current task, he would not release the keys. It has been postulated that the repeated performance of a non-volitional act by a brain-injured child may be attributed to the security derived from a successful achievement. Frequently, this trait is so deeply embedded psychologically that the child resists all attempts to perform new tasks due to the insecurity caused by possible failure.

Before moving on to the socioemotionally handicapped, the writer feels impelled to give a rationale for the use of perceptual-motor tasks in the D&A program. The compulsion to justify the use of visuomotor tasks, assumed to belong solely in the domain of the "academic disciples," is necessitated by some comments educators (and sometimes, regrettably, physical educators) have made about the inappropriateness of such activities being included in a physical education program.

The argument that physical education should be solely devoted to the *physical* aspects of learning reflects the archaic, indefensible philosophy of dichotomized people. A pervasive attitude that assumes that only traditional academic subjects can develop the intellect of the individual and that so-called "special subjects" can only develop physical skill competence is illogical and can be refuted in a variety of ways. For example, the assumption that intellectual or cognitive learning can only take place in a classroom environment is erroneous. *Webster's New Collegiate Dictionary* defines the development of the intellect as "the power of knowing . . . , the power of reasoning, judging, comprehending . . . ." Thus "the development of the intellect" results from the teaching method rather than merely the subject matter being presented. Expressed in another way, subject matter provides the vehicle through which learning takes place, whereas the teaching methodology used is the "driver," or the means of guiding the learner. The development of the mental faculties does not imply rote learning but rather development via student learning experiences designed to enhance the process of inquiry. What area can be more fertile for the attainment of these goals than physical activity?

Just as the present lock-step arrangement of scheduling students by grade level is being questioned because of its impractical approach to education (and its inconsistency with what we know regarding how learning takes place), so teaching based on the separation of disciplines is being questioned by scholars and educational researchers. As one reviews the research literature, the trend toward the interdisciplinary approach is apparent. Research findings generated by behavioral psychologists have much value for the classroom teacher, regardless of the subject being taught. Conversely, research and studies in specialized areas such as physical education should be reviewed by all educators so that important findings can be extrapolated for general usage. After all, as educators we have a common goal—maximizing the physical, mental, and socioemotional growth of all our students.

An example of a text that should be read by all educators is Mosston's book *Teaching Physical Education: From Command to Discovery.*[19] The writer clearly illustrates that "the structure of teaching behavior" (methodology) is the determinant of the types of learning behavior that will be manifested. Radler and Kephart[20] theorize that all learning is founded on motor development. Such a theory has valuable import for the classroom teacher and the physical educator. They reason that a child first learns motor patterns before he perceives stimuli, or learns to develop his powers to reason. If we as educators are to achieve our common goal, we must review all literature that pertains to education and apply techniques, such as those mentioned, that have merit.

[19] Muska Mosston, *Teaching Physical Education: From Command to Discovery* (Columbus, Ohio: Charles E. Merrill Books, Inc., 1966).
[20] D. H. Radler with Newell C. Kephart, *Success Through Play* (New York: Harper & Row, Publishers, 1960), pp. 27–29.

In summation, physical educators should avail themselves of the latest research findings and materials for use with mentally handicapped children. Appropriate materials should be adopted or modified, according to the situation that prevails.

Socioemotional Handicapped

The socioemotionally handicapped child may exhibit many characteristics similar to the mentally handicapped child, thus necessitating a somewhat similar developmental program.

The identification and classification of socioemotionally disturbed children is the prime responsibility of the school psychologist (as in the case of the mentally retarded). Such children may exhibit many characteristics similar to the mentally handicapped, thus necessitating a somewhat similar developmental program. However, their performance may be much more erratic! They may have physical or mental problems, but on most occasions their maladjusted behavior will be due to an inability to cope with daily living. The underlying problems of these children who form the core of juvenile delinquents and school drop-outs should be identified by the school psychologist. In addition, the physical educator should attend all child study team meetings that relate to the socioemotionally handicapped who are to be scheduled in the D&A program to gain some insight into the existing problems and thus be able to design meaningful individualized programs.

Stone[21] compiled the following list of psychological characteristics displayed by the emotionally disturbed child:

distractibility
tuning out
inappropriate peer interaction
odd mannerisms
disruption
difficulty in handling independent tasks
inability to accept direction
inaccessibility
short attention span
academic blocks
go-go jet propulsion
frozen silence
impulsive hitting out
breaking or taking other children's possessions
running away

disrupting class routine
defying the teacher
poking and teasing other students
not standing in line
throwing food in the lunchroom
blank expression
temper outbursts
destructiveness
unpredictability
variability in performance
surprising streaks of information
excitability
silly laugh
disorientation
imaginary tales
rudderlessness

[21] Reprinted from Thomas E. Stone, Ph.D., *Organizing and Operating Special Classes for Emotionally Disturbed Elementary School Children* (West Nyack, N.Y.: Parker Publishing Co., Inc., 1971), pp. 17, 32–33, by permission of the publisher. Copyright © 1971 by Parker Publishing Co., Inc.

Their behavior can be at the opposite pole:

withdrawal into a shell
ghostly appearance
lack of communication
distance from teachers and classmates
averted look
backing away if a friendly hand is placed on the shoulder
a wall of silence
a separate island

The diverse behavior patterns listed by Stone provide the teacher with some insight regarding the difficulty of identifying children with socio-emotional problems because many "normal" children manifest similar characteristics. The identification, classification, and prescription for these handicapped children must be determined by the school psychologist. However, the physical educator plays an important role in the learning process since he will be teaching these children. Thus he should possess knowledge related to behavior patterns of the atypical (and possible causes) and counseling techniques. Morse stresses the importance of the diagnostic ability of the teacher when he states:

The behavior symptoms a child displays are not an automatic revelation of the causes of that behavior. To plan effectively for a disturbed child, the teacher needs not only to see accurately what the youngster does but to understand why he does it. This requires the teacher to do some diagnostic thinking and to gain the ability to see life through the eyes of the pupil.[22]

The physical educator who teaches the disturbed child must demonstrate the ability to establish rapport with and empathy for him so that he can possibly identify the underlying causes of bizarre behavior patterns.

Summary

The identification of students in need of adapted physical education is the responsibility of the school physician, family physician, and/or the school psychologist. It is recommended that the physical educator classify those so identified for instructional purposes as physically handicapped, mentally handicapped, or socioemotionally handicapped. Once the students have been identified and classified, the teacher is urged to use the following suggestions as guidelines for aiding in the identification process:

 1. Following medical identification and classification, determine the developmental needs of each student. When necessary, subcategorize students; for example, direction will be given to teaching the physically handicapped if they are further

<hr>

[22] William C. Morse, "Disturbed Youngsters in the Classroom," *Today's Education*, LVIII, No. 4 (April, 1969), 31.

identified in terms of communicative disorders, motor disabilities/limitations, and circulorespiratory restrictions.

2. Design behavioral objectives that stress the importance of how a student "feels" toward his peer group, changes in attitude, and enhancement of self-concept.

3. Devise instruments to assess auditory, visual, tactile, gustatory, and kinesthetic senses so that programs can be planned accordingly to aid the child with a communication disorder to make successful compensatory adjustments.

4. Measure pre- and post-muscle group strength so that a sound exercising regimen can be implemented for the child with a motor disability or limitation; the regimen should be made more demanding as the Strength Decrement Index approaches 0 percent.

5. Utilize a flexometer, goniometer, or athrodial protractor to measure range of motion of those students displaying joint limitations.

6. Develop an exercising program for children afflicted with breathing allergies; measure pre- and post-tolerance limits and assess progress.

7. Become familiar with psychological aberrations that may be displayed by children with mental deficiencies attributable to brain injury or disease—the characteristics of hyperactivity, dissociation, figure-background disturbance, and perseveration. Devise instruments to aid in the identification of these traits.

8. Review the latest findings of all disciplines, particularly the behavioral sciences, and extrapolate those materials that may prove valuable in aiding the mentally handicapped child.

9. Be able to identify those students in the D&A program who exhibit socioemotional characteristics that conceivably may be indicative of potential juvenile delinquents or school drop-outs.

10. Register for additional course work in Special Education so that you gain some insight into the cause(s) of the symptoms manifested by each disturbed child and thus be better able to establish rapport with and empathy for the atypical.

Annotated Bibliography

AMERICAN ASSOCIATION FOR HEALTH, PHYSICAL EDUCATION AND RECREATION, UNIT ON PROGRAMS FOR THE HANDICAPPED. *The Best of Challenge.* Washington, D.C.: AAHPER, 1201 Sixteenth Street, N.W. 20036. A compilation of the best articles from the past issues of *Challenge*, AAHPER's newsletter for special educators. The material may be used as a basic or supplementary text for college/university courses in physical education, recreation, special education, and related areas; resource for agencies, organizations, institutions, or individual libraries; and references for workshops, clinics, seminars, and similar in-service and preservice programs.

————. *Guide for Evaluating Motor Development and Physical Performance of the Mentally Retarded.* Washington, D.C.: AAHPER, 1201 Sixteenth Street, N.W. 20036. 3 pp. Mimeographed. Provides specific guidelines (in the form of questions) for assessing the movement patterns, motor ability, and physical skills of the mentally retarded, ages 6–12. Free upon request.

————. *Information Sheet: Adapting the Special Fitness Test for Trainable Mentally Retarded*. Washington, D.C.: AAPHER, 1201 Sixteenth Street, N.W. 20036. 4 pp. Mimeographed. Provides guidelines for modifying the AAHPER/Kennedy Foundation Special Fitness Test so that attainable fitness goals can be established for the trainable retarded child. Free upon request.

————. *Information Sheet: Physical Education and Recreation Programs for the Emotionally Handicapped, Mentally Ill, Seriously Maladjusted and Emotionally Disturbed*. Washington, D.C.: AAHPER, 1201 Sixteenth Street, N.W. 20036, 18 pp. Mimeographed. Includes a list of over two hundred articles and books. Also provides the addresses of the major journals and periodicals and a list of key resource persons that may be contacted for additional information. Free upon request.

CRUICKSHANK, WILLIAM M. *The Brain-Injured Child in Home, School and Community*. Syracuse, N.Y.: Syracuse University Press, 1967. A text for families and teachers of the brain-injured. Discusses the symptoms of brain damage, recommends diagnostic procedures and personnel, and describes classroom and home techniques that have proved effective. Profusely illustrated with visuomotor materials and activities for classroom use.

————, ed. *Psychology of Exceptional Children and Youth*, 3rd ed. Englewood Cliffs, N.J.: Prentice-Hall, Inc., 1971. An excellent resource book for the teacher of the handicapped. Includes articles dealing with the varied handicapping conditions written by a group of eminent psychologists.

————, ed. *The Teacher of Brain-Injured Children*. Syracuse, N.Y.: Syracuse University Press, 1966. A book of readings regarding the preparing of qualified teachers to work with brain-injured children. Of particular interest to the physical educator would be the articles relating to cognitive, perceptual, and motor competencies; the development of visuomotor skills to enhance academic performance; specialized information on perception; and motor training.

DANIELS, LUCILLE, MARIAN WILLIAMS, and CATHERINE WORTHINGHAM. *Muscle Testing*, 2nd ed. Philadelphia: W. B. Saunders Company, 1956. Step-by-step explanation of techniques of manual muscle examination (346 illustrations). Explains how to determine the degree of weakness caused by disease, injury, or disuse.

VALETT, ROBERT E. *The Remediation of Learning Disabilities: A Handbook of Psychoeducational Resource Programs*. Belmont, Calif.: Fearon Publishers, 1967. Fifty-three resource programs. A text for the special educator, physical educator, or other specialists working with children with learning disabilities. Stresses diagnosis and evaluation of specific learning and/or behavioral problems in an effort to provide individualized instruction. Excellent variety of illustrations which depict various activities to enhance gross motor skills, sensory-motor integration, perceptual-motor skills, language development, conceptual skills, and social skills.

Who Is the Visually Handicapped Child? New York: American Foundation for the Blind, n.d. 9 pp. Gives an overview of the scope of the problem, educational objectives for visually handicapped children, types of educational programs and professional preparation programs for teachers of the visually handicapped. Free upon request.

5

statistical procedures and assessment of student status

The concept of developmental education implies the use of techniques to identify, classify, and assess the status of the student—the product of education. Chapters 3 and 4 were devoted to identification and classification of the handicapped child. Chapter 5 will deal with the procedures that are necessary to assess the initial status of the child who has been so identified and classified.

To assess the status of the individual, one must have a starting point—standards or norms with which to compare the child so that strengths and deficiencies can be determined. Normative data must thus be available, or prepared.

Although there are norms available in many measurement texts, teachers can prepare their own norms. Such an assumption immediately disturbs the classroom teacher because the implications are that he must have some in-depth knowledge of statistics. This is not so; the teacher need only be familiar with the rudiments of statistics—the determining of a mean score, standard deviation score, standard score, and the establishment of norm scores.

One might well ask, "Why must norms be established when texts are replete with normative data?" First, standards need not be established if text standards available satisfy the designs of the program planned. However, there are several valid reasons why the teacher should be able to prepare his own norms. For one, it may be that the standards you would like to use are only expressed in percentiles. Percentiles serve one primary function, an assessment of student rank in comparison with classmates; they cannot be used additively or for comparative purposes because the individual units of measurement are not equal in size. Thus, if a student ranks at the 10th percentile in arm strength and the 90th percentile in sit-ups, we can neither logically state he has an average of 50 for the two tests nor assume that his abdominal strength is nine times as great as his arm strength.

Another justification for the ability to design norms is that the teacher may want to design his own test battery which would not already have accessible norms. The establishment of tests and a normative scale based on the program's anticipated student behavioral outcomes is essential if one wants to develop a valid measurement and evaluation instrument. This rule is frequently violated by educators; objectives and content are expressed explicitly, but results are contaminated by incorrect test application.

A third point to support the argument for designing one's own norms is based on logic. Norms or standards are standardized scores based on a specific population. The scores of the population (those whose results were used to compile the norms) were influenced by heredity and environmental factors. To assume that norms established for a national population or a college group of women are applicable to a given school situation is erroneous. One can make such comparisons, but it does not follow that valid conclusions can then be made.

Of course, not all tests lend themselves to objective measurement; some assessment procedures involve primarily the subjective evaluation by the tester. Thus, it would be advantageous to objectify measuring instruments so that a normative scale can be prepared, another indication of the desirability of establishing standard scores. (See Chapter 3 for an objectively oriented point scale. This procedure was attempted with Kephart's Perceptual-Motor Test Battery.)

Contrary to the beliefs of some classroom teachers, the preparation of test norms is extremely feasible. The procedure recommended does not require several courses in statistics, nor does it require the use of a calculator (unless you desire to go beyond the test objectives and conduct an experimental study). Further, the practicality of preparing norms within the classroom environs justifies their use.

The remainder of Chapter 5 presents a "cook-book" procedure for the establishment of a normative scale. A basic understanding of the mathematical concepts involved will only be provided in those instances in which it is felt such an explanation is germane to the assessment procedure. (The reader interested in a more detailed discourse is referred to the reference related to the specific topic.) To make the statistical process as meaningful as possible, a series of hypothetical raw scores pertaining to a fitness test battery will be used and carried through the necessary intervening steps to the development of a normative table. The final section will present some guidelines for assessing student status and concludes with an explanation of how somatotyping can aid in the assessment process.

Raw Score Compilation

The raw score data provided below were the results of the administration of the standing broad jump to 39 girls with a chronological age of six. (*Note:* Test reliability increases with an increase in raw scores; the ultimate goal is to develop norms on the basis of 500 or more subjects. The small sample has been used to minimize the computations, but the procedure is exactly the same for a large sample.)

Test Item: Standing broad jump
Factor Measured: Explosive leg strength
Sex: Female
Age: 6

47	49	(54)			
30	40	36	37	34	29
(25)	38	27	33	42	39
40	41	42	42	41	43
40	35	43	37	44	41
35	31	36	43	44	38
44	40	42	41	45	53

A step-by-step approach to the statistical procedure will be used. Reference to Table 5–5 (p. 115) will aid the reader in understanding the processes involved in computing the mean, standard deviation, and percentiles. Texts by Smith,[1] Garrett,[2] and Barrow and McGee[3] will serve as excellent referential material (see Fig. 5–1).

[1] G. Milton Smith, *A Simplified Guide to Statistics for Psychology and Education*, 3rd ed. (New York: Holt, Rinehart & Winston, Inc., 1962).

[2] Hennry E. Garrett, *Statistics in Psychology and Education*, 6th ed. (New York: David McKay Company, Inc., 1966).

[3] Harold M. Barrow and Rosemary McGee, *A Practical Approach to Measurement in Physical Education* (Philadelphia: Lea and Febiger, 1964).

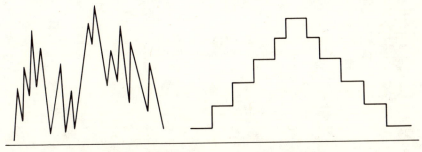

FIGURE 5–1   Converting raw data to grouped data.

Step #1: Converting raw data to grouped data

a. Prepare a grouping data sheet as illustrated in Table 5–5 (see p. 115). Typing a stencil or a duplicating master is recommended so that the teacher can reproduce a supply sufficient for his needs. After testing your students, you can immediately calculate the mean, standard deviation, and percentile scores on the form without any additional aids.

b. Determine the number of step intervals to be used. The number and size of step intervals are based on the range of scores (highest to lowest scores). Note that the raw scores 54 and 25 have been circled; by subtracting, we get a range of 29. Ten to twenty step intervals are recommended to give the best picture of the "spread" of the scores. If we were to select a step interval size of three and divide the range by the step interval, we would get nine intervals. In Table 5–1, a step interval of two was used, necessitating fifteen step intervals. (*Note:* If possible, select odd-numbered intervals such as 1, 3, 5, or 7; the reason will be explained during the discussion on mean computational process.)

c. Record the step intervals on the tally sheet. Starting with the score of 24 to include the lowest raw score of 25, step intervals of two were recorded up to the 54–55 interval so that the highest raw score of 54 was included. (*Note:* Make sure that the bottom score of the lowest step interval is divisible by the size of the interval.)

Since errors are frequently made in discerning step interval sizes, a brief explanation will be given. There are *whole number* and *real interval* limits; the 24–25 step interval refers to the whole number limits. In this case it appears that the interval size is 1, but that is not so. To determine the step interval size, you must locate the "real" limits; the real limits in the case of the 24–25 illustration would be a lower limit of 23.5 and an upper limit of 25.5. Thus the size of the 24–25 step interval is 2. Another way of checking interval size is to check the lower and upper whole numbers from the bottom up; thus, you get 24, 26, 28, etc., and 25, 27, 29, etc. Note that each step is 2, the size of the interval. This procedure is also recommended to insure the recording of consistent interval sizes since a slight error will negate the value of all subsequent efforts.

TABLE 5–1 Procedure for Grouping Raw Data

S.I.		f
54–55	/	1
52–53	/	1
50–51		
48–49	/	1
46–47	/	1
44–45	////	4
42–43	⫟⫟⫟ //	7
40–41	⫟⫟⫟ ///	8
38–39	///	3
36–37	////	4
34–35	///	3
32–33	/	1
30–31	//	2
28–29	/	1
26–27	/	1
24–25	/	1
		$\Sigma f = 39$

d. The final step in the grouping process requires the recording of a tally mark for each raw score in the frequency column (*f*). The raw score of 47 would he placed under the frequency column in the 46–47 step interval. After all tallies are recorded, place the numerical values to the right of the column and record the "Σ*f*" (the sum of the frequencies) at the bottom. In the illustration the total of 39 is consistent with the number of raw scores (another important check). (*Note:* If you are working with scores whereby the smaller scores are indicative of greater achievement, be sure to place the smallest score in the top step interval and then work down; all scores based on time would require that adjustment.)

By grouping the data in this fashion, the individual scores become more meaningful. For example, hold Table 5–1 sideward so that the step intervals are closest to the floor. You can see how the tally marks are starting to assume a "normal curve" distribution. You can further observe that the majority of the students recorded jumps of 34 to 45 inches with a *mode* (interval with the greatest number of frequencies) of 40.5 inches.

Computing the Mean

The arithmetic *mean* can be determined by adding all raw scores and dividing by the number of scores. In the example listed, the procedure does not take too much time. However, when working with 100 or more scores, a calculator is needed. The recommended procedure eliminates the need for a calculator regardless of the number of scores involved. Furthermore, once you gain experience you can compute the mean as quickly as you can with a calculator. Most important, you will not be sacrificing mathematical accuracy because the illustrated method seldom deviates from the arithmetic mean by "one integer." (In two years of teaching statistics to high school seniors, the author has never experienced a situation in which the deviation was more than .5.) The only conceivable way the deviation could be greater than the whole number 1 would be if one or more scores were a great deal above or below the pattern.

The close proximity of the score attained by the two methods is not attributable to chance, but rather to a mathematical principle which states that the best estimate of a group of scores in an interval is the midpoint of that interval. Although all scores will seldom cluster at the midpoint, scores above and below the midpoint seem to counterbalance one another. In addition, an increase in the number of scores in an interval reduces the chance of error.

Let us try an experiment with the illustrated data. The sum of the 39 raw scores is 1,541; by dividing by 39 (and carrying out the remainder three decimal places and rounding off to two places) we get an arithmetic mean of 39.51. Now let us compute the mean by the step interval method (see Fig. 5–2).

90 + 70 + 60 ... = Raw Scores

Total Raw Scores   Number of Students   Arithmetic Mean

FIGURE 5–2   Computing the arithmetic mean.

Step #2: Step interval method for computing the mean

a. Select the "assumed mean" step interval (the interval you believe contains the arithmetic mean). In Table 5–2 you will note that the 36–37 interval was selected as the assumed mean interval. You might well state that the 40–41 interval looks more appropriate and you are right. However, it is a good practice to select an assumed mean interval one or two steps below where you feel it should be. To put it another way, be sure that *more* than 50 percent of the raw scores are above the assumed mean to avoid an error in mathematical computations. For example, assuming one selected a higher interval for the assumed mean, the algebraic sum of the *fd* column (Σfd) conceivably would be negative. The negative score could thus require the changing of the sign of the mean formula to

$$\text{Mean} = A.M. - \left(\frac{\Sigma fd}{n} \times S.I.\right).$$

With the above change, your answer would be correct, but why not avoid the possibility of error and select the assumed mean interval well below the midpoint?

In actuality, you may select any interval for the assumed mean; in every case regardless of the interval selected, the mean score will be exactly the same. You may want to try that experiment on your own. Select an interval other than the one selected in Table 5–2 and go through the computations—it will be good practice.

In the formula for computing the mean (Table 5–2) you will note that the assumed mean was recorded as 36.50—the midpoint of the interval. In this instance the midpoint was relatively easy to determine; what would the midpoint be if the interval had been 36–40? Is it 38 or 38.5? Determining the interval midpoint can sometimes cause error unless you have a definite procedure for determining it. Follow this simple procedure and you will always be right. Subtract the whole number limits (40 − 36 = 4); add 1 to include real limits (4 + 1 = 5, the size of the step interval); divide by 2 (5 ÷ 2 = 2.5); and add 2.5 to the real lower limit of the interval (35.5 + 2.5 = 38.0). You will note that the midpoint is 38.0, a whole number.

Earlier, reference was made to the preferability of selecting odd-numbered step intervals; the rationale is that if you select an odd-numbered interval your assumed mean will be a whole number. In some cases, as in the illustration, you may have to select an even-numbered interval; in those instances, the midpoint will be a whole number plus .5 (the assumed mean in Table 5–2 is 36.5).

b. Record the deviation scores (*d*). Place a zero under the *d* column in the 36–37 step interval. Going above zero, record deviation scores 1, 2, 3, etc.; below zero,

TABLE 5-2   Step Interval Method for Computing the Mean

S.I.	f		d	fd	Symbols
54–55	/	1	9	9	S.I. = step interval
52–53	/	1	8	8	Σ = the sum of
50–51			7	0	f = frequencies
48–49	/	1	6	6	A.M. = assumed mean
46–47	/	1	5	5	d = deviations from the assumed
44–45	////	4	4	16	mean
42–43	⫫⫫ //	7	3	21	fd = frequencies × deviations
40–41	⫫⫫ ///	8	2	16	Σfd = the sum of the f's × d's
38–39	///	3	1	3	n = number of raw scores
36–37	////	4	0	84/−26	Formula: Mean = $A.M. + \left(\dfrac{\Sigma fd}{n} \times S.I.\right)$
34–35	///	3	−1	−3	$= 36.50 + \left(\dfrac{58}{39} \times 2\right)$
32–33	/	1	−2	−2	
30–31	//	2	−3	−6	$= 36.50 + (1.49 \times 2)$
28–29	/	1	−4	−4	$= 36.50 + (2.98)$
26–27	/	1	−5	−5	Mean = 39.48
24–25	/	1	−6	−6	Arithmetic Mean = 39.51
	Σf's = 39			Σfd = 58	

scores are recorded as -1, -2, -3, etc. (*Note: Deviation scores* refer to the deviation of the specific step interval you are working with from the assumed mean interval. For example, the 48–49 step interval is 6 steps above the assumed mean.)

c. Record the frequency times deviation scores (*fd*). Table 5–2 indicates that the 38–39 step interval has an *f* of 3 and a *d* of 1, thus an *fd* of 3. All other *fd* scores are recorded in a similar manner, by multiplying the *f*-scores times the *d*-scores. Note that below the assumed mean interval all *fd* scores have a negative value since a positive value times a negative value will always result in a negative score. Sum up all *fd* scores; you will obtain 84 and -26. Record them as illustrated. Algebraically sum up the two scores (84 plus -26) and record them at the bottom of the *fd* column as Σfd (58). You now have all the data necessary to compute the mean.

d. Apply the data to the formula:

$$\text{Mean} = A.M. + \left(\frac{\Sigma fd}{n} \times S.I.\right),$$

where: $S.I.$ = size of the step interval.

Basically, the formula provides a correction factor $\left(\dfrac{\Sigma fd}{n} \times S.I.\right)$ for any error in assuming the mean. By substitution we get:

$$\text{Mean} = 36.50 + \left(\frac{58}{39} \times 2\right)$$
$$= 36.50 + (1.49 \times 2)$$
$$= 36.50 + (2.98)$$
$$= 39.48.$$

If you recall, our arithmetic or true mean was 39.51, or only .03 greater than the mean computed by the step interval method. If you are not yet convinced of the accuracy of this method, replicate the procedure with a set of raw data from a test you administered.

Computing the Standard Deviation

Whereas the mean provides the single most reliable score of a group of scores, the *standard deviation* (σ) indicates the amount of variability that exists in the population. Once the standard deviation is determined, you are in possession of all the information necessary to establish a norm table based on standard scores. There are, however, other excellent reasons for computing the mean and standard deviation; they may be used to group students on the basis of similar abilities, or to determine student grades objectively. Both procedures will be discussed during the section relating to the development of standard scores (see Fig. 5–3).

Step #3: Step interval method for computing the standard deviation
a. Determine the fd^2 scores. The formula for determining the standard deviation,

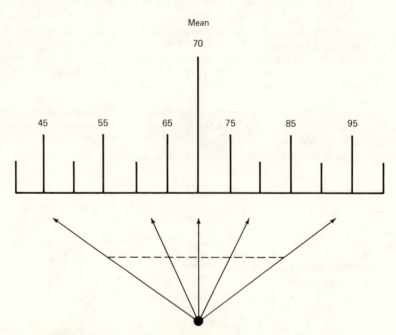

FIGURE 5-3 Standard deviation: a measure of variability. Each area between arrows represents one standard deviation (σ) above or below the mean.

$$S.D. = S.I. \sqrt{\frac{\Sigma fd^2}{n} - c^2},$$

requires only substituting scores for Σfd^2 and c^2. Table 5–3 indicates that $c^2 = \left(\frac{\Sigma fd}{n}\right)^2$; thus, since we have 1.49 for the $\frac{\Sigma fd}{n}$, we merely square 1.49 to solve for c^2. To record the fd^2 scores, simply perform the following computations for each interval: multiply the d score times the fd score and place the result in the fd^2 column. For example, the step interval 40–41 has a d score of 2 and an fd score of 16; thus, the fd^2 score is 32. Be sure to avoid the pitfall that has befallen many others; *do not* square the fd score to get the fd^2 score. If you square the fd score, the result is f^2d^2, not the fd^2 that we are looking for. One further reminder is in order at this time: remember that when you multiply two negative numbers, your answer is positive. Thus, in the 24–25 interval, we are multiplying -6 times -6 with a resultant $+36$. Finally, sum up all of the fd^2 scores and record them at the bottom as Σfd^2 (470).

b. Apply the data to the formula:

$$S.D. = S.I. \sqrt{\frac{\Sigma fd^2}{n} - c^2}.$$

By substitution we get:

$$S.D. = 2\sqrt{\frac{470}{39} - (1.49)^2}$$

$$= 2\sqrt{12.05 - 2.22}$$

$$= 2\sqrt{9.83}$$

$$= 2 \times (3.14)$$

Standard Deviation $= 6.28$.

A good "rule of thumb" to remember when computing the standard deviation is that the ratio of the range of scores to the standard deviation is seldom smaller than 2 or greater than 6. In the above example the real range was 30 (54.5–24.5) and the standard deviation was 6.28, a ratio of slightly less than 5:1. When ratios tend to exceed these limits, it is advisable to review your standard deviation computations.

For those who have difficulty extracting square roots, either of two procedures is recommended: the use of a slide rule or a text with prepared square root tables. Arkin and Colton[4] have prepared an inexpensive paperback with a table of squares (100–1,000) and a table of square roots (1,000–10,000). Twenty-five other frequently used tables are also provided. Explanations and instructions accompany each table.

For those who would like to review and master the computation of

---

[4] Herbert Arkin and Raymond R. Colton, *Tables for Statisticians*, 2nd ed. (New York: Barnes and Noble, Inc., 1963).

TABLE 5-3 Step Interval Method for Computing the Standard Deviation

S.I.	f	d	fd	fd²
54–55	1	9	9	81
52–53	1	8	8	64
50–51		7	0	0
48–49	1	6	6	36
46–47	1	5	5	25
44–45	4	4	16	64
42–43	7	3	21	63
40–41	8	2	16	32
38–39	3	1	3	3
36–37	4	0	84/−26	0
34–35	3	−1	−3	3
32–33	1	−2	−2	4
30–31	2	−3	−6	18
28–29	1	−4	−4	16
26–27	1	−5	−5	25
24–25	1	−6	−6	36
			$\Sigma fd = 58$	$\Sigma fd^2 = 470$

Symbols

$S.I.$ = step interval
Σ = the sum of
$A.M.$ = assumed mean
d = deviations from the assumed mean
fd = frequencies × deviations
Σfd = the sum of f's × d's
n = number of raw scores
fd^2 = d's × fd's
Σfd^2 = the sum of d's × fd's
c^2 = correction factor squared $\left(\dfrac{\Sigma fd}{n}\right)^2$
$S.D.$ = standard deviation

Formulae:

$$\text{Mean} = A.M.\left(\frac{\Sigma fd}{n} \times S.I.\right)$$
$$= 36.50\left(\frac{58}{39} \times 2\right)$$
$$= 36.50(1.49 \times 2)$$
$$= 36.50(2.98)$$
$$\text{Mean} = 39.48.$$

$$S.D. = S.I.\sqrt{\frac{\Sigma fd^2}{n} - c^2}$$
$$= 2\sqrt{\frac{470}{39} - (1.49)^2}$$
$$= 2\sqrt{12.05 - 2.22}$$
$$= 2\sqrt{9.83}$$
$$= 2 \times (3.14)$$
$$\text{Standard Deviation} = 6.28.$$

square roots, the following detailed explanation, provided in Barrow and McGee's text *A Practical Approach to Measurement in Physical Education*,[5] is offered:

Step 1 $\sqrt{24.60\ 16\ 00}$

1. Mark off by 2's from either side of the decimal mark.

Step 2

$$\begin{array}{r} 4 \\ \sqrt{24.60\ 16\ 00} \\ 16 \end{array}$$

2. Select the largest number that will go into 24 squared (4) and place it first in the answer.

Step 3

$$\begin{array}{r} 4 \\ \sqrt{24.60\ 16\ 00} \\ 16 \end{array}$$

$$8\,?\ |\ 8\ 60$$

3. Drop the next two numbers into place by the 8 and double the partial answer to start a new divisor.

Step 4

$$\begin{array}{r} 4.\,9 \\ \sqrt{24.60\ 16\ 00} \\ 16 \end{array}$$

$$89\ |\ \begin{array}{r} 8\ 60 \\ 8\ 01 \\ \hline 59 \end{array}$$

4. Estimate how many times 8? will go into 860 and use this number (9) in the answer and in the divisor to replace the ?. Whatever number goes in the new divisor must also go in the answer.

Step 5

$$\begin{array}{r} 4.\,9 \\ \sqrt{24.60\ 16\ 00} \\ 16 \end{array}$$

$$89\ |\ \begin{array}{r} 8\ 60 \\ 8\ 01 \end{array}$$

$$98\,?\ |\ 59\ 16$$

5. Double the 49 for the new divisor. Drop the next two numbers into the dividend.

Step 6

$$\begin{array}{r} 4.\,9\ \ 6 \\ \sqrt{24.60\ 16\ 00} \\ 16 \end{array}$$

$$89\ |\ \begin{array}{r} 8\ 60 \\ 8\ 01 \end{array}$$

$$986\ |\ \begin{array}{r} 59\ 16 \\ 59\ 16 \end{array}$$

6. Estimate how many times 98? will go into 5916 and fill in this number (6) into the answer and into the divisor.

Continue no further because the answer comes out even.

Table 5–3 indicated the need for extracting the square root of 9.83 ($\sqrt{9.83}$); compute it mathematically and see if your answer is 3.14.

Percentile Rank Scores

Percentile rank scores indicate the location of a single score in comparison with a series of scores listed in a continuum, from the lowest to the highest.

---

5 Barrow and McGee, *op. cit.*, pp. 69–70.

Percentile
Scores

Standard
Scores

FIGURE 5–4 Percentile rank scores compared to standard scores. Note the differences in score dispersement.

Although these scores serve no function in the establishment of a normative table based on standard scores, they do aid in the interpretation of a student's achievement in relation to his peer group. Upon completion of a test, a student usually asks, "How does my score compare with those of others who have taken the test?" Like standard scores, the preparation of a percentile rank table can be accomplished by use of the step interval procedure. It is recommended that percentile rank tables be developed for each test item since they can be easily interpreted to the student, parent, and community (see Fig. 5–4).

Step #4: Step interval method for computing percentile ranks
If we look at Table 5–4 we can see that we must merely establish the step intervals and determine cumulated frequencies to compute a percentile rank table (other scores have been computed in previous steps).

a. Establish step intervals.

b. Record cumulated frequency scores. By referring to the lowest interval (24–25), you will note that there is 1 tally in the f column; 1 tally in the 26–27 interval; 1 tally in the 28–29 interval; etc. Cumulated scores are recorded by starting at the bottom and entering the sum of the tallies as you progress upward. Thus, under the cf column in the 24–25 interval you would record 1, since the total number of tallies at this point is 1. In the 26–27 interval, you would record 2— the sum of the one tally in that interval, plus the one below. Continue the process until you have recorded all tally scores, 39 in this case. Incidentally, make sure your top f score corresponds with the sum of the f scores—another important check.

c. Determine P_p—the percentage of the distribution you are seeking. Let us assume we are seeking the median score (that point at which 50 percent of the scores will fall above and 50 percent below); our P_p would then be recorded as P_{50}.

d. Determine C_s, the number of cases sought. If we are seeking P_{50}, we must ascertain that point in the continuum up to where 50 percent of the cases would be located. Thus, to determine C_s we would multiply .50 times the total number of scores (.50 × 39) and get 19.5; if we desired P_{10}, our cases sought would be .10 times 39, or 3.9.

TABLE 5–4   Step Interval Method for Computing Percentile Rank Scores

S.I.		f	d	fd	fd²	cf
54–55	/	1				39
52–53	/	1				38
50–51						37
48–49	/	1				37
46–47	/	1				36
44–45	////	4				35
42–43	‖‖ //	7				31
40–41	‖‖ ///	8				24
38–39	///	3				16
36–37	////	4				13
34–35	///	3				9
32–33	/	1				6
30–31	//	2				5
28–29	/	1				3
26–27	/	1				2
24–25	/	1				1
		$\Sigma f = 39$				

Symbols:

$S.I.$ = step interval
cf = cumulated frequencies
P_p = percentage desired
LL = real lower limit of P_p interval
C_s = number of cases sought
C_b = sum of the scores below real lower limit
C_w = number of scores within interval containing P_p

Formula:

$$P_p = LL + \left(\frac{C_s - C_b}{C_w} \times S.I. \right)$$

$$P_{50} = 39.50 + \left(\frac{19.5 - 16}{8} \times 2 \right)$$

$$= 39.50 + \left(\frac{3.5}{8} \times 2 \right)$$

$$= 39.50 + (.44 \times 2)$$

$$= 39.50 + .88$$

$$P_{50} = 40.38.$$

e. Determine *LL*, the real lower limit of the P_p interval. If we are seeking P_{50}, which involves the location of the point where 19.5 cases are situated, we have but to refer to the *cf* column and locate the interval 19.5. In Table 5–4, note that there is no 19.5 listed; our *LL* would be located between the 38–39 interval, which has a *cf* of 16, and the 40–41 interval, which has a *cf* of 24. An important rule to remember is that if the C_s (in this instance, 19.5) is only slightly greater than the *cf* score in an interval, you would select the next highest step interval as containing *LL*. Thus, 19.5 is greater than 16 and, as a consequence, *LL* would be recorded as the real lower limit of the 40–41 interval. Had the C_s score been 16.1, the result would have been the same—the location of *LL* as the real lower limit of the 40–41 interval.

If you recall, step interval limits are expressed as whole number limits and real interval limits. In the problem at hand, the whole number limits are 40–41;

the real interval (fractional limits) are 39.5–41.5. Since the *LL* we are seeking is the real lower limit of the cases sought interval, *LL* would be recorded as 39.5.

f. Determine C_b, the sum of the scores below *LL*. By reference to the *cf* column we note that there are 16 cases below the interval we have selected; thus our C_b is 16.

g. Determine C_w, the number of cases within the interval selected. The 40–41 interval has 8 tallies within its bounds; thus C_w is 8.

h. Apply the data to the formula:

$$P_p = LL + \left(\frac{C_s - C_b}{C_w} \times S.I.\right).$$

By substitution,

$$P_{50} = 39.50 + \left(\frac{19.5 - 16}{8} \times 2\right)$$

$$P_{50} = 39.50 + \left(\frac{3.5}{8} \times 2\right)$$

$$P_{50} = 39.50 + (.44 \times 2)$$

$$P_{50} = 39.50 + .88$$

$$P_{50} = 40.38.$$

Thus the P_{50}, the median score, is 40 (rounded off). (If the distribution of a group of scores is such that a "perfect" normal curve were attained, the mean, median, and mode would be exactly the same. It is interesting to note how closely the data we have been using approach this utopian situation; our scores are mean, 39.48; mode, 40.50; and median, 40.38. The consistency of scores is especially significant in light of the use of only 39 scores.) Another important check at this point would be to compare the score attained with the *real* interval limits. Since the limits of the P_{50} interval are 39.5–41.5 and the cases sought are located within that interval, the percentile rank score must also be located within those bounds. By comparison, the score 40.38 is near, but below, the upper limits of the interval (41.5); thus, one can be reasonably sure the answer is correct. For interpretive purposes, a student attaining a standing broad jump score of 40 inches would have achieved a percentile rank of 50. In other words, his score was such that he would have achieved better than 50 percent of the six-year-old boys or, conversely, 50 percent of the boys achieved better than he did.

By use of the same procedure, a percentile rank table can be prepared for class use. Table 5–5, a composite of all previous calculations, provides percentile rank scores for P_p intervals of 5. Intervening raw scores can be interpolated or further computed by determining P_1, P_2, P_3, etc.

TABLE 5–5 Step Interval Method for Computing the Mean, Standard Deviation, and Percentile Rank Scores

S.I.	f	d	fd	fd²	cf
54–55	1	9	9	81	39
52–53	1	8	8	64	38
50–51	0	7	0	0	37
48–49	1	6	6	36	37
46–47	1	5	5	25	36
44–45	4	4	16	64	35
42–43	7	3	21	63	31
40–41	8	2	16	16	24
38–39	3	1	3	3	16
36–37	4	0	84/−26 0	0	13
34–35	3	−1	−3	3	9
32–33	1	−2	−2	4	6
30–31	2	−3	−6	18	5
28–29	1	−4	−4	16	3
26–27	1	−5	−5	25	2
24–25	1	−6	−6	36	1
	$\Sigma f = 39$		$\Sigma fd = 58$	$\Sigma fd^2 = 470$	

	Standing broad jump		Event
	Explosive strength		Factor
	6.28		Standard Deviation

		X Girls	6 Age	2 S.I.
Boys				
	39	Number		
	39.48	Mean		
	(25–54) 29	Range		
	40.38	Median		

Symbols:

$S.I.$ = step interval
Σ = the sum of
f = frequencies
$A.M.$ = assumed mean
d = deviations from assumed mean
fd = frequencies × deviations
Σfd = sum of the f's × d's
n = number of raw scores
fd^2 = d's × fd's
Σdf^2 = sum of d's × fd's
c^2 = correction factor squared $\left(\dfrac{\Sigma fd}{n}\right)^2$
$S.D.$ = standard deviation
cf = cumulated frequencies
P_p = percentage desired
LL = real lower limit of P_p interval
C_s = number of cases sought
C_b = number of the cases below LL
C_w = number of cases within interval containing P_p

Formulae:

$$\text{Mean} = A.M. + \left(\frac{\Sigma fd}{n} \times S.I.\right)$$
$$= 36.50 + \left(\frac{58}{39} \times 2\right)$$
$$= 36.50 + (1.49 \times 2)$$
$$= 36.50 + 2.98$$
$$\text{Mean} = 39.48.$$

$$S.D. = S.I.\sqrt{\frac{\Sigma fd^2}{n} - c^2}$$
$$= 2\sqrt{\frac{470}{39} - (1.49)^2}$$
$$= 2\sqrt{12.05 - 2.22}$$
$$= 2\sqrt{9.83}$$
$$= 2 \times (3.14)$$
$$S.D. = 6.28.$$

Determining percentile rank:

$$P_p = LL + \left(\frac{C_s - C_b}{C_w} \times S.I.\right)$$
$$P_{50} = 39.50 + \left(\frac{19.5 - 16}{8} \times 2\right)$$
$$= 39.50 + \left(\frac{3.5}{8} \times 2\right)$$
$$= 39.50 + (.44 \times 2)$$
$$= 39.40 + .88$$
$$P_{50} = 40.38.$$

Percentile rank table:

P_{99} =	P_{65} =	P_{30} =
P_{95} =	P_{60} =	P_{25} =
P_{90} =	P_{55} =	P_{20} =
P_{85} =	P_{50} = 40	P_{15} =
P_{80} =	P_{45} =	P_{10} =
P_{75} =	P_{40} =	P_{5} =
P_{70} =	P_{35} =	P_{0} =

Standard Scores

The preparation of valid norm tables presupposes the use of the mean and the standard deviation. By using the mean score as the midpoint and variations of the standard deviation as consistent units of measurement, we can devise tables that can be used to accurately assess the individual's status in comparison to the group. Comparisons can be made in terms of individual test items and on the basis of the composite test battery. In addition, profiles can be constructed whereby each scale score can be recorded for comparative purposes. Thus one may compare components such as a student evidencing a dynamic strength that is doubly superior to his cardiorespiratory endurance. Such information is vital for the prescription of individualized activities.

Earlier we mentioned that the mean and standard deviation could provide a means of ability grouping students and determining grades. (The procedure is very simple, so with the indulgence of the reader a small digression is in order.) Let us assume you would like to form four ability groups in class based on explosive leg strength. With a mean of 39.48 and a standard deviation of 6.28, proceed as follows: divide 4 (the four groups you wish) into 6 (the total number of standard deviations in the normal curve); multiply the resultant 1.5 times the standard deviation (6.28); and determine group ranges by adding the sum 9.42 to the mean to establish two upper intervals and by subtracting 9.42 from the mean to establish two lower intervals.

Mean = 39.48   *S.D.* = 6.28   1.5(*S.D.*) = 9.42

group	*scores*	*rounded off*
Group *A*	58.32	58
	48.90	49
Group *B*		
	39.48 mean	39
Group *C*		
	30.06	30
Group *D*		
	20.64	21

Thus, you would include in Group *A* (the top ability group) those students whose scores were 49 inches or greater; in Group *B* those students whose scores were 39–48 inches, etc.

The procedure would be the same if you wanted to issue four grades. However, let us assume you wanted five groups or grades; then, two adjustments would be needed. Since you used five categories, you divide the six standard deviations by five (6/5) and multiply the resultant 1.2 times 6.28 (7.54). The second change is necessitated by the odd number five. Since we cannot evenly place the five scores above and below the mean score, we must initially place one-half of the 7.54 (3.77) above and below the mean score and then add or subtract the full 7.54 two additional times.

Mean = 39.48   *S.D.* = 6.28   1.2(*S.D.*) = 7.54 $\frac{1}{2}$(7.54) = 3.77

group or grade	scores	rounded off
A	58.33	58
B	50.79	51
	43.25	43
C	39.48 mean	
D	35.71	36
	28.17	28
E	20.63	21

To be assigned to the top group, or to achieve an *A*, a student would have to jump 51 inches or better; Group *B* classification would be a score of 43–50; Group *C*, 36–42; Group *D*, 28–35; and Group *E*, 21–27.

You may have noted that in both of the illustrated examples the limits attained for grouping (58 and 21) exceeded the actual high and low range scores (54 and 25). Such a situation leads us directly into an explanation of the three most commonly used standard scores: *Sigma scale*, *T-scale*, and *Hull scale*. All three scale scores are determined by placing the mean score opposite the score of 50 and then making slight variations in the standard deviation scores. The scale score that you select should be dependent upon the population you are testing; if it is an atypical group, you would want to use a T-scale. With a fairly homogeneous group you can either use Sigma or Hull scores. An illustration will help to clarify the selection of the proper scale by computing the 40–60 decile range for each of the three standard scores.

To compute the sigma scale, place the mean (39.48) opposite the scale score of 50. Multiply the standard deviation (6.28) by .6 (3.77), add to the mean score for a scale score of 60, and subtract from the mean score for a scale score of 40. To determine T- and Hull scale scores follow the same procedure with one exception; for T-scale add the entire standard deviation score as the decile unit, and for the Hull scale multiply the standard deviation by .7. Note the ranges of the following scale scores:

Mean = 39.48   *S.D.* = 6.28.

	Sigma scale .6(*S.D.*) = 3.77	Hull scale .7(*S.D.*) = 4.40	T-scale 1(*S.D.*) = 6.28
60	43.25	43.88	45.76
50	39.48	39.48	39.48
40	35.71	35.08	33.20

You can see how the range of the scale scores increases: Sigma scale, 35.71–43.25; Hull scale, 35.08–43.88; and T-scale, 33.20–45.76. Thus, the T-scale would include more divergent scores. However, some statisticians maintain that the T-scale is not practical because it includes scores that are not attainable by the population and as a result are not realistic. As previously mentioned, you should attempt to select that achievement scale that establishes realistic limitations for the population with which you are working.

Establishing Norms

Now that all of the preliminary work has been done, the preparation of normative tables merely necessitates the use of an adding machine. However, as a refresher, let us review the procedures involved:

1. Determine the mean and the standard deviation (39.48 and 6.28).
2. Order a column of numbers from 1–100 and place the mean score of the data opposite 50.
3. For decile intervals, multiply the standard deviation by .6 (Sigma scale), .7 (Hull scale), and 1 (T-scale). To set up intervals based on hundredths, multiply by .06, .07, and .10.
4. Consecutively add the modified standard deviation to the mean for scores 51–100 and subtract for scores 0–49.

See Table 5–6, which is patterned after a scale score procedure designed by Mathews.[6]

[6] Don Mathews, *Measurement in Physical Education* (Philadelphia: W. B. Saunders Company, 1963), p. 39.

TABLE 5–6   Calculation of Sigma, Hull, and T-scales
for the Standing Broad Jump[a]

Mean = 39.48   Standard Deviation = 6.28

Scale score	Sigma scale .6 S.D. = 3.77		Hull scale .7 S.D. = 4.40		T-scale 1 S.D. = 6.28	
	computed	rounded off	computed	rounded off	computed	rounded off
100	58.33	58	61.48	61	70.88	71
90	54.56	55	57.08	57	64.60	65
80	50.79	51	52.68	53	58.32	58
70	47.02	47	48.28	48	52.04	52
60	43.25	43	43.88	44	45.76	46
50	39.48	39	39.48	39	39.48	39
40	35.71	36	35.08	35	33.20	33
30	31.94	32	30.68	31	26.92	27
20	28.17	28	26.28	26	20.64	21
10	24.40	24	21.88	22	14.36	14
0	20.63	21	17.48	17	8.08	8

[a] The scores have been expressed in deciles to facilitate the presentation.

Compare the range of the raw scores (25–54) with the range of the scores on the three scales. In this case, the Sigma scale seems most practical. For years, most statisticians prepared norms based on T-scales but the present trend seems to favor the more realistic Hull scales, since in most cases they establish attainable, yet inclusive, upper and lower limits.

It is recommended that the necessary standards be prepared so that you can assess a child's status and thus provide the basis for individualized programming. The next section of the chapter will furnish examples of how the student's status can be assessed on the basis of some of the recommended developmental test items.

Assessing Student Status

To best assess student status we must convert all raw scores to standard scores or replicate the statistics listed in the previous sections so that test battery achievement scales can be prepared. With this information we can determine a test battery cut-off score—that arbitrary point for determining whether or not students are assigned to D&A. For example, in Chapter 3, one of the behavioral outcomes states that a student can attain a minimum average standard score of 40 on the Physical Fitness Test Battery, with no single component score of less than 10. A student who scores below 40 on the total battery or below 10 on any single item would be assigned for special instruction.

Determination of a Cut-off Score

As an example, let us assume we would like to establish a procedure for determining which students should be classified as evidencing low physical vitality. Let us further assume that students so classified would be those who score in the bottom 10 percent of the population. The first step would be to convert all raw scores to standard scores. Then, proceed by taking the first student's scores and getting a single representative, mean average standard score. For example, John achieved standard scores of 40, 30, 20, 50, 30, and 10; his mean average standard score would be 30 (180 divided by 6). Proceed in a similar manner until a mean average standard score has been determined for each student in the population.

Using the recommended step interval procedure, compute the mean and standard deviation based on the mean average standard scores (arbitrary scores are mean, 52; and standard deviation, 9). With this information we can determine that score below which 10 percent of the population will fall.

Next, let us refer to a normal probability chart, which can be found in any statistics text. (It is important, at this point, to note that this entire procedure is based on the assumption that the data approximates a normal distribution.) Since all data furnished in the chart refers to distances from the mean, we must locate that point from the mean which includes 40 percent of the scores (4,000); the closest figure recorded is 3,397, or 33.97 percent of the scores. By noting the column and row figures that intersect at that point, we locate 1.28, the number of standard deviation units that 33.97 percent of the scores are removed from the mean score. Figure 5–5 will help clarify the explanation. Note that standard deviation units are reflected in both positive and negative terms; therefore, 1.28 can be used to reflect that point on either side of the mean. Since we desire the lowest 10 percent of the scores, we would be interested in the value of -1.28 because anything below -1.28 would include the bottom 10 percent of the scores.

The final step in determining our cut-off point would be to multiply -1.28 times the standard deviation (9.00) and to subtract the product (-11.52) from the mean score of 52.00 (40.48). Thus, in this example, a student who attains a mean average standard score on the Physical Fitness Test Battery of less than 40.48 would be identified as scoring in the bottom 10 percent of the population. Furthermore, for the purposes of this test he would be classified as evidencing low physical vitality and would be scheduled for developmental physical education.

You probably realize that once one has determined the mean and standard deviation for the composite scores, any desirable cut-off point can be located. If we only wanted to include the bottom 5 percent of the population, we would locate 4,500 (half of 90 percent); scores of 4,495 or 4.505 may be used since they are equidistant from 4,500. Using 4,495, we arrive at 1.64 standard deviation units. Multiplication of -1.64 times the standard deviation of 9 gives us a product of -14.76. Subtracting -14.76 from the mean score of 52.00 results in the 5 percent cut-off score of 38 (38.24). Thus, one can use the standard score procedure to identify students for program placement.

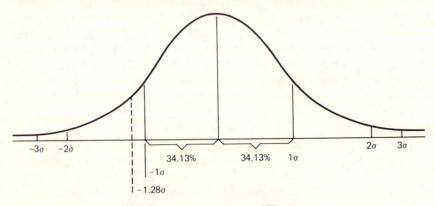

FIGURE 5–5   Normal probability curve.

Assessing Individual Student Abilities

One of the primary values of standard scores is that they permit the teacher to add raw scores that are based on different units of measurement, e.g., inches, pounds, and seconds, which provides a composite, representative score for the student's ability on selected test batteries.

Of equal and possibly greater significance, standard scores permit the instructor to compare the student's ability on various tasks. By virtue of the statistics involved in computing these achievement scales (starting with a uniform midpoint of 50 and being modified in terms of deviation units), scores of the same individual, or individuals taken from the same population, are comparable.

Figure 5–6 provides a replica of the Motor/Perceptual Progress Profile sheet used during the 1971 summer school program. The test battery represents a composite of motor skill, physical fitness, and perceptual-motor test items. A necessary prerequisite to using the sheet is the identification of specific factors hypothesized to be measured by each test item; this will provide the instructor with the information necessary to assess and prescribe subsequent exercises, tasks, or activities. For example, the *endurance index* (the ratio of speed to "staying power") was used to assess circulorespiratory endurance. Therefore, a student's score on the endurance index provides a basis for prescribing aerobic activities.

With the profile presented in the figure, the assessment of Jane's individual abilities is made relatively easy. In terms of her mean average standard score she would not be assigned to D&A since her score of 43 is above the cut-off point of 40. She would be classified as borderline. You may recall, however, that it was recommended that a cut-off score of 40 be used in conjunction with a single component cut-off score of 10 or less. It may be noted that Jane scored 10 on arm strength and endurance and would thus be admitted to the program.

The profile chart provides the teacher with the information necessary to make the following assessments:

1. Relative superiority on gross coordination tasks
2. Poor general body strength (as indicated by arm, leg, and back strength scores of 10, 20, and 30)
3. Hand/eye accuracy which is three and a half times superior to foot/eye accuracy (a normal tendency)
4. Above average speed, but poor endurance (note a speed score of 60, endurance score of 20, and an endurance index of 10)

It is obvious that other assessments could be made of Jane's ability in a more detailed report.

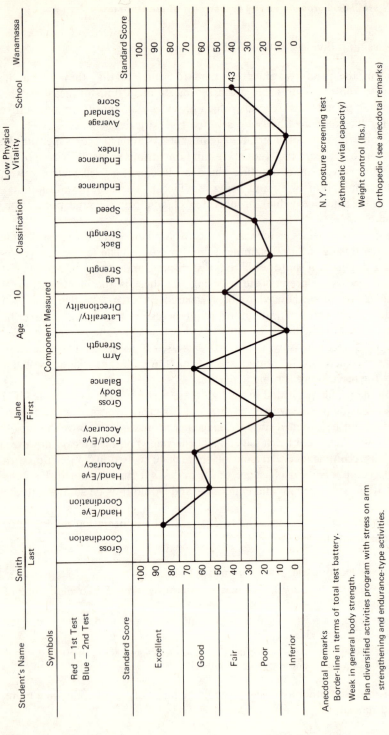

FIGURE 5-6 Motor/perceptual progress profile.

In the chart as shown, that portion entitled "Anecdotal Remarks" should be used to indicate general and specific assessments. Further, it would be advantageous to add comments of a psychological/social nature such as, "the child appears to be fearful of height," or "doesn't appear to associate with members of her peer group."

It is recommended that a battery of this type be administered to all students who have been recommended as potential candidates for the D&A program, regardless of their handicap. The child with a cerebral palsied condition obviously cannot perform all test items, but he can perform many of the tasks with reasonable competency. The important thing to remember is that he is participating in the same activities as his peer group and those test items that he *can* perform will give the instructor some basis for assessment. The author vividly recalls an incident in the summer program that highlights the value of testing all students on the Motor/Perceptual Battery:

John was assigned to the program because of an orthopedic handicap, an atrophied right arm and right leg. In addition to exercises and activities designed to increase arm and leg strength, stress was placed on basic locomotor patterns to improve his ability to walk. A comparison of pre- and post-test scores on the Motor/Perceptual Battery indicated general overall improvement, but a dramatic increase in gross body balance. His scores on the tapered balance beam reflected an improvement of 60 inches. When one considers that the beam gradually tapers (requiring more finite ability), the results were even more significant. Of all his scores, his parent was most impressed by this accomplishment.

Somatotyping: An Integral Part of the Assessment Process

As a means of introduction, we will present in its entirety a learning experience provided the students of Ocean Township High School.[7]

DETERMINATION OF BASIC BODY STRUCTURE (SOMATOTYPE)

Basic body structure is inherited. We are generally aware of the different body types because we have frequently heard such remarks as, "Mary is a butterball," or "John has a build like an Adonis." One might ask the question, "Why should I have a basic understanding of my body structure?" To answer the question completely would involve a rather lengthy discourse. Basically, an understanding of one's constitutional make-up will aid in the attainment of present and future goals. One's success or failure in most future endeavors is partially contingent upon one's physical make-up because body structure influences one's personality as well as physical prowess. You have but to reflect to note how the muscular individual tends to be aggressive and the possessor of an outgoing personality (extrovert). Moreover, the frail individual tends to prefer those activities that are individual in nature and often tends to be a "loner."

And now back to the question of why one should have an understanding of

[7] Ocean Township High School, *Figure Control Program*, Oakhurst, N.J., June, 1971.

basic body structure. . . . Heredity endows one with a physical capacity—a capacity that is infrequently attained. The first step in the solution of a problem is the full understanding of the existing problem, in this case, one's physical make-up. The subsequent steps would be to select those activities (physical and mental) that evoke positive changes.

Regardless of one's basic body structure, a person's body consists of three components[8]: *endomorphy* (an excess of adipose tissue); *mesomorphy* (large muscle masses); and *ectomorphy* (thin, frail body). (*Note:* Women tend to possess more of the first component.)

Evaluate yourself on each of the components on a 1–7 scale as per the illustration (Fig. 5-7). Your rating should consist of three digits: the endomorphy rating followed by meso and ecto ratings. Example: 5 6 2, etc.

The Most Common Type 5 3 3	*The Frail Type* 1 1 7	*The Husky Type* 1 7 1	*The Soft Fat Type* 7 1 1
Extremely thin Low in fat tissue Small front to back dimensions of trunk 1 2	Average 3 4 5	Most obese Large fat deposits Thick abdomen region, cheeks, hips, thighs 6 7	
Extremely underdeveloped muscles with poor tone Muscles squeezed or pushed in contracted state—arms, buttocks, calves, thighs. 1 2	Average 3 4 5	Extremely developed muscles large and firm with good tones in biceps, buttocks, calves, thighs, abdomen 6 7	
Extremely thick and heavy bones of ankle, knee, elbow, wrist joints 1 2	Average 3 4 5	Extremely thin and frail linear skeleton with small wrist, ankle, knee, and elbow joints 6 7	

Making students aware of restrictions imposed upon them as a result of their basic body structure is extremely important. The thin, angular male must realize he will seldom, if ever, possess the potential attributes to achieve success in football. Similarly, a young lady who possesses a large, heavily-muscled body will never be a potential candidate for modeling (as long as the present vogue demands the frail, emaciated look). However, every body structure lends itself to potential in certain areas; this is one of the reasons for teacher assessment of each student's basic body structure. The teacher must recommend those activities in which the child has a reasonable chance of achieving success. For example, the ectomorphic male can be successful in most individual/dual type activities, and the mesomorphic girl can be successful in track or field and gymnastics (in fact, most athletic activities).

[8] W. H. Sheldon, *Atlas of Men* (New York: Gramercy Publishing Company, 1954), p. 337.

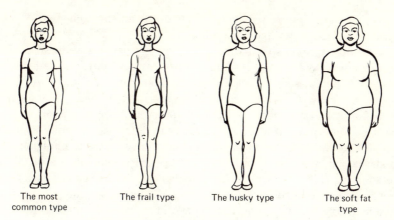

| The most common type | The frail type | The husky type | The soft fat type |

FIGURE 5–7 Somatotyping. Adapted from Janel Wessel, *Movement Fundamentals: Figure, Form, Fun,* 3rd ed. (Englewood Cliffs, N.J.: Prentice-Hall, Inc., 1970), pp. 17–18, by permission of the publisher. Copyright © 1970 by Prentice-Hall, Inc.

Somatotyping serves as a valuable adjunct to the testing program. Previously, great stress was placed on the design of fitness, motor, and perceptual-motor test batteries that incorporated built-in factors which made adjustments for individual structural differences. However, since there are few such instruments available, the physical educator must (if he wants to make a valid assessment) consider composite scores in light of an individual's basic somatotype. As an illustration, earlier reference was made to the high school student who achieved a Physical Fitness Index of at least 100, or a score consonant with his body structure. Some educators may view this means of assessment as one that provides an "easy out" for the lazy, endomorphic individual. That situation could develop if the teacher does not fulfill his role, but that is not the intent of the procedure; the intent is to design achievement goals that are attainable. Students are required to exhibit maximum effort at all times. However, this firmness must be tempered with fairness: the goals must be such that the student can achieve success. Remember, one of the basic tenets of sound teaching is to provide learning experiences so structured that each student can (with effort) achieve success.

The somatotyping procedure designed by Sheldon can be a complex, time-consuming process, one that is not feasible for use in a D&A program. The procedure we recommend is simplified so that the average teacher can somatotype 30 to 35 students in a 50-minute period. The procedure involves the identification of two basic body components, the more prominent primary and secondary components. However, prior to attempting to implement such a procedure, the teacher should familiarize himself thoroughly with *The Varie-*

ties of Human Physique.[9] Wilgoose also devotes an entire chapter to somato-typing characteristics and their implications for teaching.[10]

And now we will somatotype a student. Let us assume that a student is assigned to D&A because of low fitness and a nutritional abnormality (excess adipose tissue). A subjective evaluation of her appearance reveals that she is extremely short and heavy and possesses large bones and joints. Your initial appraisal is to identify her most prominent body component, in this case, endomorphy. At a second glance, you note that her bone structure is broad and you perceive that under the fatty tissue there is an abundance of undeveloped muscular tissue. Thus, her secondary component is identified as mesomorphic. The student so identified would, then, be classified as possessing a meso-endomorphic body structure. The secondary component is listed first to denote that it is supportive of the primary component, or grammatically that "meso" is the adjective which modifies the noun "endomorphic."

Although such an appraisal may seem much too simple to serve any value, experience has proven it to be a program asset. It has made staff members and students cognizant of the following values derived from somato-typing:

1. The teacher can evaluate test results more objectively when assessing student progress in light of body structure (functional capacity).

2. The student is intrinsically motivated to improve his performance when he realizes he is being evaluated in terms of improvement as well as achievement. (Nothing motivates a student as well as the realization that he can succeed.)

3. The teacher can truly individualize prescriptions when he is cognizant of student potentials and limitations. For example, the true endomorph could not support his body weight on various pieces of apparatus and as a consequence should be prescribed endurance activities—weight-training and other tasks that will insure improvement and success.

4. The student becomes apprised of his true self-image (especially when he is provided with opportunities to somatotype others) and establishes a meaningful aspiration level.

Summary

Providing an instructional program based on the developmental needs of students necessitates that individual strengths and weaknesses be identified. Once individual characteristics are identified, the teacher can assess student

---

9   W. H. Sheldon, S. S. Stevens, and W. B. Tucker, *The Varieties of Human Physique* (New York: Harper & Row, Publishers, 1940).

10 Carl E. Wilgoose, "The Measurement of Body Physique," *Evaluation in Health and Physical Education* (New York: McGraw-Hill Book Company, Inc., 1961), pp. 287–329.

abilities. Teacher competency in the performance of the following tasks is essential if the teacher wishes to prescribe an instructional program based on the individualized needs of each child.

The teacher should possess the ability to:

1. Develop a normative scale (achievement standards) that is consonant with the given program goals and population
2. Group raw data on the basis of the step interval procedure (which assumes a sound understanding of how to determine the number and size of step intervals)
3. Compute the mean via the use of the step interval formula:

$$\text{Mean} = A.M. + \left(\frac{\Sigma fd}{n} \times S.I.\right)$$

4. Compute the standard deviation via the use of the step interval formula:

$$S.D. = S.I. \sqrt{\frac{\Sigma fd^2}{n} - c^2}$$

5. Compute a percentile rank table via the use of the step interval formula:

$$P_p = LL + \left(\frac{C_s - C_b}{C_w} \times S.I.\right)$$

6. Prepare individual student profile charts so that assessments can be made of students' strengths and weaknesses
7. Devise ability groups on the basis of the group mean and group standard deviation
8. Determine student grades based on the group mean and standard deviation
9. Prepare Sigma, Hull and T-scale scores and know the appropriate situation for using each scale
10. Establish a specific cut-off point to identify those students who should be assigned to D&A
11. Identify the specific factors measured by each item in a test battery
12. Analyze individual student profile charts, assess status, and prescribe activities accordingly
13. Somatotype each student in terms of his primary and secondary body structure components
14. Guide the student in the selection of activities that will afford him the greatest opportunity for achieving success
15. Assess student status by utilizing test battery scores in conjunction with appraisals of body structure

Annotated Bibliography

BARNES, FRED P. *Research for the Practitioner in Education.* Washington, D.C.: National Education Association, 1964. Written primarily for teachers and administrators in the elementary schools. An attempt to bridge the gap between the need for research in the schools and teacher preparation in the use of statistical tools.

GALFO, ARMAND J., and EARL MILLER. *Interpreting Education Research.* Dubuque, Iowa: William C. Brown Company, Publishers, 1965. The text focuses on helping the teacher to read, interpret, and apply the results of research carried out by researchers via a review of typical studies in education. Also may be used as a primer for those students who plan to design original research.

GOOD, WARREN R. *An Introduction to Statistics: Emphasizing Applications to Education*, 5th ed. Ann Arbor, Mich.: University of Michigan Book Store, 1958. 48 pp. A basic manual for the teacher who is interested in statistics, or who wishes to make simple statistical analyses.

RUNYON, RICHARD P., and AUDREY HABER. *Fundamentals of Behavioral Statistics.* Reading, Mass.: Addison-Wesley Publishing Company, 1967. Devotes ten chapters to descriptive statistics which will provide the reader with the skills necessary to develop standardized norms. Includes appendices which review basic mathematics, symbols, and statistical formulas, and provides a list of tables with an explanation for usage.

TYLER, LEONA E. *Tests and Measurements*, 2nd ed. Englewood Cliffs, N.J.: Prentice-Hall, Inc., 1971. 96 pp. Includes a review of measurement principles, statistical techniques, and test construction. Provides the consumer with competency necessary to read research reports.

6

teacher and pupil role requirements for individualizing instruction

In previous chapters, repeated reference has been made to the implementation of an instructional program based on the developmental level of each child. Materials have been presented to aid in the identification, classification, and assessment of the developmental needs of the handicapped. Chapter 6 is devoted to the teacher/pupil interactions that must occur in order to initiate an instructional program geared to meet the needs of all students.

Individualized instruction may be defined as the prescription of exercises, tasks, or activities based on the results of diagnostic pretests. In addition, such instruction is presented in an environment that is conducive to the enhancement of student-teacher rapport. Learning can be maximized only if the student is totally involved in the learning process. This involvement is engendered by the provision of student learning experiences whereby the student becomes self-motivated and thus continually strives to improve.

One of the potential shortcomings of an individualized instructional unit is the possibility that the learning process becomes dehumanized to the extent that learning is negatively affected. Such was the case in research conducted by the writer.[1] In two separate experiments (physical fitness and motor learning), the Equivalent Forms of the Wear Attitude Inventory[2] were used to assess student attitudes toward physical education, before and after training regimens. The results indicated that five of the six post-test

---

[1] Thomas M. Vodola, "The Effects of Participation Time Variations on the Development of Physical Fitness, Motor Skills and Attitudes," unpublished doctoral dissertation, Temple University, Philadelphia, 1970, pp. 103–8.

[2] C. L. Wear, "Construction of Equivalent Forms of an Attitude Scale," *Research Quarterly*, XXV (1955), 113–19.

scores were lower than the pretest scores; in the fitness study, one group's score was significantly negative. It was hypothesized that the negative attitude trend was attributable to the virtual elimination of student–student and student–teacher interaction. (Interaction was minimized in an attempt to control student motivational variability.)

In a similar study, Turner[3] compared the effects of individualized and group instruction on motor fitness and attitude changes. The individualized group practiced in isolation whereas the control group was encouraged to work together. The results indicated that although both groups made significant gains in motor skills, the group instructional class made superior gains in attitude (the Acquaintance Volume Test). Brumbach[4] studied the effects of individualized instruction on the attitudes of low motor fitness subjects in a developmental class. Pre- and post-testing, via the Equivalent Forms of the Wear Attitude Inventory, revealed that personalized instruction improved student attitudes toward physical education.

Even though a few selected studies do not conclusively prove that students' attitudes are positively affected by personalized instruction, it would be fair to state that such instruction is one of the factors contributing to attitude changes. Conceivably, student attitudes are also influenced by the curriculum content. If subject matter material is made "palatable," the chances are that the student will be more receptive to learning. In the physical fitness study conducted by Vodola,[5] it was postulated that a significantly negative student attitude may have been attributable to the fact that the subjects had to repetitively practice such boring tasks as "push-ups," "spot running" and the "shuttle run." The implications of such an assumption are most significant. For example, would cardiorespiratory endurance be achieved more readily via a "figure-eight passing drill" or by dribbling drills rather than by "spot running"?

Thus, individualized instruction necessitates other than program prescriptions based on test scores; it also requires a change in teacher and student performance, topics which will be pursued in the following discussion.

Role of the Teacher

The role of the teacher is determined by the type of instruction contemplated. For example, the traditional lecture method requires the teacher to be a

[3] Edward T. Turner, "A Comparative Study of the Effects of Individual and Group Instruction on Motor Fitness Achievement of College Males," unpublished master's thesis, University of Maryland, 1965.
[4] Wayne B. Brumbach, "Effect of a Special Conditioning Class upon Student Attitudes Toward Physical Education," *Research Quarterly*, XXXIX, No. 1 (March, 1968), 211–13.
[5] Vodola, *op. cit.*, p. 106.

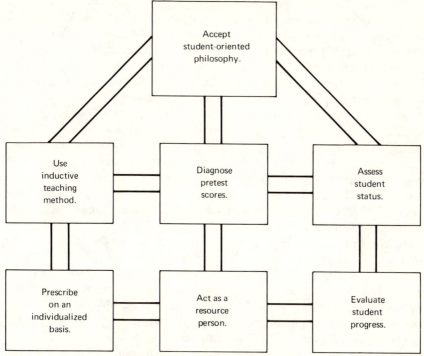

FIGURE 6–1   Teacher role requirements.

disciplinarian capable of "controlling" his students, a dynamic, oratorical spell-binder, and a curriculum master able to synthesize important facts so that they can be subsumed by the student. Individualized instruction, however, necessitates a variety of teacher competencies, some of which are not being stressed sufficiently in our teacher-training institutions. The following role requirements are essential for implementing an instructional program based on the specific needs of each child (see Fig. 6–1).

Accepting a Student-oriented Philosophy

A student-oriented philosophy can best be explained by a discussion of the component parts of education and the alternatives in terms of the interactions between the component parts. *Education* may be viewed as a triad involving the learner, the learning process, and the teacher. The general goal of education is to prepare our youth so that they can intelligently resolve the many problems they will be confronted with during their adult lives. The teacher must therefore provide the student with the tools necessary for decision-making—the ability to comprehend, to critique, to analyze, to be creative, to synthesize, etc. How can this best be accomplished?

The proponents of the teacher-centered philosophy contend that the teacher is the most important component in the educational process and that the learner is merely a "pawn" to be manipulated as necessary. This medieval philosophy stems from a time when a teacher was respected as all-knowing and the molder of young minds; the teaching method in use was primarily lecture. Of course, the interaction was in one direction only: the teacher dispensed the facts and the student absorbed (memorized) the knowledge.

A second educational philosophy stresses the importance of content per se. The educated student is one who is conversant with that knowledge which is accepted as the "truths of the day." During the era of scholasticism, the educated person was one who could recite Shakespeare, or speak two or three different languages; today, the focus is more often on competency in terms of mathematics and science. Teaching methods and teacher–learner interaction are similar to the teacher-centered philosophy: the student is the recipient of content material.

In contrast, the student-oriented philosophy views the learner as the most important part of the educational process. He is the product of education and logically the focus must be placed on him. The student-oriented philosophy places emphasis on "learning" and not on "teaching"; there is a definite distinction between the two. An effective teaching performance is worthless if the student has not "learned" that which was being taught. The teaching method used is varied; the emphasis may be placed on maximizing student involvement or on designing meaningful learning experiences. Thus, the instructional method might be class or panel discussion, role playing, experimentation, or independent study. Regardless of the method, the emphasis is placed on the total involvement of the student in the learning process. Pupil–teacher interaction is maximal with the student pursuing the goals of education and the instructor guiding the learning process.

A couple of examples might help distinguish between the teacher–content-oriented (T/C) approach and the student-centered (S/C) approach. In terms of grading, the T/C advocates are firm and adhere to strict achievement levels. If the student has not achieved the arbitrary pass-fail point, he must fail the course because he has not met the course requirements. The S/C proponents, however, tend to grade on a curve or on the basis of improvement or achievement. Their primary concern is how much the student has learned during the semester rather than how much he achieved because they fully realize that all students are different (with varied strengths and weaknesses).

Another point of distinction between the two approaches to learning regards student evaluation of teachers. The T/C group vehemently oppose being evaluated by their students because, they insist, students are not competent to evaluate a teacher's effectiveness in terms of content matter. Those who are favorably disposed to the S/C approach encourage student evaluation of the teacher because they view it as an excellent means of enhancing rapport and thence learning. Furthermore, although they might agree that students generally do not possess the expertise to evaluate a teacher's knowledge of his discipline they do feel that students certainly can tell if a teacher manifests enthusiasm for teaching, empathy, a sense of humor, and the ability to stimulate intellectual curiosity.

The author strongly recommends the adoption of the student-oriented philosophy. However, acceptance of this approach to teaching necessitates a sincere conviction that the product of education (the student) is the most important part of the educational process. We posit that one cannot be presumed capable of initiating a successful program based on the needs of each child unless he truly accepts the child-centered philosophy.

At this point, a word to administrators or department chairmen is in order. Probably the major deterrent to the achievement of justifiable educational change has been the inflexibility of staff members. Many innovative programs have been doomed to failure because of staff resistance to change. Frymier[6] maintains that many teachers are psychologically unable to change their approach to teaching. If this is true, program implementation is fraught with problems because administrators and teachers in general and physical education teachers in particular have been prepared for a teacher- or subject-centered approach. Traditionally, the teacher has been molded to be directive in his approach, to demand instant response and complete student subjugation to his whims and desires. If the reader doubts the veracity of this statement, he should note the experience listed below which, although it is a generalization, is probably applicable to a majority of administrators:

A couple of years ago, a teacher decided to attempt to individualize the pre-activity exercises in a class of 60 students. Following a pretest and student/teacher analysis and assessment of strengths and weaknesses, an individualized "circuit-training" program was devised. During the ten-minute pre-instruction period, the students rotated to six of ten stations. They were urged to constantly attempt to increase their daily circuits. Since students did vary in their abilities, class performance looked like a "three-ring circus"—students were running in every direction.

During one of the sessions, the principal walked in and commented to the instructor, "What is going on? Why all the confusion?" The teacher replied, "What do you mean? Are the students cooperative? Aren't they putting forth maximum effort?" The administrator responded in the affirmative. Finally the teacher stated, "Can you identify any two students who are identical?" The principal smiled—no more need be said.

Unfortunately, even though there are many notable exceptions to the rule such as the above example, we do generally associate conformity with acceptable teaching practices.

Although Frymier's theory undoubtedly has merit, it behooves the

---

[6] Jack R. Frymier, "Teachers: Not Will But Can They Change?" *S.E.C. Newsletter*, II, No. 6 (November, 1968), 1–4.

administrator or department chairman who hopes to initiate a D&A program to totally involve the staff in all aspects of the program. Through staff involvement in experiences related to a child-centered approach, teacher change may be elicited; certainly such an approach cannot be mandated.

The student-oriented approach also requires that the teacher manifest the following qualities or abilities: empathy toward and rapport with his students and the ability to design specific behavioral outcomes and learning experiences in terms of his students.

Using the Inductive Teaching Method

Earlier, reference was made to the fact that the "development of the intellect" implies structuring the learning process so that the student is guided toward the cognition goals of critical thinking, analysis, synthesis, creativity, etc. However, the assumption that the ability "to think" can be taught is contrary to the view of some educators who contend that cognitive skill development is merely a by-product of memorization. Others maintain that "thinking" can only be learned via the so-called academic disciplines of mathematics, science, and foreign languages. Another viewpoint proposed is that only the "gifted" child can grasp the complex skills involved in decision-making. And finally, a fourth viewpoint holds that modifying the environment to stimulate thinking is nothing more than an exercise in futility.[7]

On the other hand, research by Bruner, Goodnow, and Austin[8] and Piaget[9] suggests that cognitive skills can be learned. The author supports the viewpoint of Bruner and Piaget and contends that the development of thinking skills requires the modification of the presently accepted teaching method. We recommend *inductive teaching*—teaching students to make valid inferences of generalizations as a result of learning experiences provided.

The use of the inductive method requires the teacher to learn to develop questions and learning experiences so that the child is skillfully guided to solutions (without being told correct answers). An example of the procedure whereby the teacher "guides" rather than "tells" the pupil is given below:

Following the performance of the "Recovery Index Test" in a D&A class, a student related to the writer that his poststep-test pulse rate was lower than his prestep-test pulse rate. He indicated that he had had a discussion with a classmate regarding the validity of his finding and it was his contention that one could have a lower rate after exercise. He concluded by asking for support of his claim.

---

7 Paraphrased from Norman E. Wallen et al., *The Taba Curriculum Development Project in Social Studies* (Menlo Park, Calif:. Addison-Wesley Publishing Company, October, 1969), p. 13. Project No. 5–1314, Grant No. OE–6–10–182, Office of Education, U.S. Department of Health, Education and Welfare.

8 J. S. Bruner, J. J. Goodnow, and G. A. Austin, *A Study of Thinking* (New York: John Wiley & Sons, Inc., 1956).

9 J. Piaget, *The Psychology of Intelligence* (New York: Harcourt Brace Jovanovich, 1950).

Instead of answering "yes" or "no" the writer asked the student the following question: "By definition, what do we mean by the initial resting pulse rate (presteptest pulse rate)?" The student replied, "The lowest possible pulse rate." Another question: "Since you stated that the pretest rate is the lowest, can you now answer your original question?" Answer: "Yes, my post-test score could not be correct because nothing can be lower than the lowest score."

The writer then proceeded to pursue the problem further by asking the student, "What could have caused your inaccurate finding?" Answer: "It may be that my initial resting rate was incorrect." Question: "What do you mean?" Answer: "I may have been moving about prior to taking my initial rate causing it to rise." Question: "Good, can you think of another reason for the error?" Answer: "I could have incorrectly taken or recorded my initial and final pulse rate."

Wallen et al. give some insight into the new role of the teacher when they state:

The ability to think cannot be "given" by teachers to students. But teachers can assist in developing thinking skills in students by providing appropriate learning activities. How well an individual thinks depends on the richness and significance of the content with which he works as well as the process which he uses.[10]

Table 6–1 provides an example of how the teacher can induce the development of cognitive skills. You may note that at no time does the teacher

[10] Wallen et al., *op. cit.*, p. 14.

TABLE 6–1 Inferring and Generalizing

THIS COGNITIVE TASK REQUIRES THE STUDENT TO INTERPRET, INFER, AND GENERALIZE ABOUT DATA. THE TEACHING STRATEGY CONSISTS OF ASKING THE STUDENT THE FOLLOWING QUESTIONS, USUALLY IN THIS ORDER.

teacher asks:	*student*	*teacher follows through:*
What did you notice? See? Find? What differences did you notice (with reference to a particular question)?	Gives items.	Makes sure items are accessible; for example, chalkboard, transparency, individual list, pictures, item card. Chooses the items to pursue.
Why do you think this happened? or, How do you account for these differences?	Gives explanation which may be based on factual information and/or inferences.	Accepts explanation. Seeks clarification if necessary.
What does this tell you about ——— ?	Gives generalization.	Encourages a variety of generalizations and seeks clarification when necessary.

THIS PATTERN OF INVITING REASONS TO ACCOUNT FOR OBSERVED PHENOMENA AND GENERALIZING BEYOND THE DATA IS REPEATED AND EXPANDED TO INCLUDE MORE AND MORE ASPECTS OF THE DATA AND TO REACH MORE ABSTRACT GENERALIZATIONS.

SOURCE: Reprinted from Norman E. Wallen et al., *The Taba Curriculum Development Project in Social Studies* (Menlo Park, Calif.: Addison-Wesley Publishing Company, October, 1969), p. 18. Project No. 5–1314, Grant No. OE-6-10-182, Office of Education, U.S. Department of Health, Education and Welfare.

"tell" the student what to learn; rather, the teacher's role is to stimulate, guide, and assist in the learning process. (The reader is urged to review *The Taba Curriculum Development Project in Social Studies*[11] and *Teaching Strategies for Developing Children's Thinking: Applications to Reading.*[12]

Testing, Assessing, and Prescribing on an Individual Basis

Because the importance of testing, assessing, and prescribing has been explained in previous chapters it need not be justified here; however, its importance cannot be overlooked. A teacher cannot plan a program based on different student abilities without possessing these skills. Some teachers maintain there is no need to assess the status of each child in the class because their students have already been "tracked" or grouped homogeneously and thus evidence common abilities. Vergason[13] and Eckstrom[14] reviewed the literature and could find no evidence to substantiate the claims that so-called homogeneous grouping was superior to heterogeneous grouping. Unfortunately, the basis for grouping is usually a test score relating to only one factor, plus subjective teacher evaluations, which may account for *inter*-individual variability (variations between individuals), but what of *intra*-individual variability (individual variability within oneself)? For example, two students may be placed in the same gymnastics group because they achieved the same total number of "moves" on the apparatus. Further examination, however, might reveal that one student scored most of his points on the rings and side horse whereas the other student was weak in those areas but demonstrated competency on the parallels and high bar. Thus, we contend that individualized instruction requires the pretesting of all students so that valid assessments and prescriptions can be made.

Acting as a Resource Person

The teacher, in his new role, is viewed by his students as a partner in the educational process rather than as the leader. It is implicitly understood, however, that he is the leader, but he should teach in a manner that will motivate each student to accept more of the responsibilities involved in learning. His role is to structure the learning environment, to guide the student toward the mutually accepted goal and, when necessary, to provide

---

11 *Ibid.* (entire vol.).

12 Judy Earl, ed., *Teaching Strategies for Developing Children's Thinking: Applications to Reading* (Palo Alto, Calif.: Institute for Staff Development, 1970).

13 Glenn R. Vergason, "A Critical Review of Grouping," *The High School Journal,* XLVIII (1965), 427–33.

14 Ruth B. Eckstrom, "Experimental Studies of Homogeneous Grouping," *A Review of the Literature* (Princeton, N. J.: Educational Testing Service, 1959).

those aids that will help the student in his efforts. The instructor seldom "tells" the student the answers (unless it is expeditious); instead, he constantly stimulates the student through the provision of meaningful resource units.

Evaluating the Product of Education

The final role of the teacher is to constantly evaluate the efforts of each student in light of his personal capabilities. Even in this role, the teacher is a partner and not the sole determinant of pupil accomplishments. Further- more, "evaluation" is construed not merely as the determination of a grade, but, more important, as the assessment of the student's strengths and deficits in terms of the discipline being taught. As a result of the evaluative process, the teacher can modify prescriptions and/or his teaching so that each child can maximize his learning, within his own capabilities.

An illustration of the new role of the teacher as a partner in the learning process, from the initial planning stages through the evaluation process, is provided in an effort to clarify the concept.

The development of sportsmanship is stressed as an important objective of physical education. Most instructors state that they include this objective in their units, but they can seldom specifically explain how effective their programs are in developing sportsmanlike qualities in their students. Aware of the fact that sports- manship is a concept that cannot be taught, the writer decided to structure a 12th- grade soccer unit so that specific sportsmanlike qualities could be measured objectively. At the outset all students were required to be involved in every phase of the new unit.

One period was devoted to a class discussion of the importance of "good sports- manship" and the designing of objective situations that would indicate positive traits. By the end of the period, the following soccer unit guidelines were established:

1. No officials would be used, but all 22 players would be on their "honor" to make decisions regarding rule infractions.
2. The last person to make the ball go "out of touch" was to raise his hand.
3. "Offsides" would be determined by one of the fullbacks.
4. In doubtful situations, the person closest to or involved in the infraction would call a decision.

It was agreed that our prime consideration was the respect of individual integrity. When a decision was made by a student, it had to be accepted by all involved (in- cluding the instructor). The writer was a partner in the enterprise and to insure the success of the unit, he had to abide by the rules; only in situations of repeated flagrant violations could he make a ruling—placing the perpetrator of the infrac- tion on the sideline bench for two minutes.

Each student's sportsmanship grade was self-determined. The student was told to grade himself in light of the rules established, although the instructor had the pre- rogative of modifying any grade if his observations repeatedly indicated deviant behavior.

Was the unit successful? Was there a positive change in behavior? The answer to both questions was an unqualified "yes." In fact, the concept has been included in all 12th-grade activities for the past five years. Can you imagine a highly competitive game with no officials and no "rhubarbs"? Such has been the case. One might say that such a grading procedure cannot be successful; the following is a true experience—let the reader be the judge. When asked about what grade he should get, Mike stated he deserved an *A*. However, after class Mike requested a private conference during which he indicated that his grade should be lowered because he frequently displayed a bad temper. Such a personal evaluation by a 12th-grade student is most unusual. The writer indicated that he was aware of Mike's shortcomings, but he informed him that he would not lower the grade because Mike's admittance of his personality flaw was itself the most difficult part of the "therapy" —the rest would be easy. Consequently, Mike gained self-respect and evidenced exemplary sportsmanship (in spite of his highly competitive spirit) for the rest of the year.

The foregoing illustration incorporates most of the features of a student-centered approach to education which are necessary for the development of an individualized instructional program.

In spite of the fact that there is too much emphasis placed on student grades, they are a part of the evaluative process. Since our society demands that we attend to this matter, a description of a recommended procedure for grading all students, particularly those in an individualized program, is recommended for adoption. Baldwin[15] stimulated the development of a system with provision for evaluating a student in terms of his improvement as well as his achievement.

As an example, let us assume that we would like to grade each student during the spring of the year on physical fitness. The procedure would involve the following steps:

1. List each student's fall and spring *PFI* scores and determine his improvement, or lack thereof (fall *PFI*, 91; spring *PFI*, 100; Improvement, 9).

2. Use the step interval procedure to determine the mean and standard deviation for the spring *PFI* scores and the improvement scores.

3. Determine grade ranges for each category as listed in Chapter 5.

Table 6–2 illustrates arbitrary scores for the above three steps.

Given the following scores for John and Tom, how would you determine each student's grade? First, compare each student's spring *PFI* score with the spring group norms:

	fall PFI	*spring PFI*	*improvement*
John	128	129	1
Tom	74	85	11

[15] Discussion with Harry Baldwin, Principal, Wall Central Elementary School, Wall Township, N.J.

TABLE 6–2   Issuing Grades on an Individualized Basis: T-scores

grade	spring PFI scores (achievement) Mean = 110 S.D. = 20 1.2 S.D. = 24	improvement scores (spring PFI minus fall PFI) Mean = 8 S.D. = 2 1.2 S.D. = 2.4
A	137– up	12– up (11.7–14.0)
B	113–136	10– 11 (9.4–11.6)
C	88–112	7– 9 (6.8–9.2)
D	64– 87	4– 6 (4.4–6.8)
F	40 and below	2 and below (2.0–4.4)

and his improvement score with improvement group norms; the grade issued is the *higher* of the two scores. Let us illustrate:

	achievement	*improvement*	*grade*
John	129, *B*	1, *F*	*B*
Tom	85, *D*	11, *B*	*B*

You will note that John's improvement was only 1 but he was awarded a *B* because of his high achievement. As one "moves up the achievement ladder" learning tends to level off; therefore, it would be penalizing the high achiever to expect him to improve as much as students who achieved less. By the same token, it would be unfair to expect the child who is not endowed with the physical attributes of the more fortunate mesomorph to achieve at the same level; thus he should not be awarded a *D* for his *PFI* score of 85. He has improved his performance by 11 points and should be given a grade of *B* for his improvement in terms of his initial status.

Many physical educators have criticized the achievement/improvement grading procedure as lowering standards. Such is not the case: Tom, who improved his *PFI* score from 74 to 85, had to work as hard or harder than John, who attained a *PFI* score of 129. Besides, how can we justify grading all students on the basis of achievement in such events as running or high jumping when no consideration is given for the student's body structure?

Other critics have maintained that students can fathom the grading procedure and will put forth less effort on the pretest in order to attain a higher grade on the basis of final improvement. In fact, one student made that exact comment to the writer when the grading system was explained to the class. My response was, "You can achieve a higher grade via that subterfuge, so let your conscience be your guide—I shall respect your decision." Some educators will say that the procedure is not realistic because students will falsify their scores. This attitude of distrust is one of our many educational problems because students will generally live up to our expectations of them. If we expect them to cheat, they will cheat, but if we vest more responsibility and authority in students they will measure up to the task.

As a case in point, during a volleyball game there was a question of whether or not a student had touched the net (if he did, he was to raise his hand indicating the violation). The writer asked the student if he had touched the net (his decision would be accepted). The student, in turn, attempted to push the responsibility back on the teacher, but he was informed it was his decision to make. Finally, after some thought he answered, "I guess I did touch the net." Knowing he had to make the decision (and live with it), the student was truthful. Conceivably he had hoped the instructor would take the responsibility off his shoulders and declare that he had not committed a violation.

Unquestionably, such student-accepted responsibilities will aid in the development of a positive, internalized value system, one that will aid the student in the ethical resolution of adult life problems. It has been stated that our modern youth do not accept responsibility. It is contended that this unwillingness or inability to accept responsibility may be attributable to adult reluctance to provide students with experiences which allow them to be responsible.

For those educators who do not accept the student honor code, there is another alternative to the grading problem. By keeping cumulative scores of all students, the teacher can discern radically deviant scores so that at best students will only falsify initial scores, but not subsequent scores.

Considerable discussion has been given to the role of the teacher in planning and implementing an individualized instructional program. Specific reference was not made to the D&A program because the approach is applicable and should be used, where feasible, in the total physical education program. The degree of success attained will depend upon the degree to which each teacher accepts the role requirements.

Role of the Student

Due to the close working relationship of the student and teacher in an individualized program, the previous explanations and illustrations used in the text to explain the role of the teacher give some insight into the capabilities expected of each student. However, specific role requirements will be listed to further clarify the student's part in the learning process (see Fig. 6–2).

Developing Cognitive Skills Necessary for Partnership

The recommended program views the student as an active participant in the learning process rather than a passive recipient; thus, he should be

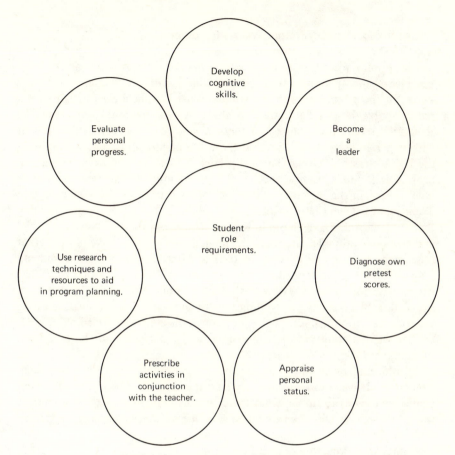

FIGURE 6–2   Student role requirements.

involved in every phase of the program. To do this effectively he should develop his cognitive powers to the fullest (e.g., comprehension, application, analysis, synthesis, and evaluation). (See Bloom's text[16] for a detailed explanation of these skills.)

The student must understand and be able to apply the scientific method to problems. He must be able to state a problem clearly, locate pertinent reference material, design an approach that makes a solution attainable, and be able to draw logical conclusions from the data available. Clearly, he must possess the ability to solve problems inductively (analyzing a series of specific facts and making a logical generalization).

[16] Benjamin S. Bloom, ed., *Taxonomy of Educational Objectives: Handbook I, Cognitive Domain* (New York: David McKay Co., Inc., 1956).

Becoming a Leader Rather Than a Follower

The pupil's role does not include asking for answers such as, "Would you please sum up your lecture?" or, "Would you please tell me what I must know for the examination?" The student must become a doer rather than a recipient, by developing leadership skills. All instructional units must be structured so that every phase of the learning process provides the student with experiences that will develop these leadership skills. For example, in the D&A classes in Ocean Township High School, as well as in the regular program, all pupils test one another. They are required to understand and be able to explain the purposes and values of each test item in their program. Traditional teachers have criticized this phase of the program, maintaining that students will make errors in testing. The rejoinder is, "So what?" Trial and error is a valuable adjunct to learning. Other teachers have objected that too much class time is devoted to testing; after all, textbooks recommend a maximum of 10 percent of the time for testing. Our explanation is, "What others refer to as tests, we view as student learning experiences." It has been found that by constantly providing the student with these types of learning experiences (responsibilities) he develops an enhanced self-image, self-confidence, the ability to make decisions, and other essential characteristics of leadership.

In addition, by having the students become doers, they develop a high degree of intrinsic motivation, a key trait that insures subsequent effort and achievement. For example, what better means is there of making a student aware of her body fat than by having her measure her own adipose tissue?

Appraising, Prescribing, and Evaluating One's Own Abilities

Student improvement and program success are enhanced if the student is knowledgeable about all phases of his individualized program. He should be able to appraise his status in terms of strengths and weaknesses, select activities as a result of his appraisal, and evaluate periodic progress. Total student involvement in all phases of individualized programming will be covered in detail in the next three chapters.

Summary

Traditionally, educational programs have been founded on the premise that the teacher is all-knowing and is the dispenser of knowledge, whereas the student must "pay the price" for acquiring this knowledge by passively, and sometimes painfully, absorbing these words of wisdom. If one is to organize a D&A program based on individualized differences, he must be aware that changes in teacher/pupil interaction are obviously necessary. Below are listed suggestions for in-service programs for staff members to enhance teaching effectiveness. To those suggestions are added essential pupil skills to give further direction to the in-service programs.

The teacher should plan in-service programs that will:

1. Devise ways and means of involving the handicapped child in the planning and implementation of D&A so that content will be meaningful and student/teacher interaction will be maximized

2. Make the staff sensitive to the individual needs of the handicapped so that they may more readily adopt a pupil-centered philosophy of education

3. Provide opportunities for the staff to share in designing behavioral outcomes and learning experiences

4. Research the area of inductive teaching and have the staff list implications and examples of how it could be applied to various phases of the program

5. Provide opportunities for the staff to test, convert raw scores to standard scores, assess and prescribe individualized programs for a random group of students

6. Stress the value of pretesting all students prior to starting the instructional program

7. Differentiate between teachers who merely "tell" and those who are resource persons

8. Have staff members design evaluative instruments which will result in grades that reflect student improvement as well as student achievement

9. Discuss the value of vesting more authority and responsibility in students

10. Explain and have staff members then develop tests and activities that will aid in the development of a student's cognitive abilities

11. Design independent study problems which must be resolved by the student via the scientific method

Annotated Bibliography

AMERICAN ASSOCIATION FOR HEALTH, PHYSICAL EDUCATION AND RECREATION, UNIT ON PROGRAMS FOR THE HANDICAPPED. *Colleges and Universities with Offerings in Adapted Physical Education* (4 pp.), *Professional Preparation Programs with Specialized Options in Therapeutic Recreation* (4 pp.), *Professional Preparation Programs in Physical Therapy* (4 pp.), and *Colleges and Universities with Offerings in Corrective Therapy Preparation* (4 pp.). Washington, D.C.: AAHPER, 1201 Sixteenth Street, N.W. 20036. Mimeographed. Lists of colleges and universities offering courses related to physical education/recreation preparation for working with the handicapped, or for an allied profession. Free upon request.

————. *Special Placement Service: For Individuals and Employers in Physical Education and Recreation Programs for the Handicapped.* Washington, D.C.:

AAHPER, 1201 Sixteenth Street, N.W. 20036, 2 pp. Mimeographed. Contains information regarding the free placement service provided by AAHPER. Also includes employment, placement, and listing services for other professional groups working with the handicapped. Free upon request.

————. *Suggestions for Students Interested in Physical Education and Recreation Programs for the Handicapped.* Washington, D.C.: AAHPER, 1201 Sixteenth Street, N.W. 20036, 2 pp. Mimeographed. Provides information regarding volunteer or part-time work experiences, organizations to contact, and high school/college preparatory requirements. Free upon request.

BERMAN, LOUISE M. *From Thinking to Behaving.* New York: Teachers College Press, 1967. 73 pp. Based on recent research, the book describes ways to help students think more effectively via a variety of learning tasks.

BRUNER, JEROME S. *The Process of Thinking.* Cambridge, Mass.: Harvard University Press, 1967. 92 pp. A classic in the field regarding teacher role, pupil role, and curriculum design. An entire chapter devoted to intuitive and analytical thinking.

Effective Teaching with Programmed Instruction. Palo Alto, Calif.: Behavioral Research Laboratories, 1970. Provides guidelines for using programmed textbooks; illustrative examples of programmed materials; reprints of noteworthy articles; and available commercial programmed materials in the varied disciplines. Free upon request.

"Individually Prescribed Instruction," *Education U.S.A.* Washington, D.C.: Education U.S.A., 1968. 32 pp. Provides a detailed explanation of the I.P.I. Program. Discusses teacher and pupil roles, fundamentals of I.P.I., teacher reactions to the program, achievement results, and a variety of other topics of interest to the teacher who wishes to prescribe instruction on an individualized basis. Charts of the complete I.P.I. mathematics and reading continuum for grades K–6 are available. Write Robert G. Scanlon, IPI Director, Research for Better Schools, Inc., 121 South Broad Street, Philadelphia, Pa. 19107.

MAGER, ROBERT F. *Developing Attitude Toward Learning.* Palo Alto, Calif.: Fearon Publishers, 1968. Includes practical approaches to maximizing student involvement in the learning process. Gives clear insight regarding the new role of the teacher.

New Approaches to Individualizing Instruction. Princeton, N.J.: Educational Testing Service, 1965. A conference report dedicated to expressions of deep concern regarding the need for individualizing instruction. Includes such topics as "Instructing the Individual in Creative Thinking," "Diagnosis and Prescription in Educational Practice," and "The Renascence of Individual Learning."

OFFICE OF EDUCATION. *Do Teachers Make A Difference?* Washington, D.C.: U.S. Government Printing Office, 1970. Consists of a series of research papers regarding teacher effectiveness. Some choice findings are: teachers are the single most important factor in the learning process; and the best measure of teacher effectiveness is the teacher verbal test score. (Request document No. 5.258: 58042; cost, 75¢.)

SCANLON, ROBERT G. *Individually Prescribed Instruction.* Philadelphia: Research for Better Schools, n.d. 16 pp. Provides an explanation of how math and reading are tailored to meet the needs of the learner. Via a question and answer format presents an overview of the IPI program and teacher functions.

THOMAS, GEORGE I., and JOSEPH CRESCIMBENI. *Individualizing Instruction in the Elementary School.* New York: Random House, Inc., 1967. The text focuses on the premise that individual differences necessitate learning experiences that should be provided so that students can progress at their own rate. Includes a discussion of old and new concepts and chapters devoted to individualizing instruction in reading, spelling, math, science, and social studies. Bibliography provides an excellent source of referencial material related to teacher effectiveness and individualized instruction.

TRUMP, J. LLOYD, and DORSEY BAYNHAM. "The School of Tomorrow," in Ronald Gross, ed., *The Teacher and the Taught.* New York: Delta Publishing Co., 1963, pp. 277–305. Discusses needed student educational opportunities: skills of independent study; developing the inquiring mind; effective discussion competencies; effective human relations; and satisfaction in learning. In-depth recommendations regarding teacher needs, curricula, and facilities.

7

individualized programming: developmental activities

Since children in any learning environment manifest a wide range of differences, educators must strive to prescribe instructional materials to meet these differentiated needs. Individualized programming is viewed as one sound approach to the problem.

The task is not a simple one because teachers are confronted with inflexible scheduling of students (grade-level placement and curricula tracks) and ever-increasing class sizes. In spite of these obstacles, however, there is little justification for exposing all students to the same learning experiences. Furthermore, there is no justification for teaching without the guidance provided by a diagnostic pretest. To do so is analogous to attempting to pilot a rudderless ship. Regardless of restrictions, some degree of individualized instruction can and must be implemented.

Many educators have been lulled into a false sense of security because their students have been grouped according to ability (homogeneous grouping), the assumption being that such grouping provides a means of better meeting the needs of individuals within different ability levels. However, some researchers such as Eckstrom[1] and Vergason[2] contend that although many schools have adopted some form of ability grouping, there is no evidence to justify its superiority over other grouping procedures. A review of the literature by the author regarding the merits of individualized instruction also revealed inconclusive results:

[1] Ruth B. Eckstrom, "Experimental Studies of Homogeneous Grouping," *A Review of the Literature* (Princeton, N. J.: Educational Testing Service, 1959).
[2] Glen A. Vergason, "A Critical Review of Grouping," *The High School Journal*, XLVIII (1965), 427–33.

The findings of the studies which supported the hypothesis that individualized instruction would enhance learning and develop positive attitudes toward education revealed: (1) individualized instruction (II) was more advantageous to slow and average pupils than to superior students; (2) II generated a more positive attitude toward reading; (3) II increased motor, auditory-language, visual, and cognitive skill development in prekindergarten children; and (4) II generated a more positive attitude toward physical education by low-motor fitness students.

The findings of the studies which did not support the hypothesis that individualized instruction would enhance learning revealed: (1) II was not superior to group instructional methods of reading; (2) II was inferior to the team approach in learning to perform the same motor task.[3]

Other studies revealed a lack of consistent evidence to support II or group instruction in terms of teaching handwriting and developing spelling principles.

It is the author's contention that the inconclusive findings are partially attributable to the inability to control teacher variability, the most important factor in learning. The studies reviewed seem to support the premise that teachers who establish rapport with their students, or who give personalized instruction (regardless of grouping procedure), will create a learning environment that results in the greatest achievement gains. Could it be that the soundest teaching strategy involves individualized instruction, coupled with a teacher who fulfills the new role requirements of the teacher listed in Chapter 6? This is the sincere conviction of the writer. One thing is certain: our present instructional methods are anachronistic and, as such, are doing a disservice to the youth of our country.

Evidence of disenchantment with present instructional methods can be gleaned from various sources. Experimentation with the ungraded school, modular scheduling, and individually prescribed instruction are three contemporary approaches to better meet the educational needs of our youth. Terms currently in vogue in education such as *relevancy, accountability, behavioral outcomes, merit pay, differentiated staffing, performance contracting,* and the *voucher plan* lend further credence to the general dissatisfaction with the teaching/learning process. Each concept has implications for providing instruction structured to meet the specific needs of the individual.

Relevancy implies that educational materials must be meaningful to the learner; the focus must be placed on student-centered rather than on content- or teacher-centered approaches. Students and parents are questioning why certain content is in the curriculum. Of what value will a particular body of knowledge be to the child in adult life? Educators must be ready to respond to these questions in terms of logic. A three-year study by the Carnegie Corp-

---

[3] Thomas M. Vodola, "The Effects of Participation Time Variations on the Development of Physical Fitness, Motor Skills and Attitudes," unpublished doctoral dissertation, Temple University, 1970, pp. 34–35.

oration[4] stressed the need for relevant curricula in a general indictment of education; it posits that public schools are all too frequently found to be grim, joyless, and oppressive.

Accountability maintains that teachers must be held accountable for their teaching. We as educators can no longer justify the rationalization that there are too many variables and that as a consequence, the product (the student) cannot be measured in terms of achievement. With the ever-increasing rise in school taxes which is primarily attributable to teacher salary increases, the taxpayer is demanding accountability. As a consequence, educators must devise procedures whereby they can determine student behavioral changes as a direct result of their teaching. Individualized instruction provides the essential ingredients for teacher accountability.

Behavioral outcomes or *performance criteria* provide means of measuring student accomplishments objectively. Specifically, the concern is, What competencies does the learner display? What changes in behavior are evident as a result of the instruction? These types of questions necessitate an instructional program based on pretests and interspersed with imbedded diagnostic tests to assess progress.

Merit pay and *differentiated staffing* are slightly different concepts but we will consider them simultaneously because both are concerned with the improvement of teaching. Merit pay stresses the need for paying teachers on the basis of learner accomplishments, or rewarding teachers for excellence. It is contended by many, including the writer, that the present system of giving all teachers (with the same professional preparation and experience) the same annual increment breeds mediocrity. The problem of determining who gets paid more for excellence is difficult, but it is one that must be resolved. Individualizing instruction would, undoubtedly, provide some of the answers because student progress can be measured.

Differentiated staffing implies better utilization of staff by designating different jobs for different levels of ability. Included in this arrangement might be teacher aides, paraprofessionals, the classroom teacher, the master teacher, and the researcher. Differentiated staffing would also provide different pay scales for each level. Even though this plan has merit, it does not resolve the problem of how to determine performance within levels.

Performance contracting is a very radical approach to education. Non-educational institutions are soliciting contracts with boards of education to provide instructional services. Basically, the contract states that the school district shall pay the contractor a sum of money commensurate with the average grade level improvement of the students involved. In addition to hundreds of districts across the country negotiating contracts, the Office of

---

4 "Study Calls Public School Grim and Joyless," *The New York Times* (September 20, 1970), pp. 1, 70.

Economic Opportunity[5] has awarded $5.6 million in contacts to industrial concerns to teach reading and mathematics to 27,000 students from low-income areas. (*Note:* Feedback from some early studies seems to indicate performance contracting is not superior to traditional teaching methods.)

The *voucher plan* is just as radical in its approach to education as performance contracting. The plan calls for the determination of what it costs to educate our young and the providing of parents with vouchers for that sum of money so that they can enroll their children in a school district that they feel will best meet the child's educational needs. The school district, in turn, receives money only for the children voluntarily enrolled within its boundaries. Unfortunately, chaos might be created by competitive bidding if this plan were generally adopted.

At this point, one may wonder why we present such a detailed elaboration of contemporary problems facing education. How does the material relate to programs for the handicapped? What does it have to do with individualized programming? The rationale for the introductory remarks is as follows:

1. The concepts mentioned are definite trends that are gaining momentum, trends that will make our present roles as teachers obsolete (regardless of our educational responsibilities) unless we make the necessary adjustments.

2. Individualized programming is viewed as a definite approach to, and solution of, many of the aforementioned problems, especially in the area of teaching the handicapped. Due to the variety of handicaps evidenced by students within a school district and the restricted facilities, it is not uncommon to find students in one class evidencing a variety of handicaps that necessitate personalized instruction. (In many of the classes in the writer's district, one will find grouped together students with orthopedic handicaps, rehabilitative problems, and nutritional and postural abnormalities.) By individualizing instruction, the teacher can find time to assist each individual in the class.

The balance of Chapter 7 is divided into two phases: suggested procedures for individualizing instruction and programming activities for the developmentally handicapped.

Suggested Procedures for Individualizing Instruction

It has been constantly reiterated that individualized prescriptions should be based on an initial pretest so that relative strengths and weaknesses may be determined. Chapter 5 provided a detailed step-by-step procedure for changing raw score data into standard or percentile scores so that one has all of the essentials for programming: four procedures for individualizing instruction based on raw score data will now be presented for consideration.

[5] James Welsh, "D.C. Prospectives on Performance Contracting," *Educational Researcher*, XXI (October, 1970), 1–3.

Time Prescriptions Based on Standard Scores

Tables 7–1 and 7–2 provide illustrative examples of how to prescribe motor skills and physical fitness exercises via time prescriptions. The time prescription charts were developed by Vodola[6] in his investigation of the effects of participation time variations on physical fitness, motor skills, and attitude.

[6] Vodola, *op. cit.*, pp. 53, 66.

TABLE 7–1   Time Prescription Chart for Individualizing Motor Skill Instruction

Total deviation points below 100	215	
Total exercising time	900	
Prescription time multiplier	4	
Adjustment time	40	

Computation

$$\begin{array}{r} 4 \\ 215\overline{)900} \\ 860 \\ \overline{40} \end{array}$$ Hull Scores

Chart — Hull Scores: FG 75, BT 63, DT 45, WB 79, PC 23

	field goal	basketball throw	dribble test	wall bounce	penny cup	total
Deviation points below 100	25	37	55	21	77	215
Prescription time multiplier	4	4	4	4	4	
Subtotal	100	148	220	84	308	860
Adjustment time					40	
Total prescription time per task (in seconds)[a]	100	148	220	84	348	900
In minutes and seconds	1:40	2:28	3:40	1:24	5:48	15:00

[a] To determine prescription time for each factor: (1) find prescription time multiplier by dividing total exercising time (900 seconds) by total Hull points below 100 (drop all decimals in the multiplier); (2) multiply deviation Hull points for each factor by the prescription time multiplier; (3) add adjustment time to the lowest factor; (4) total prescription time in seconds; and (5) convert times to minutes and seconds.

The charts were used to design time prescriptions based on individual strengths and weaknesses (*I* Group) and group strengths and weaknesses (*SI* Group). The third group in the study, the control group, followed the traditional grade-level procedure—all subjects adhered to the same curriculum content for the same amount of time (*NI* Group).

To assess the relative effects of the time variations on physical fitness, motor skills, and attitudes, two variations of three treatments were administered: a physical fitness study and a motor fitness study. Based on an analysis

TABLE 7–2   Time Prescription Chart for Individualizing Physical Fitness Instruction

Total deviation points below 100	263	
Total exercising time	900	
Prescription time multiplier	3	
Adjustment time	111	

Computation

$$\begin{array}{r} 3 \\ 263\overline{)900} \\ 789 \\ \overline{111} \end{array}$$ Hull Scores

	dynamic arm strength	explosive leg strength	gross body coordination	gross body balance	dynamic flexibility	stamina	total
	DAS	ELS	GBC	GBB	DF	S	total
Deviation points below 100	66	61	15	23	38	60	
Prescription time multiplier	3	3	3	3	3	3	
Subtotal	198	183	45	69	114	180	789
Adjustment time	111						
Total prescription time per exercise (in seconds)[a]	309	183	45	69	114	180	900
In minutes and seconds	5:09	3:03	0:45	1:09	1:54	3:00	15:00

[a] To determine prescription time for each factor: (1) find prescription time multiplier by dividing total exercising time (900 seconds) by total Hull points below 100 (drop all decimals in the multiplier); (2) multiply deviation Hull points for each factor by the prescription time multiplier; (3) add adjustment time to the lowest factor; (4) total prescription time in seconds; and (5) convert times to minutes and seconds.

of the data, the author concluded that under the experimental conditions that existed:

1. Exercises or tasks based on individual or group-assigned time variations will improve physical fitness or motor skills.

2. Exercises or tasks based on individualized time variations will improve the development of separate physical fitness or motor skill components.

3. Exercises or tasks based on group-assigned time variations will improve the development of separate physical fitness or motor skill components except for areas of extreme weakness.

4. Exercises or tasks based on individual or group-assigned time variations will not effect positive attitude changes.

5. Exercises based on group-assigned time variations (subjects devoted equal time to each exercise) will effect a negative attitude response toward physical fitness.

6. Exercise based on individualized time variations is not superior to exercise based on group-assigned time variations for the development of physical fitness.

7. Tasks based on individualized time variations are superior to tasks based on group-assigned time variations for the development of motor skills.

8. Exercises or tasks based on individualized time variations are not superior to exercises or tasks based on group-assigned time variations for the development of positive attitudes toward physical education.[7]

The following "implications for teaching" were derived from the study cited and were presented at a Research Section Meeting of the New Jersey Education Association.[8]

IMPLICATIONS FOR TEACHING

1. Pretest all students prior to the start of new units to ascertain strengths and weaknesses so that more activity time can be prescribed for areas of group weaknesses. *Rationale:* A physical fitness study revealed that the group which devoted equal practice time to each exercise (*NI* Group) was the only group that did not improve arm strength (its weakest area) as a result of the training program. *Example:* Gymnastic unit: Administer pretest and have students devote more practice time on those pieces of apparatus on which the group fared poorly. *Example:* Pre-activity conditioning unit: Vary exercises based on group needs.

2. When feasible, prescribe each student's program on the basis of his individual strengths and weaknesses (devoting proportionately more practice time to areas of weakness than to areas of strength). *Rationale:* A motor skill study revealed that significantly greater gains were attained by those subjects who practiced skills based on individual strengths and weaknesses than on group needs or grade level requirements. *Example:* Individual and dual activities: Tennis, golf, track and field, wrestling, etc.

7 *Ibid.*, pp. 99–108.
8 New Jersey Association for Health, Physical Education and Recreation, Research Section Meeting, N.J.E.A. State Convention, November, 1969.

3. Motivation is the key to learning. Motivate students by assisting and guiding rather than telling and lecturing. Provide learning experiences that maximize student involvement—through such meaningful involvement your students will become intrinsically motivated. *Rationale:* Five of the six post-test scores (in both studies) on the Equivalent Forms of the Wear Attitude Inventory were lower than the pretest scores (the *NI* Group in the fitness study had a significantly negative attitude). Although practice sessions were individualized to different degrees, student/student and student/teacher interaction were virtually eliminated in an attempt to minimize student motivational variability. *Example:* Weight training unit: Have students design their own programs, test each other, prescribe (with the assistance of the teacher), etc. In other words, maximize student involvement.

4. Present unit content so that it is interesting and meaningful to the class. *Rationale:* Negative significant attitude in the fitness study was not observed in the motor skill study. This could be attributable to the fact that the motor skill study involved such tasks as dribbling, passing, and shooting, whereas the fitness study involved push-ups, a flexibility exercise, running, etc. *Example:* Tennis, archery unit: Minimize lectures on history and rules, mimetic drills; involve the students in "stroking the ball" and shooting as soon as possible. Provide instruction on basic fundamentals during "teachable moments."

Although all data did not substantiate the superiority of *I* Group, the results were very encouraging. Furthermore, it was found that prescribing on the basis of standard scores is feasible. The initial task of establishing standard scores is time consuming, but once it is accomplished the scores can be used for many years (unless there is a great variation in terms of program or population). Once the standard scores have been established, the teacher can convert the raw scores for a class of 35 to 40 students to individualized time prescriptions in two to three hours. (The teacher can be relieved of this task if he is fortunate enough to work in a school district which has a computer that can be programmed to handle the data.) The total prescription time for the data in Tables 7–1 and 7–2 was fifteen minutes for each table. (The time factor can be varied according to the length of the class period and other factors that might necessitate a change.) In the illustrations listed, raw scores were converted to Hull (standard) scores since the author felt that the population tested was relatively homogeneous. If the target population has extremely divergent scores, the T-scale would be more appropriate because the norms would better cover the spread of scores.

In Table 7–1 a student has achieved the following Hull scores: field goal shooting, 75; throw for accuracy, 63; dribble test, 45; wall-bounce test, 79; and penny cup test, 23. An analysis of the time prescription chart reveals that the subject evidences extreme deficiency in reaction time (the factor measured primarily by the penny cup test). The recommended computational procedure provides a sound basis for prescribing activities commensurate with the evidenced needs. For example, a score of 79 necessitates 1:24 seconds of practice, whereas a score of 23 necessitates 5:48 seconds of practice. (It is important to note at this time that students should always be provided with practice time for the skills at which they are most competent because they need the reinforcement provided by such success.)

In Table 7–2 a student has achieved the following Hull scores: dynamic flexibility, 62; gross body balance, 77; gross body coordination, 85; dynamic arm strength, 34; explosive leg strength, 39; and stamina, 40. Time prescriptions for physical fitness exercise ranged from a high of 5:09 to a low of 0:45.

To illustrate the importance of individualized programming, an actual incident that occurred during the fitness study will be related.

To make the incident meaningful, the design of the study must be explained. Subjects were randomly assigned to three groups within the class, regardless of pretest scores: the three groups were referred to as the nonindividualized group (*NI*), the semi-individualized group (*SI*), and the individualized group (*I*). The *NI* group represented traditional teaching, all students practicing the same material for the same amount of time; thus, each student practiced each of the six exercises for 2 minutes and 30 seconds (2:30)—a total of 15:00. The *SI* group was representative of ability or was homogeneously grouped in that the entire group practiced the same exercises for the same amount of time. The distinguishing feature of this group was that the time prescriptions were based on the mean average score for the entire group on each test item. The subjects in the *I* group practiced their exercises in accordance with their individualized time prescriptions. To minimize motivational variability and to control for the Hawthorne Effect (gains attributable to being in a novel situation), students were not informed as to what group they were in.

During the first week of the practice sessions the investigator visited one of the classes in the experimental study. John, who was exercising feverishly, asked why he had to practice push-ups for six minutes when he had achieved the highest pull-up score in the class? A check of his file revealed he had been assigned to the *SI* group and that although his score was the highest, the group average on dynamic arm strength was the lowest; as a consequence all members of the group had to devote maximum prescription time to push-ups, regardless of individual attainment.

An attempt was made to pacify John by informing him that his personal prescription would maximize his physical fitness level. (Of course the researcher knew this was not true, but the statement was made to control motivational variability. Regardless of grouping assignments, all subjects were told the same rationale for their prescriptions.)

Although there is no question that having a student devote most of his study time to his areas of greatest strength is illogical, present instructional methods (teaching at one level) enhance such a possibility. How many of our students are "turned off" by education, or become disruptive elements in our classes because of such situations? It is postulated that if more time is devoted to areas of *weakness* (structuring the content from the simple to the complex), learning will be accelerated due to the intrinsic motivation factor.

The time prescription procedure can be utilized in individualized programming for the handicapped child. The basic prerequisite is that diagnostic tests be designed so that they can be measured objectively (in terms of raw scores). All data must then be converted to some form of standard scores. For example, the Motor/Perceptual Test Battery referred to in Chapter 3 can be used to individually program activities for students with motor and/or perceptual problems. Similarly, the procedure can be adapted to prescribing activities for other disabilities.

Time Prescriptions Based on
Percentile Rank Scores

For those teachers who would like to utilize the time prescription procedure in a less sophisticated manner, even though it is mathematically less accurate, the use of percentile rank scores is recommended. (See Fig. 5–4 on p. 112. Can you determine why percentile rank scores are less accurate?) Individualized programming via this method merely requires the establishment of percentile scores rather than mean, standard deviation, and standard scores. Time prescriptions can then be determined by establishing each student's percentile rank for each of his raw scores, plotting the data on a time prescription chart, and making the necessary mathematical computation.

If one wishes to program on the basis of percentile rank scores, one should be aware of the limitations. There is a loss of mathematical accuracy, especially with the extreme scores (above 85 percent and below 15 percent) due to the unequal size of intervals. One cannot make comparisons between percentile rank scores because they are not based on a common denominator, unlike standard scores. Finally, if the programmer contemplates further study, percentile rank data cannot be used for research purposes due to the same mathematical inaccuracies which arise.

Time Prescriptions Based on Stanine Scores

The use of stanine scores to prescribe individualized programs is somewhat similar to the percentile rank method. The term *stanine* is derived from a standard score of nine units. However, "it is now used almost exclusively as a normalized standard score (i.e., a score which is computed like a percentile rank score but is expressed like a standard score)."[9] A simplified procedure for determining stanine scores would be to arrange all students' raw scores in order from the highest to the lowest and to use the illustration provided[10]:

Stanines	1	2	3	4	5	6	7	8	9
Percent in stanine	4	7	12	17	20	17	12	7	4

Thus, the top 4 percent of the scores would be assigned a 9, the next 7 percent an 8, etc. Every effort should be made to assign stanine values as closely as possible to the listed percentages.

[9] Howard B. Lyman, "Talking Test Scores: The Stanine," *N.C.M.E. Measurement News*, XIII, No. 4 (October, 1970), 4.
[10] *Ibid.*

TABLE 7–3   Stanine Profile of Motor Skill Test
Battery Items

Field goal test	1	2	3	4	5	6	7	8	⑨
Basketball throw	1	2	3	4	5	6	7	⑧	9
Dribble test	1	2	3	4	⑤	6	7	8	9
Wall-bounce	1	2	3	4	5	6	7	8	⑨
Penny cup test	1	2	3	④	5	6	7	8	9

Table 7–3 provides an example of a profile of the Motor Skill Test Battery based on stanine scores. Analysis of the scores reveals that the student is very competent in field goal shooting, the basketball throw, and wall-bouncing. Areas of evidenced weaknesses would be dribbling and the penny cup test. If one were to use this procedure, the teacher would subjectively assign practice time prescriptions only after analysis of the scores. For example, the prescriptions for the scores attained might be as follows (based on a total of 15: 00): field goal shoot, 1: 00; basketball throw, 2: 00; dribble test, 5: 00; wall-bounce, 1: 00; and penny cup test, 6: 00.

Prescriptions Based on Teacher Evaluation

In situations wherein normalized data are not available, students should have their programs prescribed on the basis of the teacher's subjective evaluation. (In fact, teacher evaluation should also play an important adjunctive role in individualized programming regardless of the prescription procedure used.) This is especially important when working with students in the adapted phase of the program for the handicapped in such situations as: prescribing aerobic activities for the asthmatic child; designing exercises to strengthen atrophied muscles of the orthopedically handicapped; or planning a bowling or archery unit for the blind or partially sighted. In each of the above situations, prescriptions must necessarily be based on an analysis of the individual's performance and unique needs. The child who cannot supinate the hand must have exercises (prescribed by the physician) to increase his range of motion. The asthmatic child's exercises should be prescribed on the basis of his vital capacity scores, the weather, and the season of the year. Thus, each child with a medically oriented problem must be programmed in terms of his specific need(s).

It is imperative that the teacher work very closely with the school and/or family physician and school psychologist in arriving at prescriptions for the handicapped. The ideal situation would be to have the physician state the medical implications and limitations so that the physical educator can prescribe the correct activities. In any event, one must remember that all prescriptions for the students in the adapted phase of the program must be approved by the medical authority involved.

Note: The four procedures suggested for individualizing instruction have been field-tested by the writer and have been found to be practical for implementation. However, further research is needed to determine the values of individualized physical education (in both the unrestricted and D&A classes). Regardless of existing problems the teacher is confronted with (class size, limited facilities), he is urged to pretest all students and to attempt to individualize instruction, even if only on a limited basis. Experience has proven that a gratifying resultant feedback from students will motivate the teacher to further increase his efforts in terms of personalizing instruction.

**Programming Activities for
the Developmentally Handicapped**

Regardless of the method one uses for prescribing individualized activities, the basic approach should be the same. Successful individualized programming should include exercises, tasks, or activities that meet the following criteria:

1. Prescriptions based on pretests which are indicative of specific needs
2. Prescriptions that have high factorial validity (items that will ameliorate specific problems)
3. Prescriptions designed to insure success via the proper sequence (success at each level)
4. Prescriptions which include diagnostic tests to assess behavioral changes
5. Prescriptions based on individual strengths to enhance students' self-image

The following forms and activities are recommended for consideration in individually programming for the developmentally handicapped child. All forms and materials have been field-tested in the Township of Ocean School District and modified periodically. They will furnish the teacher who would like to start a D&A program with some essentials. As one gains experience, he will undoubtedly add, delete, and modify according to his teaching situation.

Test for Low Physical Vitality, K–8

A review of the K–8 Basic Motor Skill Test and Physical Fitness Test Forms in Appendix A reveals that the test batteries have been designed to assess the following factors: gross motor skills; hand/eye and foot/eye coordination; balance and postural orientation; hand/eye and foot/eye accuracy; gross body balance; arm strength; abdominal strength; explosive leg strength; and cardiorespiratory endurance. A prescriptive list of skills and activities are listed for programming purposes.

I. COORDINATION
  A. Gross motor skills
    a. Crawling
    b. Skipping
    c. Hopping
    d. Throwing underhand
    e. Throwing overhand
    f. Jumping
    g. Pushing
    h. Pulling
    i. Lifting
  B. Gross motor activities: individual, dual, and team
    a. Forward roll
    b. Log roll
    c. Backward roll
    d. Monkey roll (partners)
    e. Marching
    f. Hop scotch
    g. "Simon Says"
    h. "Jumping Jacks"
    i. Cable jump
    j. Rope-skipping
    k. Rhythmics
    l. Lay-ups
    m. Shot-putting
    n. Hurdling
  C. Hand/eye coordination
  1. Skills
    a. Bat stationary ball with hand.
    b. Bat moving ball with hand,
    c. Bat stationary ball with bat.
    d. Bat moving ball with bat.
    e. Catch a bounced ball.
    f. Catch a rolling ball.
    g. Catch a thrown ball.
    h. Dribble a ball.
  2. Activities: individual, dual, and team
    a. "Keep up" a balloon.
    b. Catch a ball with a partner.
    c. Catch a ball thrown against a wall.
    d. Bat softball off "tee" into net.
    e. Play quoits, shuffleboard, horseshoes.
    f. Play tetherball, table tennis.
    g. Play paddle ball, handball.
    h. Dribble basketball, volleyball, etc.
    i. Play dodge ball, newcomb.
    j. Pick up "jacks."
  D. Foot/eye coordination
  1. Skills
    a. Kick stationary ball.
    b. Kick rolling ball.
    c. Kick with instep.
    d. Pass a ball inside and outside of foot.
    e. Trap a rolling ball with the sole of foot.
    f. Drop-kick a ball.
    g. Punt a ball.
    h. Pick up a ball with feet (stationary).
    i. Pick up a rolling ball with one foot.
  2. Activities: individual, dual, and team
    a. Kick a ball with a partner or against a wall.
    b. Take part in dribble races.
    c. Kick a ball with a partner or against a wall.

  d. Take part in passing drills in set formations.
  e. Play goal line soccer.
  f. Drop-kick a ball for distance and accuracy.
  g. Punt a ball for distance and accuracy.
  h. Play a game of speedball.
  i. Play kick-ball.
  j. Run through staggered tires.

II. BALANCE AND POSTURAL ORIENTATION

 A. *Skills*
  1. Walk (observe cross-pattern).
  2. Walk forward, backward, sideward/toe-heel.
  3. Stand on both feet, eyes open, closed.
  4. Stand on right/left foot, eyes open, closed.
  5. Hop on both feet.
  6. Hop on one foot.
  7. Hop on alternate feet.
  8. Do forward roll.
  9. Jump from stall bench and balance.
  10. Do backward roll.
  11. Balance with head/hand (tripod position).
  12. Squat with hand balance.
  13. Do forearm balance.
  14. Do hand balance.

 B. *Activities: individual, dual, and team*
  1. March.
  2. Walk a straight, curved line, beam.
  3. Take part in potato race.
  4. Run in relay race.
  5. Hop in and out of tires.
  6. Take part in forward roll relays.
  7. Take part in jump/forward roll relays.
  8. Take part in backward roll relays; in combination of forward and backward roll relays.
  9. See "who can maintain balance longest" (tripod position).
  10. See "who can maintain balance longest" (squat hand balance).
  11. See "who can maintain balance longest" (forearm balance).
  12. See "who can maintain balance longest" (hand balance).
  13. Take ball balance test.
  14. Walk forward, backward, sideward around tires; hop in and over tires.

III. ACCURACY

 A. *Hand/eye accuracy learning experiences*
  1. Individual and dual activities
   a. Quoits, horseshoes, shuffleboard
   b. Archery, bowling, clock golf
   c. Serve tennis and volleyball.
   d. Bat softball off "tee" into net.
   e. Bat softball into right, left, and center fields.
   f. Throw basketball for accuracy.
   g. Shoot basketball from foul line.
   h. Perform basketball lay-ups (30 seconds).

B. *Foot/eye accuracy learning experiences*
   1. Individual and dual activities
       a. Kick stationary ball into net.
       b. Kick rolling ball into net.
       c. Drop-kick ball over target.
       d. Kick up ball to teammate.
       e. Kick ball to predetermined area.

IV. *STRENGTH DEVELOPMENT*
   A. *Explosive strength/agility* (*strength plus speed*)
       1. Arms
           a. Medicine ball throw
           b. Softball throw
           c. Shot-put
           d. Weight-training arm exercises involving rapidity of movement
       2. Legs
           a. Shuttle run
           b. Standing broad jump across gym
           c. Repeated vertical wall jump
           d. Hopping on one and both feet across the gym
           e. Weight-training leg exercises involving rapidity of movement
   B. *Abdominal strength*
       1. Curl-ups (hands on thighs; just raise head and shoulders)
       2. Curl-ups: touch finger tips to knee caps
       3. Sit-ups (hands behind head): knees flexed, have partner hold feet
       4. Modified leg lifts (supine position): bring knees to chest and return to original position
       5. Same as 4 except follow knees to chest with legs straight overhead, back to chest, original position
       6. Sit-ups (hands behind head and knees flexed): without partner
       7. Same as 6 on an inclined board
       8. Same as 7 with added weight behind the neck
       9. "Vee sit-ups" (supine position on mat): with arms extended overhead, simultaneously raise arms and legs, touching finger tips to toes
       10. "Rocker": from prone position on mat, grasp ankles with hands and rock back and forth
   C. *Grip strength* (*grip, wrist, forearm*)
       1. Squeeze rubber ball.
       2. Crumple sheet of paper laid flat on a table.
       3. Curl dumbbell with alternate hands.
       4. Rope curl: roll rope with suspended weight around stick held in two hands.
       5. "French curls": curl barbell with palms facing the floor.
   D. *Arm strength*
       1. Biceps
           a. Curl dumbbells
           b. Curl barbell
           c. Curl barbell with increasing weights
           d. Modified pull-ups: palms facing body
           e. Pull-ups: palms facing away from body
           f. Rope climbing: arms and legs

      g. Rope climb: arms only
      h. Rope climb: legs in pike position
      i. Pull-over: horizontal bar
      j. Static hang: chinning bar
      k. Half-inverted hang: rings
      l. Skin-the-cat: rings
      m. Leg cuts: rings
   2. Triceps
      a. Press dumbbells
      b. Press barbell
      c. Press barbell with weights
      d. Modified push-ups on knees
      e. Push-ups: legs straight
      f. Rope climbing: arms and legs
      g. Rope climb: arms only
      h. Rope climb: legs in pike position
      i. Hand walk: parallel bars
      j. Hand hopping: parallel bars
      k. Bench presses
      l. Swinging and swinging dips on parallel bars
      m. Leg cuts: side horse

  E. *Back strength*
    1. Back extension on floor: from prone position, raise head and shoulders
    2. Same as *1* but raise legs also
    3. Wrestler's bridge: supine on floor, arch back and support all weight on hands and feet
    4. Back extension with head and shoulders and waist over edge of table: hands behind neck, touch elbows to the floor and raise up to horizontal position

  F. *Leg strength*
    1. Heel raises: raise arms and rise up on toes, hold
    2. Same as *1* with added weight
    3. Bench exerciser
    4. Squats
    5. Squats with weights
    6. Leg presses (power rack)
    7. Harvard Step Test
    8. Harvard Step Test with weights

V. *CARDIORESPIRATORY ENDURANCE (STAMINA)*
    1. "Spot running": running in place
    2. Running measured distance: time constant
    3. Running measured distance: reduce the time
    4. Jumping jacks and other gross motor activities: constantly increase repetitions
    5. Same as *4* but keep repetitions constant while reducing the time
    6. Rope skipping: repetitions and time constant
    7. Same as *6* but keep "reps" constant and reduce the time
    8. Harvard Step Test: start with 30 four-count steps for two minutes; increase the time by 30 seconds until student can perform for five minutes

Township of Ocean School District   School _____

Name _____ Day _____ Period _____ Instructor _____ Classif. _____

MOTOR SKILLS	Participation Dates																
Bilaterality																	
Balance-Postural Orientation																	
Eye/Hand Coordination																	
Eye/Hand Accuracy																	
Ocular Pursuits																	
Eye/Foot Accuracy																	
PERCEPTUAL-MOTOR SKILLS																	
Geometic Forms																	
Pegboards																	
Pegboard Sheets																	
Puzzles																	
Body Image Forms																	
ORTHOPEDIC PROGRAM																	
Range of Motion Exercises																	
Strength Exercises																	
DATES																	

Handedness R/L   Footedness R/L

Remarks _____

FIGURE 7–1   Individual prescription card for grades K-8.

For a specific form of listing prescriptions, refer to the format designed by Ballard and Picaroni[11] (see Appendix A).

A procedure with considerable merit is the designing of an individual prescription card for each student in the D&A program. Figure 7–1 illustrates a format that can be placed on a $5 \times 8''$ card. On the side shown, student daily achievement levels can be recorded to assess progress. On the reverse side, student prescriptions can be recorded.

Test for Low Physical Vitality, 9–12

Table 7–4 presents a prescription form that can be used with the Rogers P.F.I. Test and with other selected fitness items.

At this point we will describe the cable jump test recommended by Fleishman (see Fig. 7–2).[12] Holding the ends of a two-foot length of rope loosely in front of his body (so that both ends of the rope are visible), the student must

---

11 James Ballard and John Picaroni, "D&A Summer Program," Ocean Township High School, Oakhurst, N.J., July, 1970.

12 Edwin A. Fleishman, *The Structure and Measurement of Physical Fitness* (Englewood Cliffs, N.J.: Prentice-Hall, Inc., 1964), p. 169.

TABLE 7–4 Individually Prescribed Conditioning Program

Student's Name	Grade	Period	Day	Instructor	Somatotype

I. Test and Analysis

		PRETEST			POST-TEST		
test item	*factor measured*	*raw score*	*% rank*	*date*	*raw score*	*% rank*	*date*
Leg lift	Leg strength	___	___	___	___	___	___
Back lift	Back strength	___	___	___	___	___	___
Arm strength index	Dynamic arm strength	___	___	___	___	___	___
100-yard shuttle run	Explosive strength	___	___	___	___	___	___
Endurance index	Cardiorespiratory endurance	___	___	___	___	___	___
Flexometer	Trunk flexibility	___	___	___	___	___	___
Modified cable jump	Gross body coordination	___	___	___	___	___	___
Balance beam	Gross body balance	___	___	___	___	___	___

II. Prescribed Program

	factor	*exercise*	*basis for prescription*
1.	___	___	*1.* Prescribe one exercise for each fitness component in which the student scored below the 75th %ile (total of six exercises).
2.	___	___	
3.	___	___	
4.	___	___	*2.* Three areas below 75th %ile: Prescribe two exercises for each; two areas of weakness: prescribe three exercises for each, etc.
5.	___	___	
6.	___	___	

III. Evaluation/Recommendations

jump over the loop without releasing his grasp with either hand. The student's score for gross body coordination is the number of correct jumps out of ten attempts. Field testing revealed the test item to be too easy, thus negating its value as a test item. As a result, the test item was modified to increase the difficulty. The subject was instructed to attempt five jumps with the rope held in front of the body and five jumps with the rope held behind the body. The test item should be included in a test battery since it is a measure of gross body coordination as well as an excellent motivating, self-testing stunt.

At a past East Central District Conference of the New Jersey Association for Health, Physical Education and Recreation, Muska Mosston[13] introduced

[13] Lecture by Muska Mosston, "Styles of Teaching Workshop," Rutgers, The State University, New Brunswick, N.J., April 11, 1964.

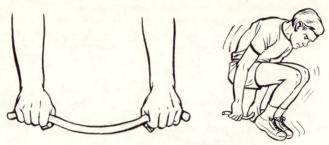

FIGURE 7–2   Modified cable jump test.

his "styles of teaching" to New Jersey teachers. Following a lecture-demonstration, the styles were applied to a variety of teaching activities.

The following list of exercises is recommended for individual programming of high school students who evidence low physical vitality. (*Note:* The levels listed are applicable to the student population in the Township of Ocean. The reader may use them as a guide, but he should design levels based on the population he is working with. Mosston's text,[14] *Developmental Movement*, provides the reader with a series of sequentially structured developmental activities.)

LEVELS OF ACHIEVEMENT (CIRCLE)

I. *Dynamic arm strength*

Pull-ups (palms in)	5	10	15	20
Pull-ups (palms out)	5	10	15	20
Pull-ups (palms in, 20 seconds)	5	10	15	20
Push-ups (to limit)	20	40	60	80
Push-ups (20 seconds)	5	10	15	20
Bent arm hand (palms out)	15 sec.	30 sec.	45 sec.	60 sec.
Dips (to limit)	5	10	15	20
Dips (20 seconds)	5	10	15	20
Hold half push-up	15 sec.	30 sec.	45 sec.	60 sec.
Rope climb (arms and legs)	15 sec.	12 sec.	9 sec.	6 sec.
Rope climb (arms only)	20 sec.	16 sec.	12 sec.	8 sec.
Rope climb (arms and legs)	$\frac{1}{4}$	$\frac{1}{2}$	$\frac{3}{4}$	1
Rope climb (arms only)	$\frac{1}{4}$	$\frac{1}{2}$	$\frac{3}{4}$	1
Peg board (ladder climb up and down)	1	2	3	4
Inverted push-ups	2	4	6	8

II. *Leg strength*

Squats (weights)	100 lbs./ 10 reps.	100 lbs./ 15 reps.	100 lbs./ 20 reps.	100 lbs./ 25 reps.
Presses (power rack)	200 lbs./ 10 reps.	200 lbs./ 15 reps.	200 lbs./ 20 reps.	200 lbs./ 25 reps.
Squats (without weights) (45°)	15 sec.	20 sec.	25 sec.	30 sec.
Squats (without weights) (45°)	15 reps.	20 reps.	25 reps.	30 reps.
Squats (without weights) (90°)	15 sec.	20 sec.	25 sec.	30 sec.
Squats (without weights) (90°)	15 reps.	20 reps.		

14 Muska Mosston, *Developmental Movement* (Columbus, Ohio: Charles E. Merrill Books, Inc., 1965).

LEVELS OF ACHIEVEMENT (CIRCLE)

Bench exercises (bench seat is
2–3 inches above knees)[a]

Full knee extension	15 reps.	30 reps.	45 reps.	60 rep.
Return to sitting position	60 sec.	120 sec.	180 sec.	240 sec.

III. *Abdominal strength (30 sec.)*

Curl-ups (hands on thighs, legs extended	15 reps.	20 reps.	25 reps.	30 reps.
Curl-ups (hands behind neck, knees flexed)	15 reps.	20 reps.	25 reps.	30 reps.
Repeat curl-ups with weight behind neck	15 reps.	20 reps.	25 reps.	30 reps.
Repeat above three on an inclined board	15 reps.	20 reps.	25 reps.	30 reps.
Leg lifts: back on floor, knees flexed; straighten both legs and return to floor (45° angle)	15 reps.	20 reps.	25 reps.	30 reps.

IV. *Explosive leg strength*

100-yard shuttle run	25 sec.	22 sec.	19 sec.	17 sec.
50-yard dash	9.0 sec.	8.0 sec.	7.0 sec.	6.0 sec.
10-yard dash[b]				
10-yard shuttle run[b]				
Standing broad jump	5′0″	6′6″	8′0″	9′6″
Standing broad jump (length of floor)	20 sec.	18 sec.	16 sec.	14 sec.
Vertical wall jump	14″	18″	24″	28″
Vertical wall jump (30 sec.)	20	30	40	50
Dodge run around cones: number of cones passed in 30 sec.[b]				
Circle run (12′ diameter): number of revolutions in 20 sec.[b]				

V. *Flexibility*

Push-up to standing position	5	10	15	20
Hurdler's position (touch toes)	5R&5L	10R&10L	15R&15L	20R&20L
Hurdler's position (chest to thigh)	5R&5L	10R&10L	15R&15L	20R&20L
Stall bar bench toe touch	touch toes	touch 1″ below	touch 2″ below	touch 3″ below
Bend, touch-twist, touch (30 sec.)	10 reps.	15 reps.	20 reps.	25 reps.
Alternate toe touching (feet apart)	5R&5L	10R&10L	15R&15L	20R&20L
Toe touching (feet together)	5	10	15	20
Palms on floor	5	10	15	20
Grasp ankles (chest on thighs)	5	10	15	20
Hip position (feet to floor)	5	10	15	20
Twist and touch	5R&5L	10R&10L	15R&15L	20R&20L

VI. *Gross body coordination*

Modified cable jump	5/10	7/10	8/10	10/10
Cable jump forward	7/10	8/10	9/10	10/10
Cable jump backward	5/10	7/10	8/10	10/10
Rope skipping (30 sec.)	30	60	90	120
Figure-8 pattern (hands and feet on floor) (30 sec.)[b]				

[a] Increase work load by leaning rearward.
[b] Levels have not been established yet.

	LEVELS OF ACHIEVEMENT (CIRCLE)			
Stick jump	5R&5L	10R&10L	15R&15L	20R&20L
Varied jumping jacks: establish levels based on the complexity of the task.				

VII. Gross body balance

T-BALANCES (STATIC)

Right foot, lengthwise (eyes open)	5 sec.	10 sec.	15 sec.	20 sec.
Left foot, lengthwise (eyes open)	5 sec.	10 sec.	15 sec.	20 sec.
Repeat above with eyes closed	5 sec.	10 sec.	15 sec.	20 sec.
Right foot, cross-balance (eyes open)	5	10	15	20
Left foot, cross-balance (eyes open)	5	10	15	20
Repeat right foot cross-balance and left foot cross-balance (eyes closed)	5	10	15	20

DYNAMIC EXERCISES: BALANCE BEAM

Up and back (walking forward, eyes open)[b]				
Up and back (walking forward, eyes closed)[b]				
Up and back (walking backward, eyes open)[b]				
Up and back (walking backward, eyes closed)[b]				
Tapered balance beam (eyes open), average 3 attempts	150″	175″	200″	233″
Tapered balance beam (eyes closed), average 3 attempts	150″	175″	200″	233″
Tapered balance beam (backward, eyes open)	150″	175″	200″	233″
Tapered balance beam (backward, eyes closed)	150″	175″	200″	233″

VIII. Cardiorespiratory endurance

Harvard Step Test (30 sec.)	30R	40R	50R	60R
Rope skipping (30 sec.):				
Two legs (forward)	40R	50R	60R	70R
Two legs (backward)	20R	30R	40R	50R
Alternating legs	40R	50R	60R	70R
Spot running: count every time right foot strikes floor (30 sec.)	40R	50R	60R	70R
Back extensions, hands behind neck (30 sec.)	10	15	20	25
Back extensions, weight behind neck (30 sec.)	10	15	20	25
Wrestler's bridge (30 sec.), support weight with feet and hands	10	15	20	25
Straddle bend (with hands locked behind neck and elbows back)	10 sec.	20 sec.	25 sec.	30 sec.
Trunk parallel to ground, straddle bend with arms forward	10 sec.	20 sec.	25 sec.	30 sec.
Same as straddle bend with arms forward holding a medicine ball	10 sec.	20 sec.	25 sec.	30 sec.

[b] Levels have not been established yet.

Nutritional Deficiencies

The developmental activities prescribed for students who evidence nutritional deficiencies are based on the assumption that the problems are caused by improper dietary habits, a lack of physical activity, or a combination of both. (The reader is urged to procure a free copy of "Exercise and Weight Control" for an excellent explanation of the prevalent weight control fallacies and the advantages of exercise.[15])

Chapter 3 recommends that students who are 20 percent above or below predicted body weight should be programmed for developmental activities. The following procedure is recommended for programming those students with nutritional deficiencies.

1. Determine true weight, predicted weight, nutritional index, skinfold, and muscle girth measurements (see Chapter 3 for explanation). Skinfold and muscle girth measurements are recommended so that the student can objectively identify and periodically reassess his body composition in terms of these two components. For example, there will be occasions when an obese student either maintains or increases body weight, following a week of accelerated activity. This individual may consider his program a failure because he will equate a successful program solely in terms of a weight loss. Although it is true that a weight loss is indicative of improvement, many students during the initial phase of the program (the first week or two) may not experience any noticeable weight loss due to either retention of body water or an increase in muscle tissue with a comparative decrease in fatty tissue deposits. Skinfold calipers and girth measurements (chest, waist, upper arms, and thighs) would indicate such a change in body composition.

2. Discuss weight control fallacies, proper dietary habits (balance of carbohydrates, vitamins, and minerals), and the effects of physical activity on weight control with each individual. The malnourished and the obese have a common problem in that their food intake is imbalanced, leading to a loss or gain in weight. The malnourished may have to increase protein intake in his diet; the obese may have to reduce carbohydrate intake.

3. Have each student prepare his own weight motivation chart.[16] Figure 7–3 illustrates the procedure for plotting one's weekly weight. In the illustration the subject's true weight is 210 pounds and his predicted weight is 200 pounds; thus, he would like to lose 10 pounds. The solid line indicates his objective, to lose 1 pound per week; the dotted line indicates his

15 Committee on Exercise and Physical Fitness of the American Medical Association and the President's Council on Physical Fitness in Cooperation with Lifetime Sports Foundation, "Exercise and Weight Control," Washington, D.C. (n.d.), 10 pp.
16 As proposed by Arne L. Olson, "Theory and Practice of Physical Conditioning," course taught at Temple University, Philadelphia, fall, 1963.

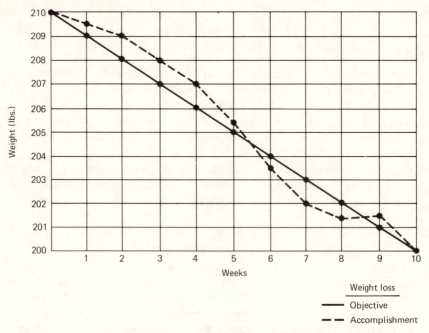

FIGURE 7–3 Weight reducing motivation chart. Reproduced from chart suggested by Arne L. Olson in course on theory and practice of physical conditioning, Temple University, fall 1963, by permission of Arne L. Olson.

actual accomplishment for the ten-week period. We can see that the subject lagged slightly behind his projected goal for the first five weeks (the adjustment phase) and attained a weight of 200.5 pounds by the end of the ten-week period. Although the chart ostensibly illustrates weekly progress, its prime value appears to be the effect it has on student self-motivation.

4. Determine student caloric and activity needs to increase or decrease body weight by 1 pound per week. You have probably noted that the prescribed goal is to increase or decrease one's weight by 1 pound per week. However, we urge that the physical educator never advise a student to diet; such a prescription should be made only by a physician. The physical educator can stress weight control via eating the proper foods and resorting to the proper exercises or activities but he ought not encourage students to lose or gain more than 1 pound per week. "Crash" diets, in addition to being detrimental to one's health, have been actually found to be only temporary adjustments of body weight which are followed by a return to the abnormal weight or even an increase in weight (obese condition). Whether the cause of the subsequent weight gain is attributable to the initial shock to the homeostasis of the body or is psychological, it has been shown that the weight adjustment is not permanent.

Opponents of the 1-pound-per-week plan have argued that such a weight control program does not provide the necessary incentive for one to reduce. Indeed, on a weekly basis, 1 pound per week does not seem significant. However, viewing the problem on a long-range basis, there are 52 weeks in a year; a weight loss of 52 pounds in one year certainly should be significant to an overweight person. Further, experience has indicated that a slower transition in body weight tends to be more lasting.

The procedure proposed for determining caloric body needs was devised by Bogert.[17] The following mathematical illustration will explain the procedure necessary for determining one's necessary daily caloric intake (*DCI*), an essential starting point for prescribing a personalized weight control program:

$$DCI = 1 \times 24 \times \text{body weight in kilograms}$$

where: a kilogram = 2.2 lbs., and
student's weight = 220 lbs.

By substitution,

$DCI = 1 \times 24 \times 100$
= 2,400 calories: basal metabolism
+500 calories: sedentary activities
2,900
+290 calories: 10% of subtotal for assimilation, digestion, etc.
3,190 total calories needed to sustain 220 lbs.

Thus, to sustain basal metabolic processes (breathing, circulation of blood, etc.) a 220-pound person requires 2,400 calories. To that figure, one must add calories in proportion to daily activity. If one is extremely active, add 1,000 calories or more. In the example, an arbitrary figure of 500 calories was added because the person did little more than expend minimal energy. (Passmore and Durnin[18] and Johnson[19] provide excellent referential material for determining the caloric cost of activity.) Finally, an additional 10 percent of the subtotal (2,900) was added to provide for caloric energy that is dissipated during ingestion. Thus, a 220-pound person needs 3,190 calories to maintain his weight.

With the information provided, the instructor can design a weight program to increase or decrease body weight by 1 pound per week. Since 1 pound of

[17] L. Jean Bogert, *Nutrition and Physical Fitness*, 7th ed. (Philadelphia: W. B. Saunders Company, 1960), p. 64.
[18] R. Passmore and J. Durnin, "Human Energy Expenditure," *Physiological Review*, XXXV (1955), 801.
[19] Robert E. Johnson et al., "Energy Expenditure by a 150-pound Person in Various Activities," unpublished paper, Department of Physiology and Biophysics, University of Illinois, 1967.

body fat is equivalent to 3,500 calories, an increase of 500 calories per day would increase one's body weight by 1 pound in one week. Conversely, one could lose 1 pound a week if the caloric intake was reduced 500 calories below the required daily needs. (In both cases, the assumption would be that the activity level remains constant.) Since, as physical educators, we are aware of the values of physical activity in a weight control program, our prescription should involve both a decrease in daily caloric intake plus an increase in physical activity. Thus, it is recommended that the 220-pound student reduce his daily caloric intake by 250 calories to 2,940 calories (3,190 − 250 = 2,940) and increase his daily physical activity by 250 calories if he wishes to lose 1 pound per week. If a student wanted to gain 1 pound per week, he would be requested to increase his daily caloric intake by 750 calories and his physical activity by 250 calories. It may seem strange to increase activity for the undernourished, but a weight gain without proper exercise will merely result in an accumulation of adipose tissue (see Appendix A for food substitution chart).

One of the questions most frequently asked by obese students is, "What types of physical activity will aid in weight reduction?" The answer is simply, "Any of a variety of aerobic activities (activities that increase the respiratory rate)." Such prescriptions might include jogging, rope skipping, or any recreational activity that stresses vigorous physical movement.

One aerobics program used with success is the "aerobics circuit." The subjects are required to perform the following exercises for a ten-minute period without any rest interval: 100 side-straddle hops; 100 hops on the right foot; 100 hops on the left foot; 100 jumps on both feet; and running in place for 100 counts (left or right foot striking the floor). Students record the whole number 1 for a complete circuit plus .2 for each exercise beyond the circuit. Thus, if a subject completes two circuits and two exercises, his score is recorded as 2.4. The exercises and time duration can be varied, but the "overload concept" must be adhered to, i.e., keeping the time constant while increasing the number of circuits.

Even though circuit training has merit in a weight reduction program, it is more advantageous to have the subject increase his caloric expediture of energy by participating in individual, dual, or team activities because these will increase his motivation. It must be remembered that if the program is to be successful a positive change in the subject's attitude toward physical activity is essential. This attitude change is enhanced if the subject is intrinsically motivated via his participation in some activity in which he achieves success among his peers. Some students have been motivated by running (running a constant distance and attempting to decrease the time), whereas others have accepted the challenge of a vigorous game of handball. Cooper[20]

[20] Ken H. Cooper, *Aerobics* (New York: Bantam Books, Inc., 1969).

has programmed a series of aerobic activities, with point values for each activity, that can be readily incorporated in a weight control program. ·

Those students who would like to increase their weight should be prescribed activities with a focus on developing muscle tissue. Aerobic activities for such students should be minimized, although not eliminated. One approach that has been found to be successful with these students has been weight training. Basically, the program involves pretesting (measuring muscle girth of wrist, arms, chest, etc.) and prescribing weight training exercises that involve a minimum of repetition with maximum weight. For, example, an underweight subject might be requested to "curl" a barbell three to six times before increasing its weight (overload principle), whereas an obese individual may be programmed for eight to fifteen repetitions prior to increasing the weight. The assumption underlying this approach is that strength development should be stressed over endurance development for the underweight individual. For the overweight individual, the object should be to develop muscle tissue and reduce adipose tissue (via an increase in repetitions).

Although weight training is recommended for prescriptive purposes, several precautionary measures should be carefully considered. One is that such a program would be contraindicated if the student has a medical history of hernia or coronary problems. Such a subject should never be permitted to lift heavy objects because the internal pressure created may seriously aggravate his condition.

Second, be sure that the subjects perform the prescribed activities properly. Detailed explanations and demonstrations should be given regarding the correct technique of lifting a weight from the floor (and relate how this is applicable to lifting any object) and performing an exercise so that stress is placed on the proper muscle group through the full range of motion. As a case in point, students will attempt to increase the amount of weight they can "curl" by not extending the weight down through the full range of motion and by bending backward when lifting. If such a technique were to persist, the student could: lose his range of motion (in terms of extension); develop less bicep strength (due to the "lift" being abetted by the rhythmic motion); and most important, injure the lower back (since stress occurs there rather than on the more appropriate biceps muscles). A simple procedure to prevent these hazards has been to have the student perform "curls" with his back to the wall and inform him that a complete repetition involves raising a weight from contact with the thighs to contact with the chest.

Finally, a distinction must be made between "weight training" and "weight lifting." Weight training implies the total development of all body muscles, whereas weight lifting is viewed as preparation for competitive lifting. Even though we do not wish to demean the values of weight lifting, we do recommend the weight training concept for use in the developmental program. Since all body muscles work in pairs (and efficiency of motion is enhanced by equal development), all subjects are required to develop both muscle groups. For example, a student who desires to develop his biceps via "curls" would also be required to perform "presses" to develop his triceps. The concept underlying weight lifting is somewhat similar, but the stress is placed on utilization of techniques that enhance the ability to perform one maximum lift. (Hooks,[21] Leighton,[22] and Massey[23] provide excellent resource materials which the reader is urged to review.)

Postural Abnormalities

Although we presented a rationale for the inclusion of a sound body mechanics unit in Chapter 3, the topic requires further deliberation because postural problems afflict from 5 to 20 percent of the school population as well as an increasing number of adults. It has been contended by some educators and laymen that since postural problems are primarily attributable to muscular imbalance, they could be resolved via a varied physical activity program. This writer's personal experience over the past fifteen years indicates that the best educational approach consists of diversified physical activity supplemented by an individualized posture improvement program which should include a detailed explanation of the values to be accrued from sound body mechanics so that the individual can modify faulty daily habits. Posture exercises will be useless unless one also applies sensible body mechanics principles twenty-four hours a day.

In addition, posture screening techniques sometimes disclose problems that require medical intervention. During the past five years, posture screening referrals to orthopedic surgeons have resulted in many students being fitted for shoe inserts (due to one leg being shorter than the other) and braces. One student even had several vertebrae surgically fused.

To highlight the importance of including a posture improvement program in developmental physical education, an incident that occurred during a summer D&A program will be presented:

Joan, an incoming 9th-grade student, was examined via the New York Posture Screening Test. Her test score was 64 and she seemingly had a spinal C curve—a dropped right shoulder and a raised right hip. Departmental policy requires that all students who evidence such problems be tested for leg length. This procedure involves measuring each leg from the head of the femur to the outer malleolus (prominent ankle bone). As suspected, Joan's right leg measured $1\frac{1}{2}''$ shorter than her left leg. Because physical educators are not qualified to diagnose or prescribe, the

[21] Gene Hooks, *Application of Weight Training to Athletics* (Englewood Cliffs, N.J.: Prentice-Hall, Inc., 1962).

[22] Jack R. Leighton, *Progressive Weight Training* (New York: Ronald Press Company, 1961).

[23] Benjamin H. Massey et al., *The Kinesiology of Weight Lifting* (Dubuque, Iowa: William C. Brown, Publishers, 1959).

parent was notified to take her daughter to an orthopedic surgeon for a thorough examination.

In a conference with the parent following the examination, the mother indicated that the surgeon had substantiated the teacher's suspicion. Joan's right leg was 1 inch shorter than her left leg, so the doctor prescribed a $\frac{1}{2}''$ shoe insert plus the addition of $\frac{1}{2}''$ to her right heel. When the parent requested exercises to alleviate the scoliotic condition, the specialist asked, "Who identified the problem?" The doctor concluded by stating that since the department possessed the knowledge to reveal the problem they must have the expertise to make the necessary prescriptions. (Even though the remark was extremely flattering, departmental policy also required that the physician approve the exercises, in writing.)

Finally, feedback revealed that the parent had written a letter to the Superintendent of Schools and the building principal commending the teacher and the department. (It should be added that the parent was at the time a member of the Board of Education.)

To avoid liability problems and to standardize operational procedures, the instructor should assign individualized prescriptions in the following manner:

1. Select a series of valid exercises, mimeograph them, and submit them to the school physician for approval (refer to Mueller and Christaldi[24] for a detailed list of prescriptive exercises).
2. Design a posture prescription form (see Table 7–5) that coincides with the mimeographed material in terms of major headings.
3. Mimeograph the forms and forward them to the school nurse so that she has them available for the school physician.

If the physical educator has screened all 9th-grade students and has forwarded a list of students with suspected problems to the school nurse (with their New York Posture Charts), he has fulfilled his responsibility. The nurse will follow up by having the students examined by the physician. If prescription exercises are needed, the physician will check the appropriate categories on the prescription form and sign it. If the problem is of a serious nature, the parents are informed by the school nurse to take their child to an orthopedic surgeon. If the abnormality is less serious the child is scheduled for D&A and the teacher refers to the approved, mimeographed exercises and programs the child.

When referral has been made to an orthopedic surgeon, the student is not scheduled until approval is granted and exercises are prescribed. Prior to their examination by the orthopedic specialist, students are given the form and prescriptive exercises for his consideration. Experience has indicated that most doctors are receptive to the plan and in some cases have prescribed their own exercises.

[24] Grover W. Mueller and Josephine Christaldi, *A Practical Program of Remedial Physical Education* (Philadelphia: Lea and Febiger, 1966).

**TABLE 7-5 Township of Ocean School District
Posture Prescription Form**

School ___Ocean Township High School___

Name ___John Doe___   Date ___November 23, 1970___

Grade Level __9__   Age __15__   Sex ___Male___

POSTURE IMPROVEMENT PROGRAM

To the physician: Please check areas in need of special exercises; comment where
necessary.

Check

__x__ A. Forward head _____

_____ B. Round upper back _____

_____ C. Unilateral shoulders snd hips _____

_____ D. Forward pelvic tilt and flat back _____

_____ E. Backward pelvic tilt and hollow lower back _____

_____ F. Hyperflexed knees _____

_____ G. Hyperextended knees _____

_____ H. Contracted arches _____

_____ I. Kyphosis _____

__x__ J. Scoliosis ____total right thoracic curve_____

_____ K. Single thoracic scoliosis _____

_____ L. Double spinal curvatures _____

__x__ M. De-rotation of lateral spinal curvatures _____

__x__ N. Lordosis _____

Physician's signature ___JOHN MALTA, D.O.___

Table 7–6 illustrates one procedure for individualizing prescription exercises. You may note that the prescribed program is based on the medical prescription (see Table 7–5) plus the findings on the New York Posture Screening Chart (if it is consistent with the medical report). Individual prescriptions are based on the severity of the posture problem. In cases with severe abnormality the student performs two exercises; with minor abnormalities, one exercise is performed.

In addition to having exercises prescribed, students are made aware of correct dynamic posture and are urged to constantly strive to maintain proper body segmental alignment during all daily activities. This development of an awareness of proper body mechanics and appropriate performance adjustment is of paramount importance. A few exercises performed daily will have absolutely no value unless the student modifies all appropriate movement patterns.

Particular prescriptive emphasis should be placed on the elimination of lateral spinal curvatures (referred to as *scoliosis*). Scoliosis may be evidenced as a "C" curve or as an "S" curve. In the illustrations in Fig. 7–4 you will note that the C curve is manifested by a dropped shoulder and a raised hip on the same side (thus the spinal curvature resembles the letter C). If the C curve is not corrected, a second compensatory curve sometimes develops so that the spinal vertabrae align themselves in a pattern that resembles an S. This abnormality is serious and most frequently results in the subject having to be fitted for a brace.

Assuming that a subject has been screened and is suspected of having a lateral spinal curvature, the teacher should use two additional follow-up procedures. First, he should determine whether the curvature is "functional" or "structural." A functional curvature is correctable because there is still flexibility in the spinal column. A structural curvature, however, indicates a definite lack of spinal flexibility with a resultant negative prognosis for remediation. A simple test is to have the student suspend his body from an

FIGURE 7–4   Scoliosis: (left) C curve, and (right) S curve.

TABLE 7–6 Individually Prescribed Posture Exercising Program Based on New York Posture Rating Chart

I. TEST AND ANALYSIS TEST ITEM	POSTURE ANALYSIS	DATE			
		TEST (SCORES)			
	anterior-posterior plane	1	2	3	4
1. Head position	Twisted, or turned (R) (L)	7			
2. Shoulder level	Drop left (L); drop right (R)	4			
3. Spinal curvature	"S"; "C"	4			
4. Hip level	Drop (R)(L)	4			
5. Foot alignment	Straight, pointed out, pronated	7			
6. Arches	High, medium, flat	7			
	lateral plane				
7. Neck position	Erect, forward, markedly forward	4			
8. Chest elevation	Elevated, slightly depressed, markedly depressed (flat)	7			
9. Shoulder position	Centered slightly forward, markedly forward (winged scapulae)	4			
10. Upper back position	Normal, slightly rounded, markedly rounded	4			
11. Trunk position	Erect, inclined rearward, markedly inclined rearward	4			
12. Abdominal posture	Flat, protruding, protruding and sagging	4			
13. Lower back position	Normal curves, slightly hollow, markedly hollow	1			
	Constant score	61			
		9			
		70			

II. PRESCRIBED PROGRAM EXERCISE

1. Supine, toe touch over head.
2. Supine, roll knees to chest, extend.
3. Lateral swinging, overhead ladder.
4. Isometric neck exercise.
5. Shoulder shrug, hold.
6. Stretch right arm overhead (to left), stabilize right hip, derotate spine.

BASIS FOR PRESCRIPTION

1. Point system 7–4–1
2. Prescribe *two exercises* for each factor for which student scored 1 pt.; *one exercise* for 4 pts.

SYMBOLS:

"C" curve: dropped shoulder and raised hip on same side of body.
"S" curve: dropped shoulder and dropped hip on same side of body.
R: Dropped right shoulder, hip, neck, etc.
L: Dropped left shoulder, hip, neck, etc.

III. EVALUATION/ RECOMMENDATION

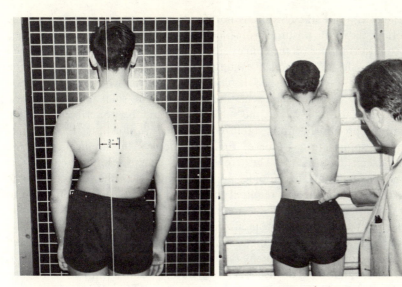

FIGURE 7–5 Scoliosis: marking vertebral prominences. Courtesy of the Township of Ocean School District.

FIGURE 7–6 Scoliosis: determining functional or structural abnormality.

overhead ladder or a stall bar so that the center of gravity pulls downward on the vertebral column.

Figure 7–5 illustrates an S curve (note that the bony protuberances of the vertebrae are marked with water-color paint to highlight the curvature). When the subject was suspended on the stall bar (Fig. 7–6), the S curve was much less pronounced, but still visible. Thus, the curvature was structural to a certain extent. Corrective exercises were prescribed for the student because the physician diagnosed the structural deformity as one that could be minimized.

The second recommended procedure for use with the student suspected of having scoliosis would be to measure leg length as previously described. This procedure is essential because postural exercises will have little, if any, value if there is a discrepancy in leg length and it is not first remedied.

If the orthopedic surgeon prescribes corrective exercises, it might be advisable to take an additional measurement. In Fig. 7–5 the distance between the innermost border of the left scapula and the vertebra in line with it horizontally has been recorded. Measurements will be taken periodically to ascertain whether the concavity is diminished as a result of corrective treatment.

Although it is not the writer's intent to describe postural exercises for all abnormalities, the basic underlying rationale for scoliotic exercises will be explained. If a lateral curvature is not due to a structural problem, then the condition, as in all posture problems, is caused by a muscular imbalance such that the muscles on the convex side of the vertebra column are stretched and the muscles on the concave side of the column are shortened. Thus, a subject with a C curve to the left (concavity to right) would have exercises prescribed to stretch the musculature on the right side, and conversely. One word of caution: When the subject performs the prescribed exercises, be sure the prominent hip is stabilized. Figure 7–7a illustrates the incorrect technique applied to a C curve; Fig. 7–7b depicts the application of the correct exercising principle. The arrows in the illustrations indicate the direction of the "pull" on the shoulder and hip. Thus, when the subject used the incorrect technique he was required to stretch his right arm over his head to raise the lowered right shoulder and modify the concavity on the right side of the body. However, by not stabilizing the right hip, this exercise would also "pull" on the right hip and increase its prominence. The correct exercising procedure should include moving the right leg to the rear, placing the weight on the toes, and forcing the heel backward and downward while stretching the right arm overhead. This same principle can be applied by having the student assume a sitting or kneeling position; the point to remember is that the prominent hip must be stabilized.

When prescribing exercises for the student with the S-type scoliotic curve, the problem is much more complex due to the addition of a second compensatory curve in the lumbar region. A difficulty is designing an exercise to minimize both curvatures without adversely affecting either one. With regard to this problem orthopedic surgeons are not presently in agreement;

FIGURE 7–7 Scoliosis exercise: C curve. (a) Incorrect technique, and (b) correct technique. Courtesy of the Township of Ocean School District.

a   b

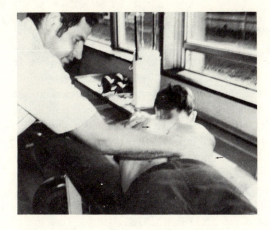

FIGURE 7–8 Scoliosis exercise: S curve. Courtesy of the Township of Ocean School District.

some advocate exercises while wearing a brace and others recommend removal of the brace before exercising. (The reader is referred to an article by Blount and Bolinski[25] for a rationale regarding the use of the Milwaukee Brace and prescribed scoliotic exercises.)

Figure 7–8 illustrates an exercise that may aid in the amelioration of an S curve. The subject in Fig. 7–5 (see p. 177) has a left dorsal (LD) and a right lumbar (RL) abnormality. The prescribed procedure would include the following steps:

1. Have the subject lie prone and diagonal on a table, with his arms outstretched, his hands grasping the upper right side of the table and the feet of his extended legs hooked on the left side of the lower left corner of the table (the purpose is to stabilize the upper and lower vertebral areas).

2. Then have the instructor apply pressure toward the convex surfaces of the spinal column (note the direction of the arrows in the illustration). The instructor should be directed to apply pressure (push and pull) on the count of "one," maintain the pressure on counts "two" and "three," and release the pressure on the count of "four."

Experience with the students in the Township of Ocean School District has indicated that hanging exercises and activities have had the most helpful effects on lateral spinal curvatures. One such activity requires the student to hang from an overhead ladder or stall bar (with the arms in a flexed or extended position) for increasing time periods. In addition to the beneficial effects the suspended body weight has on the spinal abnormalities, the student will increase the strength in his shoulder girdle, arms, and grip. To enhance motivation static hanging may be modified by having the subject "hand-

[25] Walter P. Blount and Jane Bolinski, "Physical Therapy in the Nonoperative Treatment of Scoliosis," *Physical Therapy Journal*, XLVII, No. 10 (October, 1967), 919–25.

walk" the overhead ladder. Students should be urged to increase the number of rungs they hand-walk during subsequent class periods. The activity may be modified by having the subject traverse the rungs by moving from rung to rung, swinging and grasping every other rung, and by moving sideways or backwards.

One final hanging task that is beneficial to C or S curve problems is lateral swinging. From the position depicted in Fig. 7–9, the subject should be requested to swing his body laterally (left and right). Emphasis should be placed on using the shoulders as the pivotal points rather than the hips so that total spinal flexibility is increased. To be consistent with the overload principle, repetitions should be increased on a weekly basis.

A problem concomitant with lateral spinal curvatures is the abnormal rotation of the vertebrae. As a result, those who have scoliotic problems require prescriptions to alleviate lateral and rotational deviations. To remedy rotational problems, a physician will recommend *derotational* exercises: the equal and opposite reaction to rotation. Rotation always takes place in the direction of the spinal curvature's convexity, i.e., rotation to the right in a right thoracic curvature (RD) and to the left in a left thoracic curvature (LD).

The subject in Fig. 7–10 has an LD–RL problem. As a consequence, the school physician had him maintain a stationary position while he applied pressure in the direction of the thoracic convexity. By having the subject

FIGURE 7–9   Increasing spinal flexibility. Courtesy of the Township of Ocean School District.

FIGURE 7–10   Derotation of lateral spinal curvatures. Courtesy of the Township of Ocean School District.

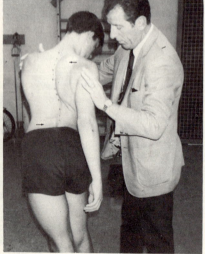

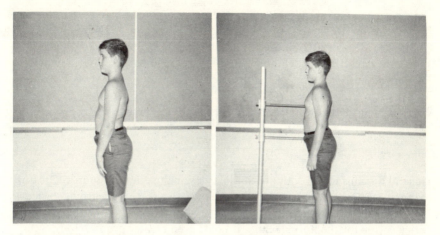

FIGURE 7–11   Modified Howland Alignometer. (left) Lordosis, and (right) developing kinesthetic awareness of proper pelvic position. Courtesy of the Township of Ocean School District.

maintain the immovable foot position, equal and opposite pressure is directed toward the lumbar convexity (note the direction of the arrows). The exercise procedure is: twist, hold, release. Repetitions should be increased periodically.

Lordosis, or a hyperconcavity of the lumbar spine, is a postural abnormality that once established carries over into the adult years. This condition worsens when women wear high heels or men carry excessive weight in the abdominal area. For both, the result is the shifting of the body's center of gravity forward, thus accentuating the "swayback" condition.

We recommend using a modification of the Howland Alignometer,[26] which allows us to objectively measure body alignment based on two anatomical landmarks—the center of the sternum and the superior border of the symphysis pubis.

Rogers[27] simplified the testing procedure, making the instrument a valuable aid for use with the D&A program. Figure 7–11 illustrates the simplicity and economy of Rogers' modification. The instrument provides an opportunity for the student to develop a kinesthetic awareness of correct anterioposterior alignment by adjusting body posture so that the upper wooden dowel makes contact with the midpoint of the sternum and the lower wooden dowel touches the upper border of the pelvic bone. Therefore

[26] Ivalclare Sprow Howland, *Body Alignment in Fundamental Motor Skills* (New York: Exposition Press, 1953), p. 78.

[27] Marion Rogers, "Conference for the Handicapped," Monmouth College, West Long Branch, N.J., November 20, 1970, p. 3. Mimeographed.

the device can and should be utilized at periodic intervals to assess personal improvement. (Refer to Appendix C for construction guidelines.)

Since lordosis is attributable to an abnormal tilt of the pelvis, a program should be prescribed to eliminate the muscular imbalance and to instill in the student an awareness of the proper "feel" of the correct pelvic position. The *Posture Exercise Handbook* by Wells[28] provides a variety of exercises to develop kinesthetic awareness of proper body mechanics.

Summary

General dissatisfaction with present instructional methods requires educators to pursue alternate approaches to enhance the teaching/learning process; individualized programming provides one sound approach to the problem. If this is true for the normal child, it holds even greater promise for developmentally handicapped children, who frequently evidence a greater disparity in abilities.

In programming developmental activities the following should be included:

1. The development of individual time prescriptions based on standard scores, percentile rank scores, stanine scores, or teacher evaluation.

2. The inclusion of exercises, tasks, or activities that are based on pretests, factorial validity, proper sequence to ensure success, periodic diagnostic tests to assess behavioral changes, and enhancement of the self-image.

3. The design of a K–12 accelerated program to meet the individualized needs of the child with low physical vitality via the provision of exercises, tasks, or activities that enhance the development of gross motor skills, hand/ and foot/eye coordination, hand/ and foot/eye accuracy, balance and postural orientation, arm strength, abdominal strength, explosive leg strength, and cardiorespiratory endurance.

4. The incorporation of a program designed to ameliorate nutritional deficiencies that are caused by improper dietary habits, a lack of physical activity, or a combination of both via learning experiences related to the determination of true and predicted body weight, a nutritional index, skinfold and muscle girth measurements, proper dietary habits, the effects of physical activity on weight control, the determination of basal caloric and activity needs, and individualized activities that focus on the loss or gain of 1 pound per week.

5. A program to eliminate postural abnormalities that are caused by muscular imbalance rather than structural problems via staff screening, school/family physician medical examinations, an individually prescribed series of exercises, and the development of sound body mechanics habits.

6. The preparation of a series of prescriptive forms so that each student's progress in the developmental program can be assessed periodically.

---

[28] Katherine F. Wells, *Posture Exercise Handbook: A Progressive Sequence Approach* (New York: The Ronald Press Company, 1963), 88 pp.

Annotated Bibliography

CLARKE, H. HARRISON. "Health-Habit Questionnaire," 2nd rev. ed. Cedar Rapids, Iowa: Nissen-Medart Corporation, 1951, 2 pp. A case study form which can be used with those students who evidence low physical vitality. Free upon request.

DIEM, LISELOTT, and RENATE SCHOLTZMETHNER. *Corrective Gymnastics and Special Exercise Classes in Schools.* Frankfurt, Germany: Decker and Wilhelm, 1963, 87 pp. Excellent resource book of developmental physical exercises to alleviate organic, muscle, and coordination weaknesses. Also includes a detailed analysis of causes and probable symptoms.

FRANKENBURG, WILLIAM K., and JOSIAH B. DODDS. *Denver Developmental Screening Test.* Boulder, Colo.: University of Colorado Medical Center, 1968, 45 pp. A standardized test for detecting developmental "lags" in the infant or preschool child. Includes the assessment of the following skills: gross motor; fine motor; language; and personal–social. Contains an appendix of norm tables based on a large cross-section of the Denver child population. Available to physicians.

LILLY, LUELLA J. *An Overview of Body Mechanics: A Student Handbook*, 3rd ed. Palo Alto, Calif.: Peek Publications, 1970, 51 pp. A workbook that could be used effectively with students who evidence low physical vitality (college or senior high school level). Provides a series of learning experiences related to basic foundations, posture, weight control, conditioning and exercise, and movement and relaxation. Also includes a list of free or inexpensive teaching aids.

LIPSITZ, LAWRENCE, ed. "Accountability in Education," *Educational Technology*, XI, No. 1 (1971), 64 pp. (whole no.). Contains current views regarding "accountability" and "performance contracting" in education.

———, ed. "Preschool Education," *Educational Technology*, XI, No. 2 (1971), 80 pp. Whole issue (fourteen articles) devoted to the education of the preschool child. The papers presented were selected because of their scientific rigor and/or their relevancy to contemporary problems.

———, ed. "Programmed Instruction Today," *Educational Technology*, X, No. 7 (1970), 48 pp. (whole no.). An analysis of programmed instruction as a viable means of individualizing instruction.

WALLIS, EARL L., and GENE A. LOGAN. *Figure Improvement and Body Conditioning Through Exercise.* Englewood Cliffs, N. J.: Prentice-Hall, Inc., 1964. Includes figure-control exercises for women and conditioning exercises for men. Exercises are grouped according to specific component needs such as endurance, flexibility, and stength. Also includes material on isometric and isotonic exercises and general misconceptions about exercise.

8

individualized programming:
adapted activities

As previously stated, the adapted phase of the program for the handicapped should include those students who evidence a medically oriented problem and have been thoroughly examined by a physician, psychologist, or psychiatrist. It is further recommended that a "total picture" of the child be obtained by using a child study team approach similar to the plan adopted by the state of New Jersey. According to the plan, diagnosis and classification of handicapped children:

> . . . shall include comprehensive medical examination, psychological evaluation, social case study and an educational assessment by approved child study team personnel functioning jointly. . . . A basic child study team acting in consultation with a physician shall consist of a school psychologist, a learning disabilities specialist, and a school social worker. A child study team may also include a psychiatrist experienced in work with children, a school administrator, a classroom teacher, a school nurse, a guidance counselor, a speech correctionist, a remedial reading teacher and other members of the school professional staff as may be recommended by the basic child study team with the approval of the chief administrator.[1]

Crystal summed it up very aptly when she stated that "no discipline can work in a vacuum if we desire to develop the whole child."[2]

---

[1] New Jersey State Department of Education, "Rules and Regulations Pursuant to Title 18A, Chapter 46," New Jersey Statutes (June 24, 1970), Title 8, Chapter 28 (Trenton, N.J.: Division of Curriculum Instruction/Bureau of Special Education and Pupil Personnel Services), pp. 1–2.

[2] Edwina M. Crystal, School Psychologist, Township of Ocean School District, Oakhurst, N.J., April, 1971.

Medical Referral

The prescription of physical activities for children with medically oriented problems necessitates the use of a medical referral form to meet the needs of the student and to avoid the possibility of teacher liability. Medical forms usually include name and sex; grade and school; address and phone number; diagnosis of condition; degree of participation permitted; and the anticipated date the student may be returned to the unrestricted program (see the medical excuse form in Appendix A). However, the form referred to as well as other forms reviewed are usually inadequate in that they list a set variety of activities and request that the physician select those that he would recommend. To be more beneficial to individualized programming, it would seem more logical if the physician explained his diagnosis in detail. What area(s) of the body should be precluded from physical activity? What area(s) should have minimal activity? What specific types of exercises would be recommended to minimize or ameliorate the disability?

The procedure presently in vogue requires that the physician diagnose and prescribe. The recommended procedure would require that the physician diagnose in detail and the physical educator then prescribe (with the approval of the physician). You may recall that this approach was referred to when we discussed prescribing postural exercises; the medical inspector diagnosed and the teacher prescribed the exercises. This procedure was accomplished by preparing in advance a series of exercises to ameliorate specific problems and submitting these exercises for approval to the school physician. A sample form distributed by the American Association for Health, Physical Education and Recreation recommends a similar approach.[3]

In Chapter 8 we will discuss some trends in physical education for teaching the handicapped child which presuppose a team diagnosis, prescriptive referral, and knowledgeable physical educators. The classification basis utilized in Chapter 4 will be repeated for simplicity (physically handicapped, mentally handicapped, and socioemotionally handicapped), but it must be remembered that students should be viewed from the standpoint of behavior manifested rather than medical categorizations.

The Physically Handicapped

For purposes of further specificity, the physically handicapped shall be subdivided on the basis of communication disorders, motor disabilities or limitations, and circulorespiratory restrictions.

---

[3] Program for the Handicapped "Sample Physical Education Referral Form, ASAW #1313–1968," American Association for Health, Physical Education and Recreation, Washington, D. C. Free upon request.

Communication Disorders

Students with sensory impairments would be classified in this category. Thus, a handicap which interferes with a child's ability to communicate (the behavior manifested) would be considered a communication disorder. As a consequence, the deaf and hard of hearing, the blind and partially sighted, the autistic and those with other speech impediments would be so classified.

Because a child with communication disorders can manifest a wide variety of behavior patterns, no single, all-inclusive prescriptive program can be written. Each individual's program must be prescribed on the basis of his medical history and a team evaluation. Moreover, the physical activities prescribed should have a dual purpose: to minimize sensory limitations and to place a focus on student capabilities.

Similarly, a blanket statement cannot be made regarding whether a handicapped child should be placed in a D&A class or in the regular physical education class. Each decision must be made in terms of what is best for the child rather than in terms of administrative feasibility. Of paramount importance is the selection of an instructional environment that is conducive to maximal learning. Experience in the Township of Ocean School District has indicated that the scheduling of the handicapped should be handled with considerable flexibility. Emphasis should be placed on integrating the child with his normal peer group as often as possible. However, whenever the student needs an individualized, remedial program, he should be scheduled in adapted physical education. The following illustrative examples will elucidate the scheduling procedures recommended.

The Blind and Partially Sighted   Research indicates that the blind and partially sighted may manifest postural abnormalities, lowered physical vitality, nutritional deficiencies (usually obesity), and restricted gross motor performance.[4] In addition, the visually impaired child evidences difficulties in participating in group games of high organization such as basketball and soccer, but can achieve very well in most individual and dual activities that have been modified to some degree.

A sound approach to scheduling the blind or partially-sighted would be to include those children in the regular program for units such as, but not limited to, weight training, bowling, archery, gymnastics, tumbling, swim-

---

[4] See Charles E. Buell, "Recreational and Leisure-time Activities of Blind Children," *The International Journal for the Blind*, XI, No. 3 (March, 1962), 1–5; Irwin M. Siegel, "Selected Athletics in a Posture Training Program for the Blind," *The New Outlook for the Blind*, LX, No. 8 (October, 1966), 248–49; Charles Buell, "Motor Performance of Visually Handicapped Children," *Journal of Exceptional Children*, XVII, No. 3 (December, 1950), 69–72; and *idem.*, "School's Responsibility for Providing Physical Education Activities for Blind Students," *Journal of Health, Physical Education and Recreation*, XLI, No. 6 (June, 1970), 41–42.

ming, and wrestling. (The reader is urged to review articles by Hyman,[5] Grosse,[6] Oliver,[7] Bolt,[8] Williams,[9] and Trevena[10] for field-tested instructional procedures for modifying the above activities.)

Too much emphasis cannot be placed on the need for integrating the handicapped child with his normal classmates as often as possible. By assigning him a "buddy" he can function effectively with a minimum of teacher assistance. For example, the blind student who ran track, referred to in an earlier chapter, was also experimentally involved in a softball unit. He was designated as the pitcher for both teams. His buddy assisted him by taking the return throws from the catcher and shielding him in the event of a line drive. The student, who was totally blind, actually developed considerable skill in throwing the ball across the plate. The direction of his toss was guided by the voice of the catcher, aided and abetted by an increasingly sensitive kinesthetic awareness of the release position of his throwing arm and hand.

During team activities the sight-handicapped individual would benefit most by being transferred to the adapted class. His individualized program should be structured so that he participates in an accelerated conditioning and posture program. In addition, he should experience a variety of movement exploratory activities—tumbling, locomotor, and balance/postural orientation skills.

The instructor should constantly strive to develop the child's tactile, auditory, and kinesthetic perceptions when teaching various movements and positions. For example, the correct upright posture position can be reinforced by having the child stand upright so that his heels, buttocks, shoulders, and head are in contact with the wall. New body positions can be visually internalized by having a buddy or instructor assume the positions and by having the sightless child "see" via his sense of touch how the parts of the body are aligned. Auditory sounds such as those emanating from a metronome "beeper" or bells inserted in balls can aid in skill development. Finally, skills should be overlearned through constant repetition so that the student can develop a kinesthetic awareness of proper body position.

[5] Dorothy Hyman, "Teaching the Blind Student Archery Skills," *Journal of Health, Physical Education and Recreation*, XL, No. 4 (April, 1969), 85–86.

[6] Susan J. Grosse, "Adapted Swimming," *Outlook*, AAHPER Unit on Programs for the Handicapped, I, No. 3 (December, 1969), 8.

[7] James N. Oliver, "Physical Education for the Visually Handicapped," *Journal of Health, Physical Education and Recreation*, XLI, No. 6 (June, 1970), 37–39.

[8] Martha Lynn Bolt, "Softball for the Blind Student," *Journal of Health, Physical Education and Recreation*, XLI, No. 6 (June, 1970), 40.

[9] F. Neil Williams, "Physical Education Adapts to the Visually Handicapped," *Journal of Health, Physical Education and Recreation*, XXXV, No. 3 (March, 1964), 25–26.

[10] Thomas M. Trevena, "Integration of the Sightless Student into Regular Physical Activities," *Journal of Health, Physical Education and Recreation*, XLI, No. 6 (June, 1970), 42–43.

We recommend for viewing a film by Buell[11] which can provide the physical educator with many ideas for adapting physical activity programs for the blind and partially sighted. This film is also valuable as a means of publicizing the benefits of physical education for the blind if shown to P.T.A. groups. The American Printing House for the Blind[12] has designed a sports kit to familiarize the visually handicapped child with baseball, basketball, bowling, football, tennis, and volleyball. Braille is utilized on six different boards to highlight the various playing fields and courts. The kit also includes various-shaped magnets to depict players, referees, balls, spectators, etc. The same source[13] has developed stationary and portable model audible goal-locators. The sounds emitted from these devices can be used as a goal-, base-, or object-locator. For example, the portable unit can be placed in the shallow end of a pool so that the blind student can constantly be oriented to the depth of the water. The Royal National Institute for the Blind[14] provides an electronic ball as well as a rubber ball with a bell inserted; both balls can be used in a variety of hand/ear coordination activities. Also available are a variety of quiet games such as playing cards, chess, dominoes, and jigsaw puzzles. The American Foundation for the Blind, Inc.[15] is a source of musical aids, measuring instruments, quiet games, and timing devices. Catalogs from all sources are available upon request.

The Deaf and Hard of Hearing   Research related to the physical capabilities of the hearing handicapped has been limited and inconclusive. However, the child can participate in all types of activities other than those activities prohibited by his natural limitations due to his hearing impediment (and concomitant communication skill problems).

By virtue of his auditory limitation, the deaf child must make maximum use of his visual apparatus. The teacher, cognizant of this fact, must face the entire class when he explains a particular skill or activity. Berges[16] suggests that another student take notes for the deaf student since the latter cannot lipread and write simultaneously. It probably would be more advantageous if the teacher duplicated all lecture materials for the class.

Another minor instructional change that should be considered would be

11 Charles Buell, "Physical Education for Blind Children" (16 mm. sound, color, 20 minutes), 42 Heather Road, Long Beach, Calif. 90808. (Purchase $150; rental $6.00 plus postage.)

12 *Staley Sports Field Kit* (Louisville, Ky.: American Printing House for the Blind), 1839 Frankfort Avenue, P.O. Box 6085, Louisville, Ky. 40206. 3 pp. Free upon request.

13 *Stationary and Portable Model Audible Goal-locaters*, American Printing House for the Blind, 3 pp. Free upon request.

14 *Apparatus and Games for the Blind* (London: The Royal National Institute for the Blind, April, 1969), 224 Great Portland Street, Win, 6AA. Free upon request.

15 *Aids and Appliances*, 16th ed. (New York: American Foundation for the Blind, July 1970–June 1971), 15 West 16th Street. 46 pp. Free upon request.

16 Shirley A. Berges, "The Deaf Student in Physical Education," *Journal of Health, Physical Education and Recreation*, XL, No. 3 (March, 1969), 69–70.

to assign a buddy to the deaf child, or brief the entire class on how to assist him in those situations when he cannot hear the whistle. For example, during a basketball or soccer game the nearest player could touch the student when the whistle is blown for an infraction of the rules.

A major consideration should be to preplan all activities to minimize accidents. A review of the literature indicates that more deaf students than blind students are injured in physical education. This is probably due to the fact that programs for the visually handicapped are highly structured, whereas deaf students are integrated with little or no program modification. Consequently, physical educators are urged to heed the following recommendations:

1. Have students remove hearing aids prior to all physical activity.
2. Assign at least one designated buddy, especially when presenting a swimming unit.
3. Maximize use of visual aids and the principle of overlearning since the instructor is unable to communicate with the deaf child once he starts to perform a skill. (Keffer[17] presents a safe means of introducing deaf preschool children to swimming.)

It is recommended that the deaf or hard-of-hearing individual not be removed from the unrestricted activity program unless he evidences a problem that necessitates individualized teaching. By interaction with his peer group, he is being provided with those experiences that will enable him to cope with adult life with a minimum of difficulty.

The Autistic and Those with Other Speech Impediments   The child with a speech impediment (of a physical nature) should not be excluded from the regular physical activity program. However, when the cause of the impediment is diagnosed as either a mental or socioemotional problem the child should be placed in a D&A class.

How to program for autistic children poses a dilemma because medical authorities have not been able to ascertain the specific cause(s) of the handicapping condition(s). It is recommended that autistic children be tested extensively for motor and perceptual motor skills and that individualized programs be prescribed based on evidenced needs. The teacher should also take note of mental or socioemotional aberrations and plan his program accordingly. (See the following discussion of programming for the mentally or socioemotionally disturbed.)

Physical educators or recreators who are interested in obtaining state or federal funds are urged to design proposals related to programming for autistic children. Such proposals would be given careful consideration because of the virtual void in this area.

17 Louis Keffer, "Introduction to Swimming for the Deaf," *AAHPER Unit on Programs for the Handicapped*, I, No. 1 (August, 1969), 3.

Motor Disabilities or Limitations

For purposes of classification, children with motor disabilities or limitations caused by a physical impediment or by other medical problems are included in this category. Thus, regardless of the causative factor, the prime determinant for classification is the child's imperfect motor performance. Planning a program for the motorically handicapped, however, should include the consideration of all potential causative factors—physical, psychological, or social—so that motor performance can be improved.

There are presently at least two prevailing theories regarding programming for those with motor restrictions: development of the physical (rehabilitative exercises) and development through the physical (participation in modified games and activities). Both approaches have considerable merit, but it is the contention of the writer that all too frequently an overemphasis has been placed on the rehabilitative approach which results in the virtual neglect of the participation theory. This may be an unfair assessment of present practices because it may well be that facility restrictions and the limited number of students with severe motor problems presents scheduling difficulties. However, the present trend in physical education for the handicapped is to provide individualized experiences that will afford each child the opportunity to focus on his strengths.

The recommended approach would be to utilize both practices because they both have inherent value. However, the prime consideration is to plan a program on the basis of each individual's needs. For example, a student assigned to the D&A program due to repeated shoulder dislocations should devote all of his initial sessions to strengthening the shoulder girdle, whereas the student with an atrophied arm should devote a portion of the period to rehabilitative exercises and the balance of the period for activities that emphasize the use of both arms. The remainder of this discourse related to motor disabilities and limitations will consist of suggested prescriptive programs based on rehabilitative exercises and modified games and activities.

Rehabilitative Exercises   At this point it could be said that the presentation is contradictory because earlier in the text we stated that the physical educator does not have the legal right to diagnose or to prescribe exercises or activities for those students with medically oriented problems. The foregoing is true, but there is no liability if the instructor follows the guidelines below in programming exercises. The recommended procedure would be to have the department chairman/supervisor:

1. Prepare a list of orthopedic conditions that restrict motor performance
2. Prepare a list of commonly accepted exercises in terms of each of the conditions mentioned in item *1*

FIGURE 8–1 Quadriceps setting (isometrically), advanced stage. Courtesy of the Township of Ocean School District.

3. Provide room in each category for the physician/orthopedic surgeon to list additional exercises

4. Develop a standardized form which can be submitted to the school/family physician for his consideration

It is important that the prepared materials be expressed so that they clearly indicate they comprise suggested, generally accepted exercises. In all cases, the medical examiner will make a final decision based on the individual needs of his patient.

The following illustrations will present some suggested sequential exercises for orthopedic problems with which the physical educator is commonly confronted. Doolittle[18] prepared the materials for use with students taking adapted physical education at Pennsylvania State University. Some exercises have been modified so that a minimum of expensive equipment is needed.

EXERCISES FOR ORTHOPEDIC PROBLEMS[19]

1. Knee injury
   a. Quadriceps setting by firming the quadriceps with no movement involved (see Fig. 8–1)
   b. Straight leg lift from a supine position
   c. When the prescription calls for quadriceps exercises, use an iron boot or

[18] John H. Doolittle, "Exercises for Orthopedic Problems," *Physical Education 10: Adapted Physical Education Handbook* (University Park, Pa.: The Pennsylvania State University, n.d.), pp. 5–8. Mimeographed. Reprinted by permission.

[19] Exercising regimens should not be prescribed until the medical inspector signs a clearance. However, exercises should be prescribed for other than the injured area(s) to minimize general body atrophy.

sandbags attached to the foot of the injured leg. The weight should be such that the student is able to perform ten to twelve repetitions through the full range of motion. Stress maximum extension at the knee joint with each repetition and a dorsi-flexed ankle to stretch the gastroc-soleus. Progressively increase resistance until the student can perform two to three sets of ten to fifteen repetitions with a maximum resistance of 50 to 60 pounds.

  d. Development of the hamstrings can be accomplished by having the student flex the knee through the full range of motion from a prone position on a mat or a table.

  e. Bicycling: the range of motion may be controlled by raising and lowering the seat.

2. *Sprained ankle.* The recommended exercises deals with inversion-type sprains since they occur most frequently.

  a. Passive dorsi and plantar flexion, followed by inversion, eversion, and circumduction.

  b. Apply the overload principle to exercises in item *a* by strapping an iron boot or sandbag to the foot. *Note:* Eversion and dorsi flexion are the most important exercises.

  c. As the student progresses, jogging and rope-skipping may be included in the program

3. *Dislocated shoulder*

  a. Stimulate flexion, extension, adduction, abduction, and circumduction and minimize the possibility of tightness and contractures by having the subject bend forward at the waist, place his uninjured arm on a table or chair, and allow the affected arm to perform relaxed pendular movements (side to side, back and forth, and circling).

  b. Repeat item *a* holding a light weight to increase resistance.

FIGURE 8–2 Shoulder adduction (front). Courtesy of the Township of Ocean School District.

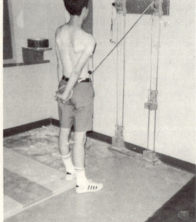

FIGURE 8–3 Shoulder adduction (rear). Courtesy of the Township of Ocean School District.

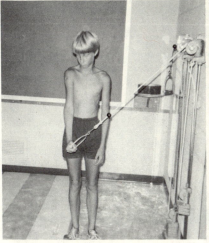

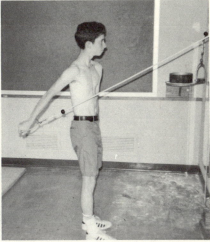

FIGURE 8–4 Horizontal abduction. Courtesy of the Township of Ocean School District.

FIGURE 8–5 Shoulder extension. Courtesy of the Township of Ocean School District.

c. Exercises with pulley weights:

    (*1*) Shoulder adduction (pectoralis major): Start at arm's length with the affected shoulder toward the pulley weights. Grasp the handle and pull across the chest and down to the opposite hip (see Fig. 8–2).

    (*2*) Shoulder adduction (deltoid, latissimus dorsi, teres major): From the same position as in item (*1*), pull down and behind the back to the opposite hip (see Fig. 8–3).

    (*3*) Horizontal abduction (deltoid, latissimus dorsi): Stand with the affected shoulder away from the pulley weights. Reach across the chest, grasp the handle, and pull across and down (see Fig. 8–4).

    (*4*) Shoulder extension (latissimus dorsi, teres major): Stand facing the pulley weights. Reach forward, grasp the handle at shoulder height, and pull down and behind the hip (see Fig. 8–5).

    (*5*) Shoulder adduction (latissimus dorsi, teres major, pectoralis major): Stand with affected shoulder toward the pulley weights. Grasp the handle at shoulder height and pull down to the side (see Fig. 8–6).

d. Exercises with dumbbells:

    (*1*) Shoulder flexion (deltoid, coracobrachialis): Flex the upper arm to shoulder height with the elbow fully extended (see Fig. 8–7).

    (*2*) Upper arm hyperextension, shoulder extension (latissimus dorsi, teres major): Starting with the arm at the side, hyperextend the upper arm through the full range, about 45 degrees (see Fig. 8–8).

    (*3*) Shoulder abduction in the horizontal plane (deltoid, supraspinatus): With the arm at the side, abduct the upper arm to about 90 degrees. Increase the range as the student's recovery progresses (see Fig. 8–9).

    (*4*) Shoulder circumduction (deltoid, supraspinatus): With the upper arm abducted to 80 to 90 degrees, circumduct the arm. Increase the size of the circles as the student's recovery progresses.

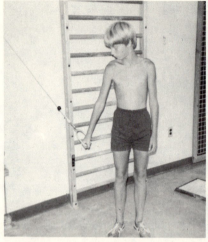

FIGURE 8–6 Shoulder adduction (affected shoulder facing pulley weight). Courtesy of the Township of Ocean School District.

FIGURE 8–7 Shoulder flexion. (left) Starting position, weight at side; (right) exercise position. Courtesy of the Township of Ocean School District.

FIGURE 8–8 Upper arm hyper-extension, shoulder extension. (left) Starting position, weight at side; (right) exercise position. Courtesy of the Township of Ocean School District.

FIGURE 8–9 Shoulder abduction, horizontal plane. (left) Intermediate position; (right) fully abducted position. Courtesy of the Township of Ocean School District.

(5) Internal and external rotation of the upper arm (infraspinatus, teres major, subscapularis): Supine lying position with the upper arm abducted to 90 degrees and the elbow flexed to 90 degrees. Lower the dumbbell by external rotation, then raise the dumbbell to the starting position and lower it by internal rotation at the upper arm. *Note:* This exercise should be assigned when it is felt the shoulder is healing well. When the exercise is introduced, guards should be required in front and back to limit the range of motion because excessive rotation might be contraindicated.

(6) Elbow flexion (biceps): With the entire arm supported on a table, perform one arm dumbbell curls. Number to be performed: These exercises may be prescribed in sets of two, three and sometimes four, with ten to fifteen repetitions to a set. Begin with light weights, both on the pulleys and with the dumbbells and increase the amount as the student's recovery progresses.

4. *Exercises for low back pain.* Low back pain is usually the result of pressure in the lumbar region created by overdeveloped back muscles and underdeveloped abdominal muscles, although there are other possible causes. Therefore, students with low back problems should be referred to a physician for medical examination and clearance. McNeil Laboratories, Inc. has provided useful advice for the care and prevention of low back pain (see Fig. 8–10).

Crutch and Cane Walking   The physical educator can provide a very meaningful service to those students who are required to use a cane or crutches by providing them with an explanation and demonstration of correct usage. Doolittle[20] utilizes the following material to provide laboratory experiences for his students:

Cane walking:

The cane is not a weight-bearing device but rather a supportive or balance aid; therefore, it should be held in the hand *opposite* the injured extremity. This technique facilitates the normal cross-patterning of the arms and legs while walking and establishes a good three-point base providing greater stability.

For proper fitting, the cane should reach from the floor to the top of the greater trochanter. The end of the cane should be equipped with a rubber tip.

Crutch walking:

1. Common types of crutches:
   a. Axillary—those which fit up under the arm (axilla)
   b. Lofstrand—for those who do not require underarm support. A cuff fitting around the forearm and a handgrip provide support.

2. Fitting axillary crutches: The length of the crutch should permit two fingers to be placed between the crutch pad and axilla. The handgrip should be adjusted to allow some flexion of the elbow. Be sure the end of the crutch is equipped with a good sized rubber crutch tip to provide good traction and shock absorption.

---

[20] John H. Doolittle, "Cane and Crutch Walking," *Physical Education 400: Laboratory Exercise 5* (University Park, Pa.: The Pennsylvania State University, n.d.), 2 pp. Mimeographed. Reprinted by permission.

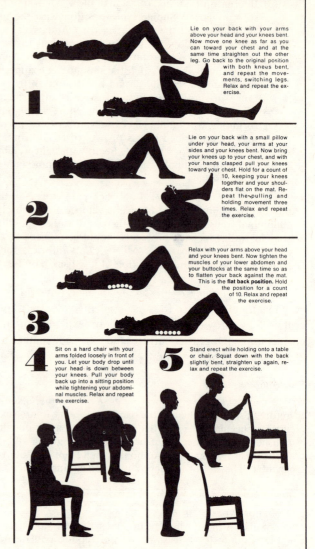

Exercises for low back pain

General Information:

Don't overdo exercising, especially in the beginning. Start by trying the movements slowly and carefully. Don't be alarmed if the exercises cause some mild discomfort which lasts a few minutes. But if pain is more than mild and lasts more than 15 or 20 minutes, *stop* and do no further exercises until you see your doctor.

Do the exercises on a hard surface covered with a thin mat or heavy blanket. Put a pillow under your neck if it makes you more comfortable. Always start your exercises slowly—and in the order marked—to allow muscles to loosen up gradually. Heat treatments just before you start can help relax tight muscles. Follow the instructions carefully; it will be well worth the effort.

Do exercises marked (**X**)

in numerical order

for _____ minutes

_____ times a day.

Take the medication

prescribed for you

_____ times daily

for_____

1 Lie on your back with your arms above your head and your knees bent. Now move one knee as far as you can toward your chest and at the same time straighten out the other leg. Go back to the original position with both knees bent, and repeat the movements, switching legs. Relax and repeat the exercise.

2 Lie on your back with a small pillow under your head, your arms at your sides and your knees bent. Now bring your knees up to your chest, and with your hands clasped pull your knees toward your chest. Hold for a count of 10, keeping your knees together and your shoulders flat on the mat. Repeat the pulling and holding movement three times. Relax and repeat the exercise.

3 Relax with your arms above your head and your knees bent. Now tighten the muscles of your lower abdomen and your buttocks at the same time so as to flatten your back against the mat. This is the **flat back position.** Hold the position for a count of 10. Relax and repeat the exercise.

4 Sit on a hard chair with your arms folded loosely in front of you. Let your body drop until your head is down between your knees. Pull your body back up into a sitting position while tightening your abdominal muscles. Relax and repeat the exercise.

5 Stand erect while holding onto a table or chair. Squat down with the back slightly bent, straighten up again, relax and repeat the exercise.

FIGURE 8–10   The care and prevention of low back pain. Distributed to physicians by McNeil Laboratories, Inc., Fort Washington, Pa. Reprinted by permission.

3. Types of crutch gaits:
    a. Four-point—a nonweight-bearing gait used by people with extreme ambulation difficulties. One crutch moves forward followed by the opposite foot. Then the other crutch moves forward followed by the other foot. Right crutch, left foot; left crutch, right foot.

How to get along with your back

Sitting: Use a hard chair and put your spine up against it; try and keep one or both knees higher than your hips. A small stool is helpful here. For short rest periods, a contour chair offers excellent support.

Standing: Try to stand with your lower back flat. When you work standing up, use a footrest to help relieve swayback. Never lean forward without bending your knees. Ladies take note: shoes with moderate heels strain the back less than those with high spike heels.

Sleeping: Sleep on a firm mattress; put a bedboard (¾″ plywood) under a soft mattress. Do not sleep on your stomach. If you sleep on your back, put a pillow under your knees. If you sleep on your side keep your legs bent at the knees and at the hips.

Driving: Get a hard seat for your automobile and sit close enough to the wheel while driving so that your legs are not fully extended when you work the pedals.

Lifting: Make sure you lift properly. Bend your knees and use your leg muscles to lift. Avoid sudden movements. Try not to lift anything heavy over your head.

Working: Don't overwork yourself. If you can, change from one job to another before you feel fatigued. If you work at a desk all day, get up and move around whenever you get the chance.

Exercise: Get regular exercise (walking, swimming, etc.) once your backache is gone. But start slowly to give your muscles a chance to warm up and loosen before attempting anything strenuous.

See your doctor: If your back acts up, see your doctor; don't wait until your condition gets severe.

McNEIL LABORATORIES, INC., Fort Washington, Pennsylvania 19034

FIGURE 8–10 (cont.)

b. Three-point—a very common gait used by people with a single leg involvement such as sprained ankle, broken leg, or amputation. The crutches are placed forward, taking all weight off the injured extremity. The unaffected leg swings through and forward. In time the injured extremity may move forward with the crutches accepting partial weight.

    c. Two-point—often used when there is involvement of both legs and a compromise can be made between speed and stability. One crutch and the opposite foot are placed forward at the same time, followed by the other crutch and foot. The cross-pattern of walking is employed.

    d. Swing-through—used by people with extreme involvement of both legs and some involvement of the trunk so that the legs cannot be moved independently. The crutches are placed forward, then both legs swing through and forward of the crutches accepting the weight of the body, thus permitting the crutches to be moved forward once again. These people wear leg braces and have been taught how to accept their body weight.

4. Stair-climbing:

    a. Ascending—place the unaffected foot on the tread of the step, then bring up the crutches and the injured extremity. When spotting, stand behind the student and hold his belt.

    b. Descending—place the crutches and the injured extremity on the lower tread of the step, then step down with the unaffected extremity. When spotting, stand in front of the student. Instruct the student to place his feet several inches from the riser of the step as this will provide more room for clearance, both ascending and descending.

    Modified Games and Activities   One of the basic needs of children is an opportunity for creative expression through physical activity and recreation. If such a statement can be accepted as a truism, it must follow that the handicapped have even a greater need for play because they have more time for involvement due to their restricting disabilities.

    Modified games and activities for the handicapped have definite therapeutic effects: the release of tensions and emotions and the enhancement of the child's self-image by providing him with experiences whereby he can achieve success. Activities should be provided which focus on the student's "ability" rather than on his "disability." If the handicapped child is to make a smooth transition into living in today's society, he must develop the self-realization that he can function competently in a variety of activities.

    Present interpretation of the term *adapted* is all too frequently viewed as synonymous with "remedial" or "corrective." As a result, many programs are founded on the faulty premise that all defects are amenable to correction. What about those students who have defects that are noncorrectable? To provide a truly educational experience for all children, a variety of modified games and activities must be incorporated in the D&A curriculum (along with rehabilitative exercises). Steele noted this general transition toward a wide variety of experiences for handicapped girls in the state of California. According to her survey:

    semi-active indoor games were offered by 88.4 percent of the schools sampled; table games were offered by 78.4 percent of the schools; and 76.1 percent of the schools offered individual exercises. Other activities included in the curriculum were fundamental motor skills (69.2 percent), relaxation training (40 percent), and rhythmical exercises, water exercises, and swimming (50 percent).[21]

Providing games and activities for the handicapped on an individualized basis necessitates consideration of each child's abilities and limitations so that modifications and adaptations can be made to insure safe participation. Doolittle[22] recommends the following modifications for games and activities for the handicapped:

ADAPTATION OF GAMES AND ACTIVITIES

General considerations:

1. Most children with permanent disabilities will have already developed necessary modifications to permit their participation in cèrtain activities. Allow these children to proceed at their own rate of involvement. If they experience difficulty or cannot make the necessary adjustments, step in and assist.
2. Adaptations must be made to suit the child's abilities rather than his disabilities.
3. Modification of game rules should not be discouraged and should be regulated to meet the needs of the group.
4. Try not to change a game to such a degree that the children lose sight of what they started to play.
5. When working with a new student, begin slowly and gradually introduce him to new activities. Keep in mind the child may have some fear of new experiences, may become embarrassed or display a lack of initiative.

Methods of modifying games and activities:

1. Reduce the size of the playing area:
   a. Change the boundary lines.
   b. Increase the number of players.
   c. Decrease the height of the net or goal.
   d. Use equipment that will reduce the range of play.
   e. Net-type games may be played through a hoop.
2. Use lighter equipment:
   a. Plastic bats, "wiffle-type" balls
   b. Large plastic beachballs; bladder balls
   c. Yarnballs, styrafoam balls
3. Slow down moving objects:
   a. Change the throwing style to underhand.
   b. Throw ball with one bounce.
   c. Roll the ball.
   d. Stationary ball: place it on home plate or place it on a batting T.

[21] Nancy L. Steele, "A Study of the Status of Adapted Physical Education Programs for Girls in California Public High Schools," master's thesis, San Jose State College, August, 1969.
[22] John H. Doolittle, "Adaptation of Games and Activities," *Physical Education 400: Laboratory Exercise 1* (University Park, Pa.: The Pennsylvania State University, n.d.), 4 pp. Mimeographed. Reprinted by permission.

    e. Increase the size of the ball.
    f. Decrease the weight of the ball.
    g. Decrease the air pressure within the ball.

4. Modify the rules:
    a. Sit down or lie down rather than stand.
    b. Walk rather than run.
    c. Kick rather than strike.
    d. Throw or strike rather than kick.
    e. Permit additional trials: strikes, throws, jumps.
    f. Allow for substitution.
    g. Reduce the time periods of the game.
    h. Reduce the number of points required to win a contest.

5. Provide additional rest periods:
    a. Discuss rule infractions.
    b. Discuss strategy and team play.
    c. Rotate players in and out of the game or into active and inactive positions.
    d. Reduce the time periods of the game.
    e. Provide quiet type games which may keep the student busy during rest periods: nok-hockey, box soccer, darts, ring toss, etc.

Modification of games and activities for exceptional children: As a rule, activities are selected from those which are most appropriate for various age groups of normal children. The difference lies in the application of these activities.

Adapting individual and dual sports:

Archery: use lighter bow, arrows with rubber tips. Student may sit, draw targets.
Bait-fly casting: place target boards on gym floor or field at various distances. Student may sit.
Badminton: four players on each side, each playing small zone. "Hoopbird" played with bird or yarnball.
Bowling: use plastic "gym-bowl" equipment or plastic detergent bottles. Student may bowl from a chair or sit on the floor. Roll ball through cardboard tube or box.
Croquet: use plastic mallets and wiffleballs, vary the distance to the wickets.
Gymnastics: tumbling, parallel bars, high bar, rings, side horse.
Golf: hit plastic practice ball into old tennis or volleyball nets which are faced with burlap. Putt on an old rug into a can placed on its side. Make miniature golf course from odds and ends.
Handball: one wall, use partially deflated volleyball or smaller playground ball to slow the action of the game.
Horseshoes: rubber shoes or quoits can be used in and out of doors. Throw shoes into a box.
Shuffleboard: shorten distance between scoring zones. Students may sit.
Swimming: obtain American Red Cross *Swimming for the Handicapped.*[23]
Table tennis: use larger paddles, make small table-size hoop and play as "hoopbird." Place plywood sides on the table so the ball will not bounce off the table as often; off the sides, ball remains in play.

---

[23] American Red Cross, *Swimming for the Handicapped* (Washington, D.C.: American Red Cross, 1955).

Tetherball: sit or stand, punch or kick. Make small table-size game with broomstick and small rubber ball in a silk stocking.

Quiet games: nok-hockey, table shuffleboard, pool, darts, bean bag toss games, box soccer.

Adapting team sports:

Baseball–softball-type games: use light plastic bats and wiffleballs, batting tee. Use base runners, two sets of bases (one of shorter distances), throw the ball into the field rather than bat it. Give children positions that require little movement.

Kickball: punch or throw the ball rather than kick it. Place ball on home plate rather than roll it.

Basketball type games: limit movement in the game by playing 21, Around the World, Six Court, Half-Court, Scooter Basketball, Foul Shooting, Barrelball. Have student do the foul shooting for both teams.

Soccer–hockey-type games: have student play goalie. Reduce size of goal. Scooter games: punching a playground ball. Hockey played with old brooms and volleyball. Barrelball: shooting for hole.

Volleyball-type games: deck tennis, Newcomb, use larger soft bladder ball. Have both teams sit on floor; put net at 4–5′.

We will expand upon our earlier reference to the advisability of incorporating the rehabilitative and modified games approach when working with children with motor disabilities or limitations by presenting a case study of a student scheduled in D&A due to an atrophied right arm and right leg.

Bobby was a bright and alert 5th-grade student whose only motor limitation was an inability to use his right arm and leg. He was very much in favor of physical activity (particularly basketball), but viewed any form of therapeutic exercise with displeasure. Following the medical report and consultation with Bobby and his mother, it was decided he would benefit from rehabilitative exercises and modified games.

Since Bobby disclosed he would like to play basketball in high school, it was decided to use that factor as the catalytic agent to get him to perform his individualized exercises. He was informed that if he devoted fifteen minutes to exercises to increase the strength, range of motion, and general use of his right arm and leg, he would be permitted to play a variety of games for the balance of each period.

His prescriptive exercises were: pronation and supination of the right hand with a dumbbell; wall-passing a basketball (both hands and right hand only); heel raising to develop the right calf; and wall-kicking a basketball with the right foot. In spite of his handicap, it was decided not to modify the games he participated in since that might further destroy his self-image. Activities he took part in were basketball, tetherball, bowling, table tennis, horseshoes, quoits, and badminton modified in that Bobby and his opponent each used two badminton racquets (one in each hand).

As a result of the rehabilitative/game-adapted approach, Bobby made excellent progress.

A review of the literature reveals many sources of information for adapting sports and recreational activities for the handicapped. Mason[24] describes specific adaptations of bowling in terms of the blind, orthopedically handicapped, those with advanced muscular dystrophy, and the mentally retarded. Pettit[25] describes a trampoline program for orthopedically handicapped children. He contends that even the more severely handicapped children were able to perform some basic stunts. As a result of their experiences, the children were more relaxed and confident, and less introverted. Newman[26] and Peters,[27] respectively, explain techniques for modifying swimming and archery for the physically handicapped. Other games and activity modifications for the handicapped can be obtained by reviewing *Outlook* and the *Journal of Health, Physical Education and Recreation*, both published by the American Association for Health, Physical Education and Recreation (1201 Sixteenth Street, N.W., Washington, D.C. 20036).

Circulorespiratory Restrictions

Only during the past decade has there emerged a general awareness of the values of modified physical activity for patients with circulorespiratory problems. Prior to that time, children with medical histories of cardiac abnormalities or breathing difficulties were counselled to avoid any form of strenuous activity. In fact, in many instances, they were told to avoid all physical activity.

Classic studies related to cardiovascular diseases and physical activity were conducted by the Registrar General for England and Wales[28]; with London postal clerks[29]; and with a cross-section of workers in Scotland.[30] The findings revealed a positive relationship between occupations of the highest incidence of coronary disease and minimal physical activity; three times as many heart attacks among sedentary workers as compared to laborers; and a higher recovery rate from heart attacks for those workers who were physically active as compared to those that had sedentary occupations.

---

[24] Robert D. Mason, "Bowling for the Handicapped" Milwaukee, Wis.: American Junior Bowling Congress, n.d.), 4 pp. Mimeographed. (Available free from AAHPER.)

[25] Milton H. Pettit, "A Trampoline Program for the Orthopedically Handicapped," *Outlook*, AAHPER Unit on Programs for the Handicapped, I, No. 2 (October, 1969), 3, 6.

[26] Judy Newman, "What a Difference a Year Makes," *Outlook*, AAHPER Unit on Programs for the Handicapped, I, No. 4 (February, 1970), 1, 4.

[27] Robert Peters, "Bullseye," *Outlook*, AAHPER Unit on Programs for the Handicapped, I, No. 4 (February, 1970), 3.

[28] F. F. McAllister et al., "The Accelerating Effect of Muscular Exercise on Experimental Atherosclerosis," *Archives of Surgery*, LXXX (1960), 62.

[29] J. N. Morris et al., "Coronary Heart Disease and Physical Activity at Work," *Lancet*, CCLXV (1953), 1053.

[30] S. L. Morrison, "Occupational Mortality in Scotland," *British Journal of Industrial Medicine*, XIV (1957), 130.

Vodola summarized the findings related to the effects of physical activity on cardiovascular diseases as follows:

The preponderance of evidence indicates that degenerative coronary heart disease occurs more frequently in individuals who participate in sedentary-type activities than in those who participate in vigorous physical activity.

When the disease does occur, it is not nearly as severe or fatal in the physically active workers as it is in the physically inactive workers.

Physical activity tends to reduce the blood cholesterol level if the stress factor is eliminated.

Regular participation in vigorous physical activity and the eating of high cholesterol-producing foods in moderation is the best course of action that can presently be undertaken to retard the onset of atherosclerosis.

The possibility of thrombosis, related to the rate of coagulation of the blood, may be retarded if one exercises regularly.

Physical activity develops much greater collateral circulation; thus it seems to have value as both a preventative and a remedial measure.[31]

Despite the supportive evidence of many scientific studies, most physicians were reluctant to prescribe physical activity for postcoronary cases until former President Dwight D. Eisenhower's series of coronary arrests. Dr. Paul Dudley White, the president's personal physician, recommended golf as a means of therapeutic rehabilitation. The attendant publicity of modified physical activity for the country's leading executive stimulated the development of postcoronary activity research programs at many of the leading hospitals in the United States. Although the results of these studies are not conclusive, the misconception that physical activity was to be avoided in all cases has been virtually eliminated.

The prescription of individualized physical activity programs for children with circulorespiratory problems necessitates a close working relationship with the family physician, the school physician, the child, and the parent. This relationship is essential if one is to plan a program commensurate with the varying needs of the individual. As indicated previously, most communication between physicians and physical educators is inadequate. Medical excuses which simply state that a child's activity program is to be "moderately" or "severely" restricted leave much to be desired. Effective communication requires that a physician (1) is fully informed as to the total offerings of the physical education program; (2) provides all pertinent information as to why an excuse has been issued; and (3) prescribes the intensity and duration of a specific activity.

The physical educator should also have many conferences with parents and their children to explain the values of the prescriptive programs and to

---

[31] Thomas M. Vodola, "The Relationship of Physical Activity to Degenerative Diseases of the Body," unpublished paper submitted to Temple University, Philadelphia, October 24, 1967.

recommend types of activities that can be performed at home. These conferences can do much to alleviate parental concern and enhance student progress. As an example, one parent was so impressed with the benefits his son derived from exercising on the overhead ladder in school that he constructed and installed one in his home.

All efforts will be in vain unless the student is receptive to, and sees the values of, his program. It is essential that the D&A teacher establish rapport with each and every child in his class, particularly those with circulorespiratory problems. The child must be made aware of the fact that he must make the final decision regarding his exercising regimen. It is easy to prescribe a program for an individual, but the program should never be mandated because there are too many intervening variables. For example, the asthmatic child's performance may be hindered by climatic conditions, emotional stress, or generally just feeling sub-par. (Such findings have been evidenced by plotting the vital capacity scores of students in the Township of Ocean School District. Patterns of retrogression can be predicted based on past performance scores.)

At this point, it must be obvious that there are many factors to consider before prescribing a program for a student who has been assigned to D&A because of circulorespiratory limitations. The following guidelines are recommended for careful consideration.

1. Be sure the physician is cognizant of the diversity of your D&A program (send out a packet of materials) so that he may prescribe a program based on the student's needs.
2. Plan the student's program on the basis of the medical excuse form. If the intensity and duration of the activity is not included, communicate with the physician.
3. Pre- and post-test each student on a daily basis to determine tolerance limits (review testing procedures for the asthmatic child in Chapter 4).
4. Counsel the student daily to assess progress, to help him maintain motivational level, and to modify the program when necessary.
5. Keep the family/school physician apprised of student progress so that medical prescriptions can be modified at periodic intervals.

Doolittle[32] designed the following activity program to be consistent with the American Heart Association classification for students with cardiac conditions:

Class I: Patients with heart disease whose physical activities need not be restricted. Possibly cross-country, wrestling, and certain positions in soccer would be contraindicted due to the continuous stress involved.

[32] John H. Doolittle, "Classification and Activities for Students with Cardiac Conditions," The Pennsylvania State University, 1 p. Mimeographed.

Class II: Patients with heart disease whose ordinary physical activity need not be restricted, but should be advised against unusually severe or competitive effort.

badminton	swimming
some gymnastics	tennis
kickball	tetherball
softball	volleyball
square dance	

Class III: Patients with heart disease whose ordinary physical activity should be moderately restricted and whose more strenuous habitual efforts should be discontinued.

basketball shooting games	table tennis
bowling	tumbling
golf	

Class IV: Patients with heart disease whose ordinary physical activities should be markedly restricted.

archery	deck shuffleboard
bean bag games	horseshoes
box soccer	minature golf
casting	nok hockey
croquet	riflery
dart games	

Class V: Patients with heart disease who should be at complete rest, confined to a bed or chair. These children will not be in school.

In all cases, it is important that the physical education program be approved by a physician.

The Mentally and Socioemotionally Handicapped

We previously noted that children classified by the school psychologist as either mentally or socioemotionally handicapped will manifest many of the same characteristics. Thus, for the purpose of writing prescriptive programs, both categories will be grouped together.

We have consistently recommended throughout the text that despite legislative and societal demands for classifying the handicapped categorically, the teacher should focus on the developmental approach, i.e., basing instruction on manifested needs. The developmental needs should be determined via a "team approach": examinations of and conferences with the child by the school physician, the school psychologist, the learning disability specialist, and other members of the child study team.[33] Individual physical activity programs should be prescribed by the physical educator (and approved by the team) based on the findings and recommendations of the team and the results of the administration of the Motor-Perceptual-Fitness Test Battery.

The prescription of *individualized* physical education programs must be

[33] The term "child study team" is used in the state of New Jersey to refer to those individuals who, collectively, assess the educational needs of the handicapped.

stressed at this point. Admittedly, children with learning disorders will manifest some common problems, but they will also display many disparate problems. If one is to provide meaningful educational learning experiences, the instructional program must be based on *individual* rather than *group* needs. (The author has become somewhat disenchanted with many programs for children with learning disorders, be they mental or socioemotional problems, because in most instances prescriptions have been designed on a group basis.)

To provide personalized programs, the physical educator must identify each child's specific problem(s) and plan physical activity experiences that will ameliorate these limitations. Earlier we noted that these children may evidence "hyperactivity," "dissociation," "figure-ground disturbances," and "perseveration." Other specific problems encountered might relate to perception (the ability to organize sensations); postural and spatial orientation; gross and specific body coordination; auditory, visual, and tactile discrimination, kinesthetic awareness; memory; and sequentualization (the ability to perform the parts of a task in their proper order). To this list one could add motor-patterning problems and low physical vitality. Thus, it becomes readily apparent that individualized prescriptive programs require extensive diagnostic testing via all available services.

Individualized programming for students with learning disorders provides a challenge for today's physical educator because there are so many unanswered questions. Many theories are presented for consideration, but few are founded on scientific fact. The physical educator has the task of reviewing all literature and designing a program based on the needs of the students in his school district.

The procedure recommended for providing individual prescriptive programs for the mentally and socioemotionally handicapped includes identifying specific areas of weakness via testing and other diagnostic practices and planning specific tasks and activities designed to develop generalizations, or conceptualizations in terms of the expressed need. Identification of areas of weakness has been explained in previous chapters, but it must be stressed again that the individual program will be of little value unless the prescriptions are based on valid test items. For example, does a ball-bounce test measure eye/hand coordination? It may, but it is also possible that the child who misses the ball has never learned to track an object with his eyes. Thus, if one were to prescribe eye/hand coordination tasks, it might well be that the child would make no improvement because the prescription would be based on an invalid test item.

Of equal importance in prescriptive programming is the selection of those tasks and activities that will help the child to generalize and conceptualize so that he can transfer the learning to other situations. A classic example of fragmenting the teaching/learning process would be to have a child repeatedly walk a balance beam to alleviate a postural orientation problem. Such a prescription will aid a child in walking a balance beam, but will have little effect on total postural orientation. In other words, the child would be improving a particular motor skill competency rather than a motor pattern competency. An analogous situation would be to stress the use of geometric forms to enhance a student's ability to read. The planning of a variety of experiences via the use of geometric forms will aid the child in identification of those same forms; it will not, however, aid him in reading unless the tasks are designed to enhance transferability to reading. Cratty[34] contends that after children learn to identify the various forms, they can be taught letter recognition by constructing letters with the forms; for example, placing two half-circles together will form the letter *B*.

In an effort to give the reader some specific suggestions for planning individualized programs, the remainder of the chapter shall be devoted to prescriptive tasks and activities based on hyperactivity, dissociation, figure-background disturbance, perseveration, and mental retardation.

Hyperactivity

It has been the contention of the writer that children with varying handicaps could receive individualized instruction within the same class. Experience has proven that rule to be sound except when dealing with the hyperactive child. He should not be scheduled with children with other disabilities because of his need for a teaching environment that is virtually devoid of disconcerting stimuli. The following observation is presented as a case in point showing how distracting an improper teaching environment can be. The teacher was a member of the author's own department who was teaching a group of emotionally disturbed children.

During a previous class, the D&A teacher had set up a variety of testing stations to assess eye/hand coordination. Portable cages and portable clothes racks with tires suspended from them had been used to measure student achievement. Unaware of the distractions that would be caused by the presence of such items, the teacher had not removed the testing equipment during the subsequent class.

Upon entering the class, some of the emotionally disturbed children got embroiled in the nets; others decided to use the clothes racks as vehicles for traveling around the gymnasium. Despite the valiant efforts of the teacher, she could not gain control of the class for the balance of the period.

During the conference period that followed, the teacher was extremely upset because her students had "let her down." She maintained that they had always been more cooperative in the past. The supervisor assured her that her teaching method was sound but pointed out that the equipment in the gymnasium had "triggered" the children's hyperactive behavior.

[34] Bryant J. Cratty, *Active Learning: Games to Enhance Academic Abilities* (Englewood Cliffs, N. J.: Prentice-Hall, Inc., 1971), p. 27.

The basic problem of the hyperactive child is his inability to concentrate on the task at hand. It is theorized that the child cannot selectively "screen out" those stimuli that do not contribute to the achievement of the task, for regardless of the task being performed, every individual is constantly receiving a variety of distracting sensory impulses. The normal child learns to "block out" all neural patterns that diminish the efficiency of his task completion, but the hyperactive child cannot. One could compare the movements of a child learning a new manual skill to the movement patterns of the hyperactive. In both cases, the initial performance is extremely erratic, seemingly causing tetanic contractions of all body muscles. However, after a relatively short time there will be a distinctive contrast in performance: the normal child's performance will evidence a meaningful organization of most neural impulses with a resultant smooth pattern whereas the hyperactive child will evidence little or no improvement.

If we accept this theory prescriptive programming should include activities which decelerate neural impulses and require an increasing focus of attention on the task being performed. This poses a problem because our teacher-training institutions have emphasized the stimulation of neural impulses, e.g., the development of strength, endurance, neuromuscular coordination, and other such attributes. Little or no attention has been devoted to the other end of the spectrum—the laws of relaxation and the reduction of neuromuscular tensions.

Steinhaus[35] contends that physical educators should stress the development of "muscle sense" in its entirety, from complete relaxation through maximum activity. In a review of research at clinics relating to techniques of relaxation (not induced by hypnosis or autosuggestion), he found:

1. Experimental groups—reduction in muscle tension 25–40 percent, significant at the .001 level; control group—no significant change.

2. Experimental groups—diastolic arterial pressure drop of 9 mm., significant at the .001 level; control group—no change.

3. Experimental groups reported reductions in headaches, insomnia, etc.

4. Some inclination that [by] resting vocal and visual apparatus, one could "blank the mind" and thus rest the mental processes.

Two examples from the writer's own experience might strengthen the significance of the theory of neuromuscular relaxation and its value for the physical educator:

---

[35] Arthur H. Steinhaus, "Teaching Neuromuscular Relaxation: A New Phase of Physical Education," *The Canadian Association for Health, Physical Education and Recreation*, XXXI, No. 6 (August-September, 1965), 4.

In one situation a member of the track team, who was physiologically healthy, informed me that he was always completely "bushed" following a track meet, but he never "placed." I discussed relaxation exercises with the track coach to alleviate the student's hyperactive state of muscular tonicity. It was too late in the season to compare meet results, but the student seemed to benefit psychologically.

In the other situation, a simple statement by a baseball player had profound implications. The player was informed that he was to pinch-hit with the score tied 4–4. He related to the writer (after the game) that at that moment he was extremely "tight" and "nervous" and felt he was going to strike out. Then he added that the coach called him for a conference, wrapped an arm around his shoulder and stated, "Relax and swing away as you do in batting practice." The student related that that short conference relaxed him. Outcome: He hit a home-run.

Although such outcomes could be merely coincidental, the teaching of neuromuscular relaxation can have profound implications for physical education. It certainly appears to be a fertile research area.

We recommend that hyperactive children receive at least fifteen minutes of daily instruction designed to relax neuromuscular tension. The specific instruction program is based on extensive research conducted since 1908 by Dr. Edmund Jacobson, the founder of the program, and his successors. (If the reader is not conversant with this area, he should read Dr. Jacobson's texts, *Progressive Relaxation*[36] and *You Must Relax*[37]; he should also contact the Foundation for Scientific Relaxation, Inc.,[38] a nonprofit organization, for a series of mimeographed teaching materials.)

Basically, the program involves teaching the child to identify tensions of the various muscle groups so that he can internalize the true meaning of relaxation. The two basic positions assumed by the student are lying supine on the floor (Fig. 8–11a) and sitting at a desk or on a stool (Fig. 8–11b). For the lower grades K–2, the former position would be recommended. Ask the pupils to shut their eyes (with feet apart and hands slightly removed from the body) and relax like a rag doll. Teaching techniques could be to have the students tense a right arm, right leg, etc., or the entire body. Have the children feel the tenseness and then relax. Another sound technique is to appeal to the vivid imagination of children. Request that they emulate "a snowman on a hot day," "butter in a frying pan," "a wilting flower," "a puddle of water," or other such descriptive positions. Regardless of technique, minimize instructions.

For the upper grades, a slightly more sophisticated approach is in order.

[36] Edmund Jacobson, M.D., *Progressive Relaxation*, 2nd ed. (Chicago: The University of Chicago Press, 1938).

[37] Edmund Jacobson, M.D., *You Must Relax*, 4th ed. (New York: McGraw-Hill Book Company, 1957).

[38] Foundation for Scientific Relaxation, Inc., 301 Pittsfield Building, 55 East Washington Street, Chicago, 60602.

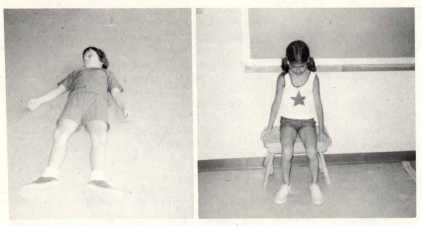

a   *b*

FIGURE 8–11   Basic relaxation positions. (*a*) **Lying on floor, and** (*b*) **sitting.
Courtesy of the Township of Ocean School District.**

From a sitting position, the students can progressively be taught to relax all of the major muscle groups. Dr. Jacobson[39] recommends the following six basic lessons in tension control:

SIX LESSONS IN TENSION CONTROL:
FOR SCHOOL CHILDREN OR ADULTS

General method: Muscles can relax far more in the working state than most people realize. For lessons, or other practice, one should be comfortable, head drooping, body well supported as in Fig. 8–12*a*. *Practice periods in school* may start with one or two minutes, gradually increased to five or more. Adults might relax ten minutes to an hour daily, six or seven days a week.

After resting a moment or longer, depending on available time, slowly contract, then relax muscles that perform a certain act (Fig. 8–12*a* to *f*). Meanwhile, note the faint control signal, the tight feeling in tensing muscles, and the fade-out as they go. After two or three brief tensions, with short rests between, keep letting go. Do not watch the clock; adults use a timer.

In relaxing, (1) *don't try to hold still*, as beginners often do. Simply (2) *don't bother to repeat the tension*; (3) *give the idle muscle group plenty of time to let go* more and more, but (4) *don't keep your mind on it*. Merely check it now and then. A fully relaxed part feels nothing at all, as if it is no longer there. A kindergarten boy described this as "melting right into the floor."

Practice scheme: Grades 2–6 may first learn to relax as in Fig. 8–12*a*. Then, each grade may practice one muscle group during rest: grade 2, Fig. 8–12*b*; grade 3, Fig. 8–12*c*; etc. Adults also practice one muscle group at a time, say one or two per week. Every third period, forget about muscles and simply rest.

---

[39] Reprinted from Edmund Jacobson, M.D., "Six Lessons in Tension Control" (Chicago: Foundation for Scientific Relaxation, Inc., 1965), 3 pp. (mimeographed), by permission of the author.

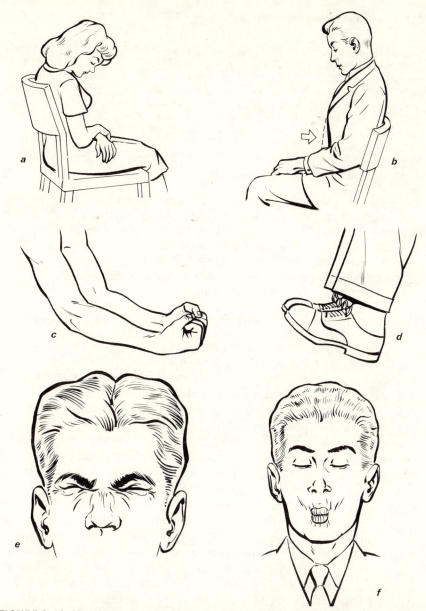

FIGURE 8–12 Muscle groups. (*a*) Relax, seated. Head droops to loosen tension at back of neck, and perhaps between the shoulder blades. Back slumps against back of seat, arms rest on thighs, feet flat on floor or back of heels. At first, stretching tendons in back of neck may hurt. Pain is relieved by holding head up a minute and disappears with practice as tendons lengthen, usually in a few days. (*b*) Pull in abdomen; tense abdominal muscles are felt most at the waistline. (*c*) Tighten both arms slowly and steadily, noting tensions from shoulder to wrist, above and below elbow, front and back. Hold and observe tension a moment, then *gradually* go to zero. (*d*) Bend feet up, tense, and relax slowly. Control signals felt along shins. (*e*) Close eyelids tightly and relax slowly. (*f*) Pucker lips, relax slowly. Adapted from Edmund Jacobson, M.D., "Six Lessons in Tension Control" (Chicago: Foundation for Scientific Relaxation, Inc., 1965), 3 pp. (mimeographed), by permission of the author.

To evaluate student progress, the teacher should look for telltale signs of existing tensions, or relaxation. Signs of *tension* would be: local or general rigidity of musculature (ascertained by touching a moving body part); restlessness; irregular, rapid breathing, with frequent sighs; an alert, expressive face; frowning and twitching of the eyes and lips; and an immediate response to command. The *relaxed* pupil evidences muscles that are limp to the touch; slow, regular breathing; a dull, vacant facial expression; and a lethargic response to a command.

Based on teacher experimentation with his method of tension control, Jacobson makes the following suggestions:

1. Start tension control programs as early as possible, as children learn more readily in the lower grades. (. . . [P]rekindergarten children, especially in the nursery schools, [could participate], as part of the daily activities include periods of rest.)

2. Tension control programs should be conducted for tense, hyperative children, as they may benefit more due to their special needs.

3. Blind children might benefit from a similar program because their lack of sight creates many tense, awkward postural problems.

4. Include neuromuscular relaxation sessions with the mentally retarded. (There is empirical evidence to indicate I.Q.'s . . . increased, subjects were learned easier, and typing ability improved as tensions were reduced.)[40]

Cratty[41] recommends the deceleration approach to physical activity. He hypothesizes that if the hyperactive child is required to perform movements as slowly as possible he may gain better control over superfluous muscle tonus. Thus, activities and tasks should be provided whereby students are requested to perform a variety of physical movements as slowly as possible. The teaching techniques could be patterned after Jacobson's method: have the students perform at full speed and then decelerate movement until they are barely moving. For example, children may be requested to run at full speed, three-quarters speed, one-half speed, and then as slowly as possible.

Distractibility, or the inability to concentrate on the task at hand, is usually associated with hyperactivity. As a consequence, classroom teachers frequently utilize small cubicles, devoid of any distractions, for instructional purposes. In addition, written assignments are concentrated on the presentation of one task. The physical educator should structure the physical activity program similarly, so that the child is required to concentrate on only one task at a time, such as walking a balance beam, executing a forward roll, or balancing an object in his hand. Experience has shown that once the child can perform a task with reasonable competency, he may revert back to his bizarre behavior. Consequently, the teacher should continually revise the child's prescription so that the tasks become more demanding (and thus,

---

40 Edmund Jacobson, "Methods of Teaching Scientific Relaxation" (Chicago: Foundation for Scientific Relaxation, Inc., 1961), p. 3. Mimeographed. Reprinted by permission.
41 Cratty, *op. cit.*, pp. 17–25.

hopefully, increase his attention span). For example, the plane of the beam can be altered (or obstacles placed on it), the number of forward rolls can be increased, or an object can be balanced while the child assumes various positions.

Dissociation

Dissociation, a problem that is manifested by most children with learning disorders, is the inability to see or to complete a task as a whole. Children with this learning disability can perform (and in many cases extremely well) a series of discrete acts, but do not seem to be able to synthesize the isolated skills into meaningful patterns. Evidence of this inability to synthesize or integrate may be found by observing students copying geometric forms; they may perceive the patterns properly but will have difficulty replicating them accurately. They may also have a *closure* problem (the inability to complete a design). Children with dissociation problems will perform simple stunts and motor skills as well as most normal children, but as soon as they are required to modify their performance slightly they will fail dismally or refuse to perform the new pattern.

Kephart[42] recommends a three-step approach for teaching the integration of skills: (1) presenting the "initial datum," or isolated skill to be learned; (2) "elaborating," or providing a variety of similar but not identical learning experiences; and (3) "integrating," or presenting the initial data in a variety of different patterns with emphasis on a *simultaneous* multisensory approach. The author[43] provides several examples for teaching one to generalize, followed by some implications for teaching.

Initial datum	*Elaboration*	*Integration*
Walking (cross-patterning).	Walk up, down incline, crab walk, etc.	Step in footprints to visually see left and right while verbalizing.
Form perception of straight and curved lines and change of direction.	Finger painting, chalkboard drills, connecting dots, puzzles, etc.	Trace, copy, draw forms with emphasis on visual, auditory, tactile, and kinesthetic senses.
Counting and adding drills.	Pegboard, locomotor drills, involving counting and addition variations.	Use of beads, abacus and grid floor patterns to count and add a variety of numbers, using multisensory approach.

---

[42] Newell C. Kephart, *Learning Disability: An Educational Adventure* (West Lafayette, Ind.: Kappa Delta Pi Press, 1968), pp. 43–72.

[43] Thomas M. Vodola, "Learning: An Integration of Experiences," *The Reporter*, New Jersey Association for Health, Physical Education and Recreation, XLIII, No. 3 (March, 1970), 18–19.

IMPLICATIONS FOR TEACHING

1. Provide learning experiences that keep the goal constant while varying the process. Movement exploration provides a sound means of achieving this objective.

2. Concentrate on the process (how the student performs) rather than on the end result. This will allow you to assess whether the child's learning tends to be fragmented or integrated.

3. When a child cannot achieve success with a particular task, reduce the task difficulty by altering the process rather than the end result. For example, if a child cannot draw a diamond, do not instead have the child attempt to draw a square, because he may still evidence the same problem: the inability to change direction. Altering the process in such a case might involve having the child "walk" a diamond marked on the floor, or trace a diamond shape with his finger or a pencil to increase the visual/tactile sensations.

4. Make all learning experiences as concrete as possible by using a multisensory approach, but make sure all senses are coordinated for the same task. For example, if the student is performing a forward roll, make sure he concentrates on his performance visually and kinesthetically; he may even say, "I am performing a forward roll."

In the final analysis, regardless of whether one is teaching children with learning disorders or normal children, the theory of learning as an integration of experiences has considerable merit. Students may achieve integration by pursuing objectives via a variety of learning experiences that utilize (wherever possible) the auditory, visual, tactile, and kinesthetic senses. Through such structuring, the teacher will be providing learning experiences as meaningful wholes.

Figure–Background Disturbances

Figure–background disturbances refer to the inability of the student to discern the task at hand (the foreground material) from the stimuli that are always present but not necessarily meaningful to the task solution (the background material). Students evidencing this problem do not seem able to mentally block out the extraneous sensory stimuli. We are all familiar with the situation whereby a batter has difficulty distinguishing a pitched baseball (foreground material) from the spectators in the bleachers (the background), especially during the summer months when the spectators are wearing white shirts. Similarly, a foul shooter in basketball must concentrate on the basket so that he is not distracted by the presence of spectators and their shouts. Children who manifest this problem in the classroom will have extreme difficulty with reading. Their performance may include hesitant reading, the omission of words and sentences, repeated loss of reading position, and general frustration. Children with this visual problem usually complain that their reading material is a mass of jumbled figures.

Prescriptive programming, regardless of whether it is in the classroom or the gymnasium, involves initial structuring of the learning experience (and the environment) so that the child's attention is focused *solely* on the task to be performed. Then, as the child achieves success, background material may be gradually added. For the teacher this means the preparation of special materials. For example, if one were to attempt to teach the addition of numbers, it is recommended that addition problems be reproduced with only one problem per page so that the child is not distracted by other problems. Similar procedures can be used in teaching letters and words. Another approach to the problem would be to increase the stimulus of foreground material by highlighting it with colors and then having the child trace the figure to develop a kinesthetic awareness.

Pegboard activities can also be utilized to prescribe activities for children with figure-background disturbances.[44] Following is the author's adaptation of Strauss and Lehtinen's Visuo-Motor Perception Test[45] (see Fig. 8-13).

THE DEVELOPMENT OF PERCEPTUALIZATION
VIA PEGBOARD USAGE

General objective: To perceive figures as a whole (figure/ground relations)
Specific objectives:

1. To determine handedness via observation
2. To enhance color discrimination via the use of different colors
3. To improve eye/hand coordination by stressing the use of both hands in inserting and removing the pegs
4. To aid in the development of mathematical concepts by having students relate how many pegs are in each line, etc.
5. To aid in the development of comparative discriminations by having the students make comparisons (such as which of two lines is longer)
6. To engender creativity and logic by having the student design a variety of patterns

Activities for use in the gymnasium or on the playing field should also be modified to accentuate the foreground object. All activities should involve eye/hand, eye/foot, and eye/body coordination and accuracy skills. Some illustrative examples follow, along with recommended modifications:

Task	*Modifications*
Catching	Use large, colored objects, with solid, contrasting background.
Kicking, or striking objects	Start with large, colored, stationary objects.

---

[44] This teaching device can also be used with children who display a wide variety of learning problems. In fact, its general use is also recommended for normal children.

[45] Adapted from Alfred A. Strauss and Laura E. Lehtinen, *Psychopathology and Education of the Brain-Injured Child* (New York: Grune & Stratton, Inc., 1967), pp. 28-33, by permission of the publisher.

1. Test on all six items, plus circle, cross, square, triangle, diamond, and horizontal diamond.

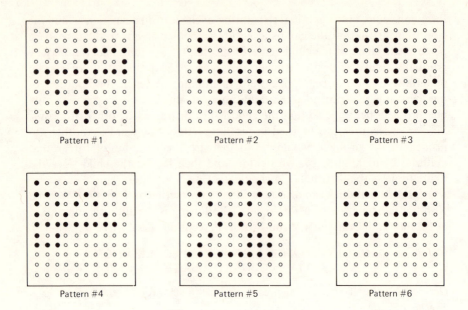

2. Diagnose patterns and prescribe activities via tracing, copying, and drawing from memory.

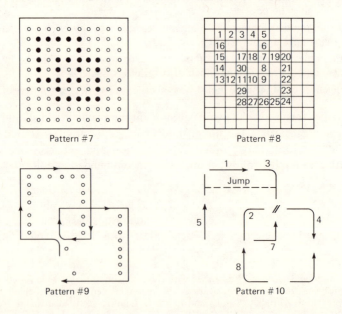

FIGURE 8–13 Visuomotor perception test: teaching procedure. Reprinted from Alfred A. Strauss and Laura E. Lehtinen, *Psychopathology and Education of the Brain-Injured Child* (New York: Grune & Stratton, Inc., 1967), pp. 32–33, by permission of the publisher.

Task	*Modifications*
Locomotor skills	Accentuate patterns by printing foot-prints and handprints on the floor.
Tumbling stunts	Demonstrate skill and have the student assume the basic position(s) to get kinesthetic and tactile reinforcement.
Throwing, batting, or kicking for accuracy	Start with enlarged target area, with solid background; decrease size as accuracy increases.

With experience the physical educator will be able to devise many other tasks and game modifications to aid the child with figure–background problems. Just keep in mind that prime consideration must be given to highlighting the task at hand while factors of secondary significance are minimized or eliminated.

Perseveration

Children who tend to "perseverate" will usually manifest the psychological characteristics of hyperactivity and dissociation and possibly even figure–background problems. Thus, their prescriptive programs should incorporate some of the previously listed activities. One additional procedure should be mentioned. Theorists contend that mentally or socioemotionally handicapped children perseverate because they have achieved success in the tasks they can perform and will repeat them for self-gratification. Moreover, these children will resist all efforts to induce them to perform new skills because of a fear of failure. Experience has shown that when this situation exists, the physical educator *must* resort to a diplomatic, but *forceful* means of having the student execute the new skill. An example of such a situation follows:

John was admitted to the summer program upon graduation from the 8th grade. In the fall of the year, he was admitted to the high school D&A program because of a request from the guidance department. Testing revealed poor posture, low physical vitality, and motor-perceptual and coordination problems.

Throughout the year, John was obsessed with the idea of playing varsity basketball. The instructor told John that it was possible for him to make the squad, but he would have to improve his coordination. John accepted tumbling as part of his prescriptive program, especially after he was informed that he could practice basketball at the end of each period.

For one entire year, John attempted a forward roll without success. The instructor demonstrated, lectured, and used every means at his disposal other than force, but to no avail. The student sincerely wanted to perform the skill, but his entire body became rigid the moment he placed his head on the mat.

Finally the instructor decided to use *diplomatic* persuasion. He placed a chair near the mat, had John extend his body face down over the chair so that his head was just above the mat, and then he forcefully carried the student through the forward roll. In a matter of days, John was executing the forward roll on his own.

This example is typical of the behavior of abnormal children who tend to perseverate. Once a new skill can be achieved in a rote pattern (in John's case, the forward roll), the constant repetition will start all over again. Thus, children who manifest this tendency must receive individual attention, must be assisted through the learning of each skill, and must be presented with variations or new skills as soon as they learn the old patterns.

The Mentally Retarded

Much has been written about teaching children who are mentally handicapped. Because of their innate limited ability to assimilate new knowledge, it is usually recommended that the teacher present new materials in a slow, methodical fashion: directions should be explicit, demonstrations should be given frequently, and learning experiences should be presented as concretely as possible. Physically, these children do not differ much from their normal peer group, although there is usually a lag of approximately two years in physical development (depending upon the level of mental deficiency). They will evidence varying discrepancies in terms of posture, physical fitness, and general motor ability.

In Chapter 3, the writer alluded to a golden opportunity available to today's physical educator to explore the perceptual–motor–cognitive area and to refute once and for all the idea that the child's learning takes place dichotomously: physically and mentally. The physical educator is also faced with the opportunity to enhance physical education as a discipline that is an essential part of the total school offering.

The teaching approach we recommend for working with the mentally retarded (and with normal children in the lower grades) is referred to as "physical education cognitively oriented activities," or simply physical activities designed so that the child is mentally as well as physically involved. In a factor analytic study Ishmail and Gruber[46] found that coordination activities correlated significantly with academic achievement. The specific test item selected involved the child's hopping on one foot for so many counts and then shifting to the other foot for so many counts and finally shifting back to the original foot for so many hops. Thus, the child not only had to perform the skill of hopping, but also had to "think" while he was performing. (If you have any doubts about the mental involvement, have a 1st-grade student perform the task of hopping alternately twice on his right foot, three times on his left foot, and two times on his right foot. Upon close observation of his eyes, you will see him "thinking.")

To validate their hypothesis that children could achieve academically with the aid of coordination activities, Ishmail and Gruber[47] conducted a

---

[46] A. H. Ishmail and J. J. Gruber, *Motor Aptitude and Intellectual Performance* (Columbus, Ohio: Charles E. Merrill Books, Inc., 1967), p. 75.

[47] *Ibid.*, pp. 179–91.

research study in which the experimental group performed those tasks and activities that involved "thinking" while the control group participated in the "traditional" program. (By "traditional" program we mean the teaching of physical education with the emphasis on developing physical and motor competencies, with a minimal emphasis on the cognitive aspect of learning.) Their initial findings were substantiated; the experimental group did achieve significantly higher academic scores than the control group.

Cratty has researched this area quite extensively. In his text, *Active Learning: Games to Enhance Academic Abilities*,[48] he provides a plethora of ideas for the classroom teacher to use in physical activity to enhance the child's ability to (1) identify symbols, letters, and numbers; (2) remember; (3) perform mathematical operations; (4) read; and (5) perform other tasks associated with cognition. Cratty cautioned, however, that such techniques are not meant as replacements for the more formal approaches to learning, but rather as supplemental aids that should be used judiciously by the classroom teacher.

During the past year, the Township of Ocean School District's elementary physical education staff has experimented with the physical education cognitively oriented approach (PECO) with grades K–3. In addition to program implementation on the playgrounds and in the gymnasia, demonstrations have been conducted for teachers, administrators, and parents. The response from all involved in the program has been extremely enthusiastic. One staff member informed the writer that he had been losing interest in teaching physical education, but had discovered a renewed zest for teaching because of the new approach. Another staff member responded by saying that although the new teaching method was demanding, it was very gratifying. As a result of the experimentation, the staff decided to write a proposal to obtain state-supported funds for a research study, which developed into "The Effects of Physical Education Cognitively Oriented Activities on Academic Achievement."[49]

To return to our discussion of Cratty's techniques, although they are valuable as supplemental teaching aids, they also present profound implications for teaching the slow learner. Many of these children respond adversely when they confront an academic learning experience in the traditional classroom. The classroom teacher will interpret their reactions as lack of attention span, very poor motivation, or extreme hyperactivity. By contrast, most mentally retarded children have always been very receptive to physical activity. Physical educators usually relate that these children are highly motivated and cooperative. Since intrinsic motivation is probably the

[48] Cratty, *op. cit.*
[49] Thomas M. Vodola, "The Effects of Physical Education Cognitively Oriented Activities on Academic Achievement," Township of Ocean School District, Oakhurst, N.J., 3 pp. Mimeographed.

prime prerequisite for learning, the physical educator (or classroom teacher, if he uses the physical activity approach to learning) has a propitious opportunity to enhance the mentally retarded child's ability to achieve academically as well as physically.

Individualized, prescriptive programming for the mentally retarded child should be based on the results of the Perceptual-Motor, Motor and Physical Fitness Test Batteries described in Chapter 3. Individualized programming involves:

1. Identification of areas of deficiency
2. Prescription of physical activities to alleviate or minimize these deficiencies
3. The simultaneous incorporation of those learning experiences that will enhance academic achievement

What experiences are necessary to stimulate academic achievement? Prime consideration must be given to *transfer of learning*. The closer the association of the learning experience with the specific objective, the greater the transfer of learning. Let us assume that two classes are playing hop scotch and that one group's grid is marked with traditional numbers but the second group's grid is marked with letters. After some play has occurred, the first group would show a superior gain in number concepts and the second group would tend to be superior in letter concepts. For both classes, the superior gain would be attributable to the structure of the learning experience. (We might add that if a third group were to hop on a grid with no symbols at all, they would develop competency in the locomotor skill of hopping— but little else.) Thus, if the physical activity learning experience is closely related to the academic skill one wants to teach, it will be successfully learned. More specifically, physical activities should incorporate the use of (1) perceptual-motor tasks (perceiving stimuli and replicating via motor activity); (2) discriminatory activities (comparing, contrasting); (3) tasks that increase one's ability to comprehend interrelationships; (4) experiences that require the retention of facts for an increasing period of time; (5) tasks designed to facilitate the proper sequentialization of discrete items into a meaningful whole; and (6) all other experiences that directly relate to academic achievement (identification of letters, numbers, reading, and mathematical concepts, etc.).

At this point the reader may be somewhat confused and feel that the PECO approach is too complex. While it is admittedly more sophisticated than the teaching of motor skill acquisition, the rewards for using it are far greater. For example, Cratty[50] conducted a study whereby slow learners practiced locomotor patterns involving letter recognition for three half-hour periods a week (experimental group); the control group received extra help in the classroom for a similar time period. Comparison of post-test scores revealed

---

[50] Cratty, *op. cit.*, p. 79.

that 70 percent of the experimental group learned the alphabet without making any mistakes, but only 30 percent of the control group achieved the same success.

Let us follow through in a hypothetical learning situation from teacher referral to program prescription. A 2nd-grade student has been referred to you by the school child study team for diagnostic screening. Your report to the team indicates that the child exhibits poor gross body balance, gross body coordination, and a distorted perception of form and directionality. A review of the child's personal history also reveals an inability to differentiate left from right, or to read and write words listed on the 1st- or 2nd-grade vocabulary list. After receiving your report, the school psychologist refers the child to the D&A program for supplementary tutoring.

Based on the foregoing information you might prescribe the following program:

Task or Game	*Objectives*
1. Pegboard games; tracing, copying, and reproducing (from memory) geometric letters of the alphabet (see Fig. 8–14). Pegboard forms can also be produced on paper.	*1.* Eye/hand coordination, conception of form, letter identification, association between forms and numbers, memorization, laterality, directionality (see Fig. 8–15).

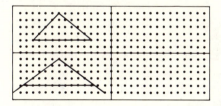

FIGURE 8–14   **Pegboard activities.**

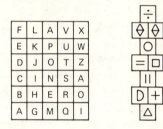

FIGURE 8–15   **Grids and patterns.**

2. Grids and various patterns painted on the playground or drawn on the gym floor with white shoe polish; a variety of locomotor patterns with the accompanying identification of symbols, letters, and the spelling of words. The students are the listen to directions and to verbalize their motor responses.	*2.* Locomotor skills, gross body balance, conception of form, letter identification, word identification, laterality, directionality.
3. Coordination-type activities: "Follow the Leader" and "Simon Says" games. For example, "let me see you touch your knees, toes, hands," or "grab your right ear with your left hand and your left ear with your right hand."	*3.* Motor skills, gross body coordination, identification of body parts, sequentialization of performance, laterality, directionality.

Task or Game	*Objectives*
4. Integrating auditory sounds with visual discrimination; discrimination of "loud" and "soft" sounds from a drum and replication by hopping on large or small geometric forms,[51] or by hopping on upper- or lower-case letters spread indiscriminately on the floor (see Fig. 8–16).	4. Locomotor skills, auditory discrimination, memorization, serial ordering, identification of forms, letters.

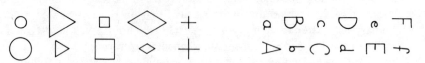

FIGURE 8–16   Integration of auditory, visual, and motor experiences.

5. Movement exploration: goal-oriented tasks wherein students are to read a series of signs and perform the tasks until they reach a goal. This activity would be for the more advanced student.	5. Movement skills, reading skills, gross body balance, gross body coordination, laterality.

Innumerable other physical education cognitive-type activities can be introduced into the program. Games can be made competitive by forming squads and using flash cards with letters or words printed on them. On command the students perform as requested, identify the symbol, letter, or word verbally, and return to their squads. Award 1 point to the team whose member responded correctly and returned to his line first. Writing can also be added to the activity program by having one partner write a word and his teammate replicate it on a grid. Once this type of program has been implemented, countless variations to those presented can be added. Furthermore, if requested, students can add many other creative experiences that will supplement the existing repertoire.

(The reader is urged to read the Cratty text previously mentioned, plus two of his other texts, *Motor Activity and the Education of Retardates*[52] and *Developmental Sequences of Perceptual-Motor Tasks.*[53] They will provide a sound theoretical and practical basis for initiating a PECO program for the mentally retarded.)

51 G. N. Getman, Lecture: "Perceptual-Motor Programming," E.D.A.–AAHPER Workshop, Philadelphia, April 1, 1971.

52 Bryant J. Cratty, *Motor Activity and the Education of Retardates* (Philadelphia: Lea and Febiger, 1969).

53 Bryant J. Cratty, *Developmental Sequences of Perceptual-Motor Tasks* (Freeport, N.Y.: Educational Activities, Inc., 1967), 88 pp.

Summary

Adapting a physical activity program to meet the needs of the child with a medically oriented problem is complex and fraught with liability problems unless the school district develops definite policies regarding scheduling, prescriptive activities, and procedures for release from the program. The role of the teacher in working with children with physical or psychological problems is strictly supportive; the school child study team is vested with the authority and the responsibility of identifying, classifying, and prescribing prescriptive programs. We do not wish to minimize the value of the classroom teacher, but rather to clearly delineate job descriptions because the over-zealous teacher (one who exceeds his authority) may negate the overall value of the program and even subject himself to a law suit.

Although the teacher role is supportive, it is undoubtedly the prime factor regarding the successful implementation of an adapted physical education program. Teacher qualities which will enhance program success are:

1. The ability to *publicize* the benefits to be derived from a physical activity program for the handicapped
2. The ability to *work effectively* with the child study team and teachers of other disciplines
3. A *sound understanding* of the latest research, studies, and knowledge related to physical activity programs for children with medically oriented problems
4. The *diagonostic ability* to analyze a series of discrete motor skills and draw generalizations in terms of motor pattern deficiencies
5. The *prescriptive ability* to develop general prescriptive materials which may be used as guidelines by the team
6. The ability to *adapt exercises, tasks*, and *games* to the varying needs of the handicapped
7. The *diligence* and *ingenuity* necessary to extrapolate materials from related disciplines and develop innovative programs based on "what research tells us" about sound theories of learning and child growth and development

Annotated Bibliography

AMERICAN ASSOCIATION FOR HEALTH, PHYSICAL EDUCATION AND RECREATION, UNIT ON PROGRAMS FOR THE HANDICAPPED. *Annotated Bibliography: Swimming for the Handicapped.* Washington, D.C.: 1201 Sixteenth Street, N.W. 20036, 6 pp. Mimeographed. Provides sources of information regarding every aspect of a comprehensive swimming program for all handicapped children. Free upon request.

————. *Guide for Programs in Physical Education and Recreation for the Mentally Retarded.* Washington, D.C.: 1201 Sixteenth Street, N.W. 20036, 1968, 80 pp.

Provides guidelines and suggestions for developing new programs or enriching and expanding already existing programs, including a self-evaluation procedure and format.

————. *Information Sheet: Adult Mentally Retarded and Contributions of Physical Education and/or Recreation to Social Development of Mentally Retarded.* Washington, D.C.: 1201 Sixteenth Street, N.W. 20036, 7 pp. Mimeographed. Extensive bibliography related to programming for the mentally retarded. Free upon request.

————. *Information Sheet: Competitive Athletic Programs for the Handicapped.* Washington, D.C.: 1201 Sixteenth Street, N.W. 20036, 2 pp. Mimeographed. Provides contacts to be made for specific information and materials about special competitive programs and athletic activities for the impaired, disabled, and handicapped. Resource materials are categorized as follows: amputees, blind, deaf, mentally retarded, and confined to wheelchair. Free upon request.

————. *Information Sheet: Dance, Music, Arts and Crafts for the Handicapped.* Washington, D.C.: 1201 Sixteenth Street, N.W. 20036, 7 pp. Mimeographed. Provides a list of resource people, books, articles, audiovisual materials, and professional preparation data. Each source is coded to identify the area to which it is applicable. Free upon request.

————. *Information Sheet: Physical Education and Recreation for the Visually Handicapped.* Washington, D.C.: 1201 Sixteenth Street, N.W. 20036, 7 pp. Mimeographed. Includes sources of information for providing a complete physical activity program for the visually handicapped. Free upon request.

————. *Physical Activities for the Mentally Retarded* (*Ideas for Instruction*). Washington, D.C.: 1201 Sixteenth Street, N.W. 20036, 1968. Provides instruction in activities promoting fundamental motor development and the exploration of general areas of skill; designed for use by physical education instructors, classroom teachers, parents, and recreation personnel.

————. *Practical Guide for Teaching the Mentally Retarded to Swim.* Washington, D.C.: 1201 Sixteenth Street, N.W. 20036, 1969. Designed to help professionals and volunteers teach the mentally retarded to swim better. Sections deal with the instructional staff, volunteers and aides, preservice and in-service training, community involvement, and includes creative approaches which have been used successfully in aquatic programs.

————. *Programming for the Mentally Retarded in Physical Education and Recreation.* Washington, D.C.: 1201 Sixteenth Street, N.W. 20036, 1968. Includes material on recreation and day care for the mentally retarded; a community recreation team approach to programming; play facilities and equipment; the role of motor activities in programs for the retarded; and recreation programming for the adult retardate.

————. *Resource Guide in Sex Education for the Mentally Retarded.* Washington, D.C.: 1201 Sixteenth Street, N.W. 20036, 1971, 56 pp. Designed to help educators, counselors, volunteers, parents, and others concerned with the growth, development, and welfare of the mentally retarded. Developed around four major topical areas: awareness of self; physical changes and understanding of self; peer relationships; and responsibility to society as men and women.

————. *Special Fitness Test Manual.* Washington, D.C.: 1201 Sixteenth Street, N.W. 20036, 1968, 56 pp. Explains the development of the test which was adapted from the AAHPER Youth Fitness Test, and describes each of the seven test items and tells how each is administered. National norms for mentally retarded boys and girls ages 8 to 18 are presented along with standards of eligibility for each award.

————. *Tin Can Craft: For Camping or Arts and Crafts Fun.* Washington, D.C.: 1201 Sixteenth Street, N.W. 20036, 8 pp. Mimeographed. Provides projects that can be incorporated in a recreation/outdoor education or classroom program for the handicapped child. Includes illustrations, lists of necessary materials, and procedures. Free upon request.

BARSCH, RAY H. "Cognitive Stress and Movement," *Enriching Perception and Cognition: Techniques for Teachers*, Vol. II. Seattle: Special Child Publications, 1968, pp. 286–97. Provides examples of integrating motor and cognitive skills.

CARLSON, BERNICE WELLS, and DAVID R. GINGLEND. *Recreation for Retarded Teenagers and Young Adults.* Nashville: Abington Press, 1968. An excellent resource book of music, games, parties, sports, handicrafts, nature interests and hobbies for the mentally retarded.

CHANEY, CLARA M., and NEWELL C. KEPHART. *Motoric Aids to Perceptual Training.* Columbus, Ohio: Charles E. Merrill Books, Inc., 1968. Presents basic motor and perceptual activities for training children with learning disorders, including the brain-injured and retarded. Includes sections dealing with the theoretical basis for such training, evaluation of behavior, and detailed descriptions of actual training activities and programs.

CRATTY, BRYANT J. *Developmental Games for Physically Handicapped Children.* Palo Alto, Calif.: Peek Publications, 1969, 52 pp. Provides a series of games modified to provide physical activities commensurate with the needs of the physically handicapped. Includes a fine selection of activities for children confined to a wheelchair.

DOOLITTLE, JOHN H. *Challenge to Change: Program Guidelines in Physical Education for the Mentally Retarded.* Harrisburg, Pa.: Pennsylvania State Department of Education, September, 1970. An easy-to-read paperback that provides the teacher with an overview of the mental retardation problem in the United States, general characteristics of retardates, teaching methods, and detailed testing and curriculum materials.

ENDRES, RICHARD W. *A Year-Round Camping and Outdoor Center for the Mentally Retarded.* Washington, D.C.: AAHPER, Unit on Programs for the Handicapped, 1201 Sixteenth Street, N.W. 20036, 45 pp. Mimeographed. A research study that provides a wealth of information regarding outdoor education for the mentally retarded. Includes a topical outline of the major areas, with the specific sources of resource materials needed (pp. 26–36). Free upon request.

FAIT, HOLLIS F. *Special Physical Education: Adapted, Corrective, Developmental*, 2nd ed. Philadelphia: W. B. Saunders Company, 1966. Provides the elementary and secondary teacher with practical methods of teaching physical education to handicapped children. Principal handicaps considered are orthopedic, neurological, postural, cardiac, visual, auditory, allergic, and nutritional.

Hunt, Valerie V. *Recreation for the Handicapped*. Englewood Cliffs, N.J.: Prentice-Hall, Inc., 1955. Practical aid for teachers, recreational personnel, or parents working with the handicapped. Provides detailed guidelines for the planning of a recreation program for the disabled.

Kelly, Ellen Davis. *Adapted and Corrective Physical Education*, 4th ed. New York: The Ronald Press Company, 1965. An excellent reference book for teachers of the handicapped. Presents theories, methods and techniques for working with the physically sub-par, physically handicapped, and those students who require adaptations of physical activity to meet their individual needs.

Klein, Karl K., and William L. Hall. *The Knee in Athletics*. Washington, D.C.: AAHPER, 1201 Sixteenth Street, N.W. 20036, 1963, 49 pp. Focuses on preventative measures and the importance of correct rehabilitative techniques. Includes an explanation and illustration of an exercise bench which can be constructed; the bench can be used to strengthen the hamstring and quadriceps muscles (see Fig. 8–1, p. 191, for a picture of the bench).

Lipsitz, Lawrence, ed. "Education of the Handicapped and Educational Technology," *Educational Technology*, X, No. 8 (1970), 64 pp. (whole no.). Reviews some of the latest advances in educational technology for working with the handicapped, such as closed circuit television for the partially sighted, region media centers for the deaf, and the work of the National Center on Educational Media and Materials for the Handicapped.

Rathbone, Josephine L., and Valerie V. Hunt. *Corrective Physical Education*, 7th ed. Philadelphia: W. B. Saunders Company, 1965. Explains the basic principles and techniques of corrective physical education. Includes programs for the physically underdeveloped and intellectually and emotionally maladjusted. Other areas dealt with are basic principles of neurology, orthopedic disabilities, and basic physical therapy.

Williams, Marian, and Catherine Worthingham. *Therapeutic Exercise*. Philadelphia: W. B. Saunders Company, 1957. Includes principles of exercise and relaxation and stretching. The 400 illustrations provide the reader with a sound understanding of the kinesiological principles which underlie prescriptive programming for the physically sub-par student.

III

AVAILABILITY AND SOLICITATION OF FUNDS FOR PROGRAMMING

9

local, state, and federal funding

Ever since our forefathers landed on the shores of America, they have clung tenaciously to their conviction that local school districts should have complete and autonomous control over the education of their young. However, the advent of the atomic age has ushered in an era of educational fermentation, an era whereby the cost of educating each pupil has skyrocketed. Thus, local municipalities have by necessity been forced to clamor for a greater share of state and federal funds. The provincialism of local school districts is abating as the present tax structure for supporting education places increasingly overburdening financial demands on the individual citizen.

To heed the outcry of the general populace for improved mass education, federal and state funds for education have been dramatically increased during the 1960s. For example, from 1963 to 1967 federal aid to education increased from $2.2 billion per year to $10.2 billion per year.[1] Educators should be cognizant of the many and diverse sources of these funds for their potential use. (Unfortunately, many school districts and states have not effectively disseminated this information to their teachers.) It is even more imperative that the physical educator or special educator be thoroughly conversant with all sources of funds because of the general public's apathy and reticence to meet their obligation to educate all handicapped children.

Knowledge of available funds is essential because agencies have realized the dire need for improving the lot of the handicapped child and as a con-

[1] Charles A. Quattlebaum, *Federal Educational Policies, Programs and Proposals: A Survey and Handbook, Part I, Background; Issues; Relevant Considerations* (Washington, D.C.: U.S. Government Printing Office, 1968), p. 3.

sequence have *specifically* appropriated funds for that purpose. For example, amendments to Title III, Elementary and Secondary Education Act (ESEA), in 1970 required that "15% of the total state allocation be expended in projects for the handicapped."[2]

In Chapter 9 we will attempt to inform teachers of the handicapped of sources of financial assistance. Reference is made to both specific and general sources of funds or services via local, state, or federal agencies.

Local Funding

Despite the urgent need for improved programming, teacher education, and research, very few school districts in the United States have made funds available at the local level. Critics of our educational system are numerous; supporters of research and innovative programs, however, are difficult to locate. Industry has always been aware of the need for continued research so that it can effectively serve mankind. However, this same attitude has not prevailed within the educational community. Only very progressive school districts will submit annual school budgets which allocate as much as 1 percent of the total expenditures for research and innovating programming (1 percent is generally accepted nationally as a minimal necessary figure).

One constant source of irritation is that teachers who want to start programs for the handicapped will often ask, "Where can I get funds to start a program?" Or they will comment, "Our school district will permit me to implement a physical education program for the handicapped if I can locate the necessary funds." Although school districts should investigate all sources of supplementary funds, it is the prime duty and obligation of every local school district to educate *all* students. State and federal authorities support the philosophy that the local communities are responsible for educating their youth, which is evidenced by the fact that most funding applications will include a clear, definitive statement that there will be a gradual "phasing out" of state- or federally-supported funds (usually a three- to five-year period). At the end of that period, it is assumed that the financial support of the program will be provided at the local level.

It often seems that there are no funds available at the local level but this is not really true; there may not be finances appropriated specifically for programs for the handicapped, but surplus funds are always available for unanticipated contingencies. The essence of the entire chapter is condensed in the next statement: anyone can get financial assistance (be it on the local, state, or federal level) if he is willing to make the necessary sacrifices in terms

---

[2] New Jersey State Department of Education, "Special Education 1970 Title III Applications" (Trenton, N. J.: Division of Curriculum and Instruction, December 3, 1970), p. 1.

of time and effort and if he conducts a comprehensive public relations campaign. One must remember that parents and administrators are vitally interested in the welfare of their youth, but they are bombarded with requests for financial assistance from many sources. The teacher who wants financial assistance to implement a program for the handicapped must make explicit the values that are to be derived by the children involved. The historical background of the Township of Ocean School District's developmental and adapted physical education program should clarify the need for tireless efforts and continual public relations.

Phase One : Funds for Postural Screening, Grades 9–12

Subjective posture screening by the physical education staff during the 1965–1966 school year revealed the possibility of an abnormally high percentage of students with postural deficiencies. With no funds available for individual screening and insufficient teaching personnel, the writer decided to submit a detailed report of his tentative findings to the superintendent of schools. He also recommended that two part-time staff members be hired to screen all the high school students. After an interview with the superintendent, $2,143 was granted to hire one part-time male physical educator for the 1966–1967 school year.

Phase Two : Funds for Identification of Students in Need of a D&A Program, Grades K–12

Although the D&A program was initially funded under Title III of ESEA, it could not be submitted to the federal government until approval was granted by the local board of education. The writer compiled student medical history data (with the assistance of the school nurses) and presented a comprehensive report to the board of education. All efforts were focused on apprising board members of the approximate number of students who had physical, mental, or socioemotional problems and thus were in need of individualized physical education programs. After careful deliberation, the physical education grant proposal "Optimum Fitness for All" (OFFA) was approved by the board of education (the salient features of the proposal will be discussed in Chapter 10). Regardless of whether a request is granted, the image of physical education and physical educators in a district will be enhanced if the proposal submitted is sound and well-documented.

Phase Three : Funds for Program Implementation, Grades 9–12

Project OFFA was conducted during the 1967–1968 school year for the purpose of identifying all the handicapped students in the district. However, the 1968–1969 continuation federal grant requested to implement the program was denied. As illustrated earlier in the text, a sound, concerted effort by all staff members working with the handicapped in the high school had convinced the high school principal of the need for the program. To keep the program running with less money, teacher assignments were adjusted and existing facilities better utilized. The initial part-time program was so successful that a regular classroom was designated for teaching D&A during the 1969–1970 school year and additional staff members were hired so that a D&A class was available for 35 of the 40 school periods each week.

Phase Four: Funds to Implement a Summer Program, Grades K–8

Several discussions between the school physicians, school nurse, and the writer resulted in a meeting with the board of education to stress the need for program expansion to the elementary level. To eliminate or ameliorate the physical, mental, and socioemotional problems afflicting the youth of the district, the physicians recommended a daily period of physical education and a summer D&A program for the students in grades K–8. The supportive evidence presented induced the board to approve the summer program as a pilot study. (Although to date, physical education is not offered on a daily basis, the board of education is aware of the need and has approved the hiring of additional physical education specialists.)

In spite of the late approval granted to conduct the summer program, it was very successful (see Appendix B for an overview of program implementation, layout of facilities, and test scores). The main contributing factor to the success of the total program was probably parental involvement. Interested parents were encouraged to assist the teachers at various teaching stations and to attend the final day which was devoted to parental conferences. The written report to the superintendent of schools and the board of education[3] is presented below in its entirety because of its inherent value as a tool for sound public relations:

SUMMER DEVELOPMENTAL AND ADAPTED PHYSICAL EDUCATION PROGRAM

As a result of the letters mailed to parents, 68 students were registered in the six-week D&A summer program. The classification of students were: postural deficiencies, 13; asthmatic, 2; orthopedic, 2; medical problems, 5; and motor–perceptual–coordination problems, 46.

Testing Program   The testing phase involved a pretest administered during the first week and a post-test conducted during the last week of the six-week

---

[3] Thomas M. Vodola, "Summer Developmental and Adapted Physical Education Program" (Oakhurst, N.J.: Township of Ocean School District, August 12, 1969), 2 pp.

program Each student was tested to ascertain his or her level (prior to and at the end of the program) in terms of gross body coordination, hand/eye coordination, hand/eye accuracy, foot/eye accuracy, gross body balance, arm strength, leg strength, abdominal strength, laterality/directionality, speed, endurance, and endurance index. Raw scores were converted to standard scores and each child's average standard score was computed.

Those students with problems other than motor–perceptual were administered the motor–perceptual battery, plus other tests specific to their needs such as posture screening and examination, etc.

Instructional Program   As a result of the pretest, each child had an individual program prescribed on a 5 × 8″ card. During the course of each period, the students rotated to areas of need, performed their tasks, and had their cards initialed by either the instructor or one of four student assistants. A high motivation level was maintained by affording each student the opportunity to participate in activities of his choice *after he completed his prescribed program.*

Prescribed programs involved ocular pursuits, peg board activities, assembling puzzles, drawing, coloring, cutting out pictures, movement exploration activities, strength and endurance activities, individual and dual games, posture exercises, and specific exercises to increase strength and range of motion in atrophied limbs.

Program Evaluation

1. Direct   All students made significant overall gains as a result of the individual programs. Group gains revealed similar results. One asthmatic child increased vital capacity by approximately 25 percent, thus allowing her to breathe easier and to withstand attacks.

An analysis of individual component scores revealed a general weakness in leg, arm, and abdominal strength and a high correlation between low abdominal and arm strength scores and postural deficiencies. It is apparent that elementary physical education curricula should be reevaluated, with consideration given to increasing time allotments.

2. Indirect   Anecdotal comments written at the conclusion of the pre- and post-tests indicated that major individual and group gains had both social and psychological implications. Comments revealed increased sociability and attention span, psychological adjustments, and enhanced self-image.

From the first day of the program, parents were invited to observe the instructional program. On August 11th (the last day of the program) a conference was held with all interested parents; approximately 40 parents attended. Student progress was reviewed and parents were informed as to what they could do to aid in the progress of their children.

Parental response to the program was extremely complimentary. Most stated that their children had been initially reluctant to attend a "remedial" physical education program, but most of the negative attitudes had changed to enthusiasm shortly thereafter. Parental remarks such as, "I have noted a definite improvement in my child's posture," were commonplace. One parent even wrote a full-page feature story for a local newspaper extolling the virtues of the D&A program.

Summary Remarks   The superintendent of schools and the board of education are to be complimented for providing a program for the handicapped children of the township. From all indications, the program was extremely successful.

By the same token, the results have reinforced the convictions of the program director and school physicians that if we are to truly meet the needs of all students in the Township of Ocean School District, we must implement all proposals submitted to the board this past June. In addition, it is recommended that the D&A program be added to our summer school each year.

Parental support of the program was concretely illustrated by over 40 letters that were written to building principals, the superintendent of schools, and the board of education. The parents thanked all involved and urged that the program be implemented in the elementary grades during the following school year. This unanimous support was acknowledged by the board of education by authorizing the chief school administrator to hire two full-time physical educators to teach the handicapped starting the following September (authorization was given in August). The foregoing illustrates just how a program for the handicapped can be successfully implemented when no funds are initially allocated. It is clear that school officials are interested in children and will provide the necessary funds if a teacher can substantiate the value of his proposal.

Additional local funds may be attained through parental associations or local committees and organizations who are interested in promoting better services for handicapped children. Most of these agencies are vitally interested in assisting the local school districts in any capacity. Although their funds are usually limited, they are very responsive to any suggestions that would enhance the educational opportunities for the atypical child. In fact, these local agencies need leadership; they are zealous in their desires and possess organizational strength, but they need someone to show them how they can be of assistance.

If one wishes to implement a program for the handicapped, one should contact all local organizations that already aid the handicapped and offer one's services as a guest speaker to apprise members of the existing situation and solicit their help. Here is a fertile field for public support. These people are vitally concerned since many are themselves parents of children with learning disabilities. The united efforts of these people may furnish the impetus necessary for program implementation.

State Funding

Prior to the 1900s states were providing very limited services for the handicapped child. These services were provided in special residential schools and were very often restricted to the blind, the deaf, and the mentally deficient.

After the turn of the century state leaders realized it would be less costly if these handicapped children were educated in the public schools, which marked the advent of special education. However, local communities resisted setting up special classes since they had to bear the cost of programs which were two or three times more expensive than the cost of educating nonhandicapped children.[4] In an effort to encourage program implementation, legislators throughout the United States sponsored legislation to provide funds to subsidize local school districts. At the present time, all states provide funds for special education (vis differing formulas) to incorporate special education programs as part of the regular school instructional program.[5] In spite of these efforts by local and state authorities (even with federal assistance), however, "a recent survey by the Bureau of Education for the Handicapped found that over 15,000 school districts across the country are offering appropriate special education services to less than half of the handicapped children within their districts."[6]

The partial subsidization of special education classes by state authorities has seldom benefitted the handicapped child in terms of his physical/recreational needs. Most legislation that has been enacted has made provisions for self-contained classrooms for teaching the "3 R's" to the mentally retarded (although recently classes have been organized for the deaf, the blind, the emotionally disturbed, and the orthopedically handicapped). Very little progress has been made in terms of providing physical education programs commensurate with the needs of the physically, mentally, and socioemotionally handicapped. California and Pennsylvania are the only two states in the country that have *explicitly* mandated physical education programs for all children in their public schools.

Careful scrutiny of the legislation enacted in the other states will reveal that, in most cases, *implicit statements* have been made in reference to meeting the total needs of the child, not just the mental needs. Such is the case with the legislation enacted in New Jersey on behalf of the handicapped. A detailed analysis (with recommendations) of present New Jersey statutes is presented to (1) provide administrators and physical educators within the state with the information necessary to justify the establishment of an individualized program for the handicapped that will be subsidized (50 percent) by state funds,[7] and (2) provide guidelines for educators in other states who are interested in pursuing similar goals. All statutes referred to may be located in Title 8, Chapter 28, of the New Jersey Administrative Code.[8]

[4] Samuel A. Kirk, "Handicapped Children," in *Notes and Working Papers Concerning the Administration of Programs Authorized Under Title III of Public Law 89–10, The Elementary and Secondary Act of 1965 as Amended by Public Law 88–750* (Washington, D.C.: U.S. Government Printing Office, 1967), p. 231.

[5] *Ibid.*, p. 232.

[6] James W. Moss, *Background Paper on Special Programs for Handicapped Children and Youth for the 1970 White House Conference on Children and Youth* (Washington, D.C.: U.S. Department of Health, Education and Welfare, Office of Education/Bureau for the Handicapped, December 1970), p. 32.

[7] It should be noted that the Township of Ocean School District is presently being funded under Title 8, Chapter 28 on a pilot study basis and has applied for subsidization on the strength of supplementary services provided.

[8] New Jersey State Department of Education, "Rules and Regulations Pursuant to Title

Introduction, Title 8, Chapter 28–1.[9] The legislation specifically requires each local public school district to identify and classify all handicapped children between the ages of 5 and 20 and to provide a special education program for them.

Comments   The law is quite specific: *all* handicapped children must be identified, classified, and provided with a special instructional program. A review of the statutes of other states will reveal similar all-inclusion statements.

General considerations, Title 8, Chapter 28–2.[10] A child shall be considered handicapped under Chapter 46 of Title 18A when he is impaired physically, emotionally, intellectually or socially to such extent that without the aid of special facilities, special professional staff, special supplies and equipment, special time schedules, and/or special methods of instruction he would not function educationally in a manner similar to that of children not so impaired.

Comments   Article 2 clearly states that any child who manifests a disability to the extent that he cannot benefit educationally from the regular instructional program shall be considered handicapped. Once again the statement is all-inclusive. The child with an impairment that precludes him from participation in the unrestricted physical education program is, thus, a prime candidate for classification. However, such classification is only justifiable if the administration provides the staff with facilities, supplies, and equipment and an individualized program. Financial support is not provided for instruction conducted within the regular physical education program.

Identification, Title 8, Chapter 28–3.[11] The identification process may involve the judgment of teachers, medical and health professionals, school administrators, special services personnel, parents, and/or agencies concerned with the welfare of children. The identification process shall include a planned screening procedure. Every effort should be made to identify the preschool handicapped child in the district.

Comments   The identification process must be very comprehensive. Examination and classification must be based on reports submitted by members of the school district's special services team: physician, psychologist, learning disabilities specialist, social worker, and other appropriate personnel (see Appendix A for a copy of a Child Study Team Referral Form). In situations wherein school districts do not have such personnel in their employ, special approval must be granted by the commissioner of education *prior* to employing the services of said professionals on a per case basis.

18A, Chapter 46, New Jersey Statutes" (June 14, 1970), Title 8, Chapter 28, New Jersey Administration Code (Trenton, N.J.: Division of Curriculum and Instruction/Bureau of Special Education and Pupil Personnel Services), 22 pp.

[9] *Ibid.*, p. 1.

[10] *Ibid.*

[11] *Ibid.*, pp. 2–3.

Classification, Title 8, Chapter 28–4.[12] Local boards of education shall provide for such diagnostic examinations as are necessary to determine the need of special education programs for pupils who manifest disabilities in one or more of the following areas:

1. Mentally retarded

2. Visually handicapped

3. Auditorily handicapped

4. Communication handicapped

5. Neurologically or perceptually impaired
  (a) Neurologically impaired
  (b) Perceptually impaired

6. Orthopedically handicapped

7. Chronically ill

8. Emotionally disturbed

9. Socially malajusted

10. Multiply handicapped

Comments   The physical educator/recreation specialist who has taught children with any of the listed learning disabilities can attest to the need for a special instructional program. To comply with state statutes the teacher should develop a course of study for the handicapped.[13] Included in the curriculum guidelines should be: specific diagnostic pretests, individualized tasks, exercises, or activities, and evaluation procedures.

Definitions, Title 8, Chapter 28–4.[14] *Orthopedically handicapped.* A child shall be classified as orthopedically handicapped who, because of malformation, malfunction or loss of bones, muscle or tissue needs a special educational program, special equipment or special facilities to permit normal learning processes to function.

Comments   Children with severe postural abnormalities such as a double spinal curvature can be classified as orthopedically handicapped. After the school physician identifies the handicap, the teacher should have the student practice the exercises approved by the physician and then apply appropriate evaluation techniques to assess student progress (see Chapter 7 for an explanation of evaluation procedures). All data pertaining to each child must be recorded and kept in an individual folder. Using a similar procedure, children with other disabilities that are in accord with the definition can be included in the state-subsidized program.

[12] *Ibid.*
[13] The author will forward a copy of the Township of Ocean's course of study, grades K–8, upon request. Write Dr. Thomas M. Vodola, Ocean Township High School, West Park Avenue, Oakhurst, New Jersey 07755.
[14] New Jersey State Department of Education, *op. cit.*, p. 9.

Definitions, Title 8, Chapter 28–4.[15] *Chronically ill.* A child who, because of illness such as tuberculosis, epilepsy, lowered vitality, cardiac condition, leukemia, asthma, malnutrition, pregnancy, or other physical disabilities which are otherwise uncategorized but make it impractical for the child to receive adequate instruction through the regular school program shall be classified under the category of chronically ill.

Comments   The category of chronically ill provides justification for including the child with low physical vitality. Recommended for inclusion would be those students who score in the bottom 5 or 10 percent of the school population in terms of muscular strength, muscular endurance and, particularly, cardiorespiratory endurance. With the addition of those students with nutritional deficiencies, breathing allergies, cardiac conditions, postoperative conditions, convalescent and other physical disabilities, this category will include the greatest portion of students in the D&A program.

Placement and programs, Title 8, Chapter 28–5.[16] Children classified as handicapped shall be the primary instructional responsibility of a teacher certified to teach pupils so disabled. Such teachers shall provide instruction designed to correct or compensate for the disability. . . .
Handicapped children may be served in an appropriate educational program on any of the following bases, but not necessarily in the order named:

a. Instruction at school supplementary to the other programs in the school whenever, in the judgment of the board of education with the consent of the Commissioner, the handicapped pupil will best be served thereby. . . .
b. Individualized instruction at home or in school whenever in the judgment of the board of education with the consent of the Commissioner it is impractical to provide a suitable special education program for a child.

Criteria for approval of special education programs, Title 8, Chapter 28–7.[17] Participation in regular school activity program shall be provided to the extent that the capabilities of the child permit as determined by the child study team. All services (e.g., shop, art, music, home economics, etc.) extended to so-called normal children shall be provided for the handicapped.

Comments   Previous reference has been made to the fact that physical educators do not need special certification to provide instructional programs for the handicapped. The standard educational preparation of the physical educator provides him with the expertise necessary to prescribe programs for students whose disabilities are caused by motor or physical fitness inadequacies. As for the handicapped classified in other categories (assuming the teacher follows the philosophy of the writer), the teacher would not prescribe for them but would guide and assist the students to perform activities recommended by members of the child study team.

[15] *Ibid.,* p. 10.
[16] *Ibid.,* p. 11.
[17] *Ibid.,* p. 15.

Physical education programs for the handicapped in New Jersey may be authorized for funding if they provide supplemental services or individualized instruction. (The program recommended in the text makes specific provisions for supplemental services and individualized instruction.) It should be obvious that the postoperative/convalescent pupil will *not* be best served either by complete inactivity or by admittance to the unrestricted program. Similarly, team games and sports are *not* designed to meet the needs of the asthmatic or the student with a severe postural abnormality.

Although no specific reference in New Jersey statutes is made to the provision of physical education for the handicapped, the Branch of Special Education and Pupil Personnel Services has established as one of their goals for the 1970s[18]:

That every handicapped child will have an opportunity to participate in all educational programs and services available to all children within a local school district *commensurate with his needs* (Vocational, Industrial, Music, Physical Education, etc.) [italics mine].

Further, in a conference with New Jersey State Senator Alfred N. Beadleston regarding state legislation for the handicapped, he stated: "As I interpret the law, every school district in New Jersey is charged with the responsibility of providing physical education programs commensurate with the needs of their handicapped."[19]

It is quite evident that although all references to a physical education program geared to meet the needs of handicapped children in New Jersey public schools are merely implied in the statutes, it is still the responsibility of each local school district to implement such programs. Further, if the districts comply with the statutory regulations in terms of staff, programming, and facilities, each district is entitled to a reimbursement of 50 percent of the expenditures for personnel and programming and 75 percent of the costs incurred for transportation.

An attempt has been made to provide the reader with excerpts from Title 8, Chapter 28, of the New Jersey Administrative Code that specifically imply that the current law mandates that each local school district in New Jersey *must* implement *total* educational programs for all handicapped children, and that such programs would be reimbursable. For a complete copy of the New Jersey Statutes pertaining to the handicapped, the reader is requested to contact the Branch of Special Education and Pupil Personnel Services.[20] These statutes are similar to those of many other states.

[18] Daniel Ringleheim, "Equal Opportunity for all Handicapped Children," in *Bureau Briefs*, II, No. 2 (Trenton, N.J.: New Jersey State Department of Education, 1970), 2.

[19] Conference with the Honorable Alfred N. Beadleston, Senate Majority Leader, Fifth District, Monmouth County, N.J., March 30, 1971.

[20] New Jersey State Department of Education, *op. cit.*

Administrators and educators who would like to implement physical education/recreation programs within their states are urged to (1) investigate their present state-mandated statutes pertaining to the handicapped; (2) design programs to comply with those rules and regulations; and (3) submit requests for state subsidization. The urgent need for such action is based on the fact that of the meager funds available for the handicapped, the local school districts and states currently provide the greatest available sources of financial aid for education.[21]

Federal Funding

Of the participants in the tripartite relationship (local, state, and federal), the federal government contributes the least amount of financial support for educational programs. Table 9–1, compiled by Moss, clearly illustrates this relationship. Even considering the dramatic increase in federal assistance from 1959 to 1969, the local/state partnership contributes almost 93 percent of the funds for public education. If one were to consider the contributory relationship of the three agencies for educating the handicapped, the total relationship would be even more disparate—with a much smaller percentage contributed by the federal government. The low financial priority which is accorded to programs for the handicapped was forcefully brought to the attention of the federal authorities by the delegates to the 1970 White House Conference on Children and Youth. Forum 12 (the committees that devoted one week to discussing the handicapped child) concluded their efforts by submitting three major recommendations for federal implementation. Of the three, one dealt with the dire need for additional funding[22]:

[21] Moss, *loc. cit.*
[22] Report of Forum 12, "Children Who Are Handicapped" (Washington, D.C.: White House Conference on Children, May, 1971), p. 6.

TABLE 9–1   Percent Contributions to Public School Funding

SCHOOL YEAR	FEDERAL	STATE	LOCAL
1919–1920	0.3	16.5	83.2
1929–1930	0.4	16.9	82.7
1939–1940	1.8	30.3	68.0
1949–1950	2.0	39.8	57.3
1959–1960	4.4	30.1	56.5
1968–1969	7.3	40.7	52.0

Source: Reprinted from James W. Moss, *Background Paper on Special Programs for Handicapped Children and Youth for the 1970 White House Conference on Children and Youth* (Washington, D.C.: U.S. Department of Health, Education and Welfare, Office of Education/Bureau for the Handicapped, December, 1970), Table 6A, p. 33.

Full Appropriation of Funds. Congress has recognized the need for these programs but has not appropriated the funds authorized. We recommend the immediate and full appropriation of these funds, especially for those programs which focus on manpower training and the provision of services for the handicapped.

In explanation of their recommendation, the delegates added:

In view of the special health service and manpower requirements of the child with developmental and acquired disabilities, we urge the immediate full funding of all authorized special programs and services. One example of a bill with a large authorization for which there is not a full appropriation is Public Law 91–517, "Developmental Disabilities Services and Facilities Construction Amendments of 1970." It provides for "interdisciplinary training programs for personnel needed to render specialized services."

Full appropriation of authorized funds as well as additional funds are necessary to achieve a high priority for child health care and to develop the recommended systems for meeting the health and other needs of all children. The United States can afford to buy what its people need and will do so if all of us join in making our needs and wishes known. Only thirteen cents of each tax dollar now goes for health, education, and welfare. Furthermore, we spend nine dollars of our national budget annually on each adult, but only one dollar on each child.

However dismal this picture may look, the future of federal funds for the handicapped is much brighter. For example, in 1959 approximately $1 million in federal funds were invested in education for the handicapped; in 1970 this figure increased to $170 million.[23] Also, since the mid-1960s funds have been made available to local school districts for establishing and improving programs for children with all types of handicaps. (Prior to that time most funds had been appropriated for research, leadership, and the establishment of an administrative hierarchy.)

The Bureau of Education for the Handicapped of the United States Office of Education is the single most important source of information for educators of the handicapped. A majority of the legislation enacted into law on behalf of the handicapped is administered or monitored by this Bureau. Table 9–2, compiled by the Bureau, has been reprinted in its entirety to provide the reader with all the necessary information for applying for federal funds.

Of particular interest is the specific reference to funds available for physical education and recreation: $300,000 for research related to the handicapped and $700,000 for training physical educators and recreation personnel for handicapped children. Not until the enactment of the Elementary and Secondary Education Act of 1965 were funds made available so that school districts could submit physical education grant requests to the federal government.

The trend toward increased funding for physical education/recreation programs for the handicapped has resulted in an increase in research, in-

---

[23] Moss, *op. cit.*, p. 35.

TABLE 9-2 Federal Programs Administered or Monitored by the Bureau of Education for the Handicapped.
U.S. Office of Education, Fiscal Year 1971 Appropriation (Total, $197, 767, 633)

TYPE OF ASSISTANCE	AUTHORIZATION	PURPOSE	APPROPRIATION FY 1971	WHO MAY APPLY	WHERE TO GET INFORMATION
Services					
Programs for the handicapped, preschool, elementary and secondary	Education of the Handicapped Act, P.L. 91–230, Part B	To strengthen educational and related services for handicapped, preschool, elementary and secondary children	$34,000,000	Local agencies apply to state departments of education.	Division of Educational Services, Bureau of Education for the Handicapped
Programs for the handicapped in state-supported schools	Elementary and Secondary Ed. Act, Title I (P.L. 89–313, amended)	To strengthen education programs for children in state-operated or -supported schools for the handicapped	$46,129,772	Eligible state agencies apply to state departments of education.	Division of Educational Services, Bureau of Education for the Handicapped
Title III, supplementary educational centers and services	Title III, Elementary and Secondary Education Act, as amended	To provide grants for supplementary, innovative, or exemplary projects for the educational improvement of the handicapped	$16,438,116 (represents 15% of state's total Title III allotment)	Local education agencies apply to state departments of education.	Division of Educational Services, Bureau of Education for the Handicapped; or Division of Plans and Supplementary Centers, Bureau of Elementary and Secondary Education
Early education for handicapped children	Education of the Handicapped Act, P.L. 91–230, Part C, Section 623	To develop model preschool and early education programs for handicapped children	$ 7,000,000	Public agencies and private nonprofit agencies	Division of Educational Services, Bureau of Education for the Handicapped
Vocational education programs for the handicapped	Vocational education amendments of 1968	To provide vocational education and services to handicapped children	$30,750,000 (represents 10% of the basic state allotment under Part B of the 1968 amendment to the Voc. Ed. Act)	Local educational agencies apply to state departments of education.	Division of Vocational Technical Education, Bureau of Adult, Vocational and Technical Education Regional Office; or Division of Educational Services, Bureau of Education for the Handicapped

Program	Authority	Purpose	Amount	Eligibility	Administering Agency
Media services and captioned film loan program	Education of the Handicapped Act, P.L. 91–230, Part F	(A) To advance the handicapped through film and other media including a captioned film loan service for cultural and educational enrichment for the deaf	$ 6,000,000	State or local public agencies and schools, organizations, or groups which serve the handicapped, their parents, employers, or potential employers	Division of Educational Services, Bureau of Education for the Handicapped
		(B) To contract for research in use of educational and training films and other educational media for the handicapped, and for their production and distribution	(included above)	By invitation	Division of Educational Services, Bureau of Education for the Handicapped
		(C) To contract for training persons in the use of educational media for the handicapped	(included above)	Public or other nonprofit institutions of higher education for teachers, trainees or other specialists	Division of Educational Services, Bureau of Education for the Handicapped
		(D) To establish and operate a national center on educational media	(included above)	Institutions of higher education	Division of Educational Services, Bureau of Education for the Handicapped
Deaf-blind centers	Education of the Handicapped Act, P.L. 91–230, Part C, Section 622	To develop centers and services for deaf-blind children and parents	$ 4,500,000	State education agencies, universities, medical centers, public or nonprofit agencies	Division of Educational Services, Bureau of Education for the Handicapped
Information and recruitment	Education of the Handicapped Act, P.L. 91–230, Part D, Section 633	To improve recruitment of educational personnel and dissemination of information on educational opportunities for the handicapped	$ 500,000	Public or nonprofit agencies, organizations, private agencies	Division of Educational Services, Bureau of Education for the Handicapped

TABLE 9-2 (cont.)

244

TYPE OF ASSISTANCE	AUTHORIZATION	PURPOSE	APPROPRIATION FY 1971	WHO MAY APPLY	WHERE TO GET INFORMATION
Programs for children with specific learning disabilities	Education of the Handicapped Act, P.L. 91–230, Part G, Section 661	To provide for research, training of personnel and to establish and operate model centers for children with specific learning disabilities	$ 1,000,000	Institutions of higher education, state and local educational agencies and other public and nonprofit agencies	Division of Educational Services, Bureau of Education for the Handicapped
Research					
Regional resource centers for improvement of education for handicapped children	Education of the Handicapped Act, P.L. 91–230, Part C, Section 621	To develop centers for educational diagnosis and remediation of handicapped children	$ 3,550,000	Institutions of higher education and state education agencies, or combinations within particular regions	Division of Research, Bureau of Education for the Handicapped
Handicapped research and related activities	Education of the Handicapped Act, P.L. 91–230, Part E, Section 641	To promote new knowledge and developments with reference to the education of the handicapped	$15,000,000	State or local education agencies and private educational organizations or research organizational groups	Division of Research, Bureau of Education for the Handicapped
Physical education and recreation for the handicapped	Education of the Handicapped Act, P.L. 91–230, Part E, Section 642	To do research in areas of physical education and recreation for handicapped children	$ 300,000	State or local education agencies, public or nonprofit private educational or research agencies and organizations	Division of Research, Bureau of Education for the Handicapped
Training					
Training personnel for the education of the handicapped	Education of the Handicapped Act, P.L. 91–230, Part D, Sections 631, 632	To prepare and inform teachers and others who work in the education of the handicapped	$31,900,000	State education agencies, institutions of higher education, and other appropriate nonprofit institutions or agencies	Division of Training Programs, Bureau of Education for the Handicapped
Training of physical educators and recreation personnel for handicapped children	Education of the Handicapped Act, P.L. 91–230, Part D, Section 634	To train personnel in physical education and recreation for the handicapped	$ 700,000	Institutions of higher education	Division of Training Programs, Bureau of Education for the Handicapped

Total $197,767,633

SOURCE: Reprinted from Bureau of Education for the Handicapped, *Federal Programs Administered and Monitored by the Bureau of Education for the Handicapped* (Washington, D.C.: Department of Health, Education and Welfare, 1971).

novative programming, and general interest in specializing in this important area. Julian U. Stein, Consultant, Programs for the Handicapped for the American Association for Health, Physical Education and Recreation highlighted the profound impact of the trend on AAHPER when he stated:

AAHPER membership has shown great interest in programs for the handicapped since 1965 when the Project on Recreation and Fitness for the Mentally Retarded started. The very fact that the Board of Directors authorized the Unit on Programs for the Handicapped with a full-time consultant in 1968 is an indication in itself of the need and interest. Prior to 1968, no mention was made of any aspect of programs for the handicapped as an area of interest on the general membership card. However, since that time this has been a category in which members designate special interest. Numbers making this designation have ranged between 3,800 and about 5,000. . . . However, our Unit does not just service Association members. Virtually all of our services are also available to nonmembers as well. For example, the *Challenge* mailing list consists of about one-third members, one-third nonmembers, and one-third libraries and agency subscriptions. Approximately 10,000 to 13,000 pieces of mail emanate from our Unit office per year, not including special mailings of various kinds and types. Another indication of increased interest and participation in programs for the handicapped is the attendance at programs at national, district, state, and local conferences and conventions on the subject. . . . Special workshops, seminars, institutes, clinics, in-service programs, classes and courses, and orientation programs are being held in these areas. Interest from other disciplines is also very high and demand for services great.[24]

One important point should be discussed regarding funding at the local, state, or federal level. Reference has been made in the White House Conference Report to the fact that not all funds appropriated for a given year have been authorized by the President for actual use. It is easy to be critical of the federal government, but in the final analysis the onus must be placed on the administrators and teachers in the profession. We must avail ourselves of all information and submit requests for existing funds. If monies that have been appropriated have not been used, it could well be that enough specific requests were not submitted. An excellent example of a lack of knowledge, or general apathy regarding the availability of materials at the federal level is that many surplus items such as computers, office equipment, tools, and a variety of supplies are eventually sold to the public because school districts do not follow simple procedures to acquire these items free of charge. (A letter to the U.S. Surplus Property Utilization Division[25] will procure all necessary information.)

[24] Personnal correspondence with Julian U. Stein, Consultant, Programs for the Handicapped for the American Association for Health, Physical Education and Recreation, Washington, D.C., August 23, 1971. Reprinted by permission.

[25] Office of Surplus Property Utilization, *How to Acquire Federal Surplus Personal Property for Health, Education and Civil Defense Purposes and Federal Surplus Real Property for Health and Educational Purposes* (Washington, D.C.: U.S. Government Printing Office, March, 1969), 12 pp. Free upon request.

To become thoroughly conversant with funds that are available, the reader should contact the sources listed below:

1. Consultant, Program for the Handicapped, The American Association for Health, Physical Education and Recreation.[26] Request materials related to existing programs for the handicapped, latest funds available, and periodical composite reprints of articles published in AAHPER's journal.

2. Department of Health, Education and Welfare.[27] Request material pertaining to the Elementary and Secondary Education Act of 1965. The packet you receive will furnish booklets relating to Title I, Better Schooling for Educationally Deprived Children; Title II, School Library Resources, Textbooks and Other Instructional Materials; Title III, Supplementary Centers and Services; and Title V, Strengthening State Departments of Education.

3. United States Bureau of Education for the Handicapped.[28] Request the brochure which describes the traineeship and fellowship programs supported under Public Law 91–230 in addition to other grant programs for the handicapped (see Appendix E). This office is the single most important source of federal funds for programs for the handicapped.

4. Joseph P. Kennedy, Jr. Foundation.[29] Request a packet of materials on special olympics for the mentally retarded.

5. State department of education (in your state). Request a copy of the existing statutes pertaining to funds available for programs for the handicapped. If you are a New Jersey teacher (or would like a copy of New Jersey laws for reference) write to the Branch of Special Education and Pupil Personnel Services.[30]

6. Defense Logistics Services Center.[31] Request the pamphlet, *How to Buy Surplus Personal Property from the Department of Defense*. The pamphlet furnishes all necessary information for soliciting free governmental supplies and equipment.

7. Office of Field Administration, Surplus Property Utilization Division.[32]

---

[26] Consultant, Programs for the Handicapped, American Association for Health, Physical Education and Recreation, 1201 Sixteenth Street, N.W., Washington, D.C. 20036.

[27] *Elementary and Secondary Education Act of 1965, Titles I–III and V* (Washington, D.C.: U.S. Department of Health, Education and Welfare, Office of Education, n.d.).

[28] Bureau of Education for the Handicapped, *Scholarshop Program*, OE-35059-71 (Washington, D.C.: U.S. Department of Health, Education and Welfare, Division of Training Programs, 1970–1971), 63 pp. Free upon request.

[29] *Special Olympics: A Guide for Local Programs* (Washington, D.C.: The Joseph P. Kennedy, Jr. Foundation, Suite 205, 1701 K Street, N.W., n.d.), 64 pp. Free upon request.

[30] New Jersey State Department of Education, *op. cit.*

[31] *How to Buy Surplus Personal Property from the Department of Defense* (Battle Creek, Mich.: Defense Logistics Services Center, June, 1969), 26 pp. Free upon request.

[32] Office of Surplus Property Utilization, *How to Acquire Federal Surplus Personal Property* (Washington, D.C.: U.S. Department of Health, Education and Welfare, Office of Assistant Secretary for Administration, 1969), 12 pp. Free upon request.

Request their publication on how to acquire federal surplus property.

8. Superintendent of Documents, U.S. Government Printing Office.[33] Request the paperback, *Federal Educational Policies, Programs and Proposals: A Survey and Handbook.* The publication furnishes an overview of the evaluation of federal policies in education, federal support to education in the states, federally operated educational programs, federal educational programs for special groups, and other materials that would furnish the reader with a sound understanding of the general role of the federal government in education.

Summary

The implementation of a program for the handicapped is a costly venture. As a consequence, teachers who wish to initiate a program should avail themselves of all possible financial assistance. This is especially important now, when local, state, and federal authorities have expressed a greater concern for the education of handicapped children and are manifesting this concern by making funds, supplies, equipment, and services more readily available. The teacher will obtain financial support for his program if he:

1. Evidences willingness to devote the time, effort, and continued public relations that are necessary for program implementation (an essential prerequisite)

2. Submits a detailed report to the superintendent of schools (via the respective building principals) of all students who have low physical vitality, poor motor ability, nutritional deficiencies, postural abnormalities, and other medically oriented problems (this report is essential because most administrators are not aware of the magnitude of the problem)

3. Addresses local civic groups and solicits their support

4. Solicits and reviews the statutes in his state which provide funds for special education (all states have passed such legislation)

5. Designs and submits a request for state subsidization of his physical education/recreation program which complies with *all* state statutes

6. Contacts the Bureau of Education for the Handicapped of the U.S. Office of Education, since the Bureau can provide information regarding all federal funds that are available directly from the federal government, or through the state agencies

7. Investigates all other sources of federal funds, supplies, equipment, and services

Annotated Bibliography

AMERICAN ASSOCIATION FOR HEALTH, PHYSICAL EDUCATION AND RECREATION, UNIT ON PROGRAMS FOR THE HANDICAPPED. *Memorandum Regarding Student Financial Assistance.* Washington, D.C.: 1201 Sixteenth Street, N.W. 20036,

---

[33] Quattlebaum, *op. cit.*

3 pp. Mimeographed. Provides federal sources of information to students in need of financial assistance for further schooling related to physical education and recreation for the handicapped. Free upon request.

"Federal Aid: New Directions for Education in 1969–70," *Education U.S.A.* Washington, D.C.: National School Public Relations Association, 1969. 48 pp. Provides excellent referential material regarding sources of funds and complimentary copies of the various Acts. Includes a section devoted to the "Handicapped Children's Assistance Act of 1968."

OFFICE OF EDUCATION. "Regulations Pursuant to Titles I, II and III of the Elementary and Secondary Education Act of 1965," *Federal Register*, XXXII, No. 27, Part II (February 9, 1967), 2724–63. Includes definitions, eligibility requirements, available grants, project applications, and duties and functions of state educational agencies

————. *School Programs for Educationally Deprived Children: Basic Facts for School Administrators.* Washington, D.C.: U.S. Government Printing Office, 1965. 16 pp. Uses a question-and-answer format to explain the Elementary and Secondary Education Act of 1965, Title I. Free upon request.

10

guidelines for submitting
a proposal for financial aid

During the past decade there has been a dramatic increase in state and federal aid to education. However, neither state nor federal agencies have developed a planned, systematic procedure for disseminating the necessary information to the local school districts. As a result, only the more opportunistic districts have availed themselves of funds that have been appropriated. One effective procedure has been to appoint or hire a coordinator of special projects who is usually required to devote his full energies to investigating available sources of funds at the state or federal level.

Teacher-training institutions have also been remiss in that they have generally not included course content related to the development of grant proposals. Since curriculum development or revision, in the public schools or teacher-training institutions, should be structured partially in light of societal changes and since all present evidence points toward a definite trend of increased state and federal funds, each institution should provide all future teachers with the background necessary to develop a sound proposal.

Chapter 10 has been prepared to fill the apparent knowledge void that currently exists. (For example, of the 839 proposals approved in 1965 under Title III of the Elementary and Secondary Act of 1965, only 9 related specifically to physical education.[1] Special education had 76 proposals approved, 14 of which related to the academically talented.) The following discussion will present a step-by-step procedure for designing a sound proposal. The

---

[1] Subcommittee on Education, *Notes and Working Papers Concerning the Administration of Programs Authorized Under Title III of Public Law 89–10. The Elementary and Secondary Education Act of 1965 as Amended by Public Law 89–750* (Washington, D.C.: U.S. Government Printing Office, April, 1967), p. 29.

format was actually used by the author to submit a Title III Planning Grant that was approved (*Optimum Fitness for All*[2]). This format has been presented because it incorporates all the features required in various proposal applications. Also included are the pitfalls that should be avoided and pertinent referential materials that will further aid the reader.

General Data

The first two or three pages of most applications request general information related to the grant proposal. The standard procedure is to request:

1. The official name and address of the local agency submitting the proposal (usually the local board of education)
2. The name, title, and address of the person authorized to receive the grant (usually the superintendent of schools)
3. The name, title, and address of the project director (the person who has written the proposal)
4. The specific grant the applicant is requesting (Title III Planning, or Operational Grant, a state mini-grant, etc.)
5. The total estimated number of students to be served by the proposed project
6. The educational and cultural needs of the group to be served
7. The total personnel to serve on the planning project
8. The estimated cost of the proposed project
9. The sources and amounts of direct federal support other than that which is being requested by the applicant
10. The sources and amounts of nonfederal support

Items 1, 5, and 7 are self-explanatory and thus shall not be elaborated upon at this point. Vodola[3] described the educational and cultural needs of the Township of Ocean students by identifying the students with physical or medical problems (based on a review of physical/medical records) and listing the following program objectives:

This program is designed to identify, classify, and formulate a developmental and adapted program for students in grades K–12 who:

1. Possess a low level of physical or motor fitness (e.g., muscular power, muscular strength, agility, muscular endurance, cardiorespiratory endurance, speed and body balance
2. Evidence faulty body mechanics and functional postural defects
3. Evidence nutritional abnormalities, i.e., malnutrition or obesity

[2] Township of Ocean Board of Education, *Optimum Fitness for All (OFFA), Planning Grant, P.L. 89–10, Title III, Form Number 4312* (Washington, D.C.: U.S. Department of Education, February 9, 1966), 19 pp. Mimeographed.
[3] *Ibid.*, p. 5.

4. Are recuperating from illnesses or operations

5. Are physically handicapped

All applications will request information regarding the cost of the proposal submitted. However, some will not ask for information related to other sources of funds. It is strongly recommended that all requests be backed up by financial contributions the school district will make toward the proposed project. This will indicate that the school district considers the problem to be of prime concern and is willing to make a financial commitment. The OFFA Proposal[4] listed a breakdown for items 8–10 as follows:

Total cost	$23,815.95
Total nonfederal support	1,500.00
Total federal support under Title III, P. L. 89–10	20,172.00
Total federal support other than Title III	2,143.00

Source and amount of direct federal support other than Title III, P.L. 89–10 to be used for financing this project: Title I, $2,143.00 for a part-time person to conduct posture screening examinations for high school students.

Source and amount of nonfederal support for this project: Ocean Township Board of Education, $1,500.00 (equipment and supplies that have been purchased this year and will be used in the project such as chinning bars, posture grids, parallel bars, and New York State Posture Rating Charts).

One final point related to project financing is worth mentioning: be sure to indicate your intent to "phase out" the need for state or federal assistance. In most instances, financial assistance is provided with the expectation that each school district will assume the full burden of the cost of the proposal within a stipulated period of time. Thus, an indication that one is aware of, and planning to fulfill this obligation will increase the probability of project approval.

When it requested a continuation grant of the OFFA Study,[5] the Township of Ocean School District listed the following adjustments that would be made over a period of years:

During the planning grant and operational grant period, the following methods and procedures are being developed to continue the project without federal support, subject to administrative and board approval:

1. Make maximum utilization of existing facilities such as gymnasiums and Township recreational areas.

2. Incorporate an additional all-purpose area in new facilities to accommodate a developmental and adapted physical education program.

[4] *Ibid.*, p. 6.

[5] Township of Ocean Board of Education, *Optimum Fitness for All, Continuation Grant, P.L. 89–10, Title III* (Washington, D.C.: U.S. Department of Health, Education and Welfare, January 14, 1967), pp. 17–18. Mimeographed.

3. Construct an all-purpose teaching station or additional gymnasium at the high school to accommodate the new program.

4. Hire additional personnel necessary to conduct the program.

It is important to note that although the continuation grant was denied, the Township of Ocean Administration and Board of Education was able to honor all commitments. Since 1967 the District has provided the following facilities, personnel, and programs for its handicapped children:

1. A high school classroom converted to a full-time D&A teaching station
2. Specifications for two D&A teaching stations in elementary schools
3. Five physical educators to teach D&A on a part- or full-time basis
4. A D&A program in all five schools for grades K–12
5. A six-week summer program for the handicapped

Abstract of the Proposed Project

Most applications will require a brief abstract of the proposal. It is essential that the writer succinctly present all the salient features of his proposal. The abstract may be compared to the preface of a book in that the reader will read the main body of the material only if his interest is aroused by the abstract. Similarly, careful consideration should be given to selecting a title for the proposal.

Statement Concerning the Nature of the Problem

The problem one desires to investigate is a major determining factor of whether a grant request will be honored. The problem should concern current educational needs of the highest priority. A propitious situation confronts the teacher of the handicapped because most funds appropriated for public school use specify that a certain portion must be devoted to programs for the handicapped. For example, the 1968 Vocational Act Amendment requires "10 percent of the monies granted through Section B of the Act to be expended on programs for the handicapped."[6] Similarly, amendments to Title III, E.S.E.A., 1970 require that 10 percent of state allocations be diverted to projects for the handicapped. (These special appropriations are in addition to monies available through the Bureau of Education for the Handicapped.)

A careful review of the literature related to the problem selected should be made in order to avoid duplication of efforts. (Although the adapting of known exemplary programs to a local school district will be given considera-

---

[6] New Jersey Department of Education, *Vocational Programs for the Handicapped* (Trenton, N.J.: Division of Curriculum Instruction, October 8, 1970), p. 1. Mimeographed.

tion, greater emphasis is being placed on the development of original research-oriented studies.) An excellent source of research and demonstration
possibilities for programs for the handicapped was identified at a conference
of the American Association for Health, Physical Education and Recreation
and the National Recreation and Park Association.[7] In their report, these
organizations listed a variety of specific problems categorized under major
areas. For example, under "Assessment and Evaluation," 69 separate topics
or problems are offered for consideration, such as, "Determine the effects
of early identification and placement of handicapped children into programs
emphasizing psychomotor development, physical activity and recreation."[8]
Problems related to interpretation, legislation, recruitment and training, and
services are also analyzed effectively.

The problem you propose to alleviate should be cause for concern in the
local district or, better yet, the entire geographic area. Be sure to indicate how
the problem relates to your specific area of knowledge and explain your
specific plans to identify its parameters. One of the weaknesses of grant proposals is that the problem to be dealt with is often too all-encompassing and
is thus not realistically achievable.

The problem we selected, optimum fitness for all (OFFA), was introduced
as follows[9]:

When discussing educational philosophy, we frequently state that our modern
educational program is superior to programs of the past based on the premise that
formerly the child was "geared" to the curriculum, whereas today the curriculum is
developed to meet the needs and interests of each child.

With the problems that face one in physical education today—large class size,
heterogeneous motor ability grouping, and students with various functional and
structural physical limitations—it is difficult to design a program which will develop
each child to his or her physical capacity.

If our planning proposal is accepted, all students in grades K–12 will be tested
to determine their physical status and potentialities so that an activities program can
be constructed to meet the needs of each child.

Prior to writing the proposal, the writer requested that the school nurses
review all student medical histories in the district. The results of the investigation were included to justify the need for the grant.

A New Jersey State mini-grant proposal submitted by Severs[10] entitled
A Pupil-Centered Drug Education Program stated the nature of the problem
as follows:

[7] AAHPER and N.R.P.A., *Physical Education and Recreation for Handicapped Children*
(Washington, D.C.: Bureau of Education for the Handicapped, Office of Education,
1969), pp. 62–75.
[8] *Ibid.*, p. 63.
[9] Township of Ocean, *Planning Grant, op. cit.*, p. 7.
[10] Reprinted from Evelyn Severs, *A Pupil-Centered Drug Education Program: Project Proposal* (Trenton, N.J.: State Department of Education, May 5, 1971) p. 1, by permission
of the author.

The magnitude of the drug problem in the United States is constantly increasing. It has been estimated by Yolles[11] that 60 million Americans are directly affected by this problem. The extent of use can be estimated in four categories:

1. Nonusers who are closely related to users/abusers, 40 million
2. Experimenters, for whom continual illicit drug use is not a part of their life styles, 7 million
3. Moderate users, who use drugs periodically within some segment of their life style, 5 million
4. Invested users, for whom illicit drugs play a central role in life styles and coping mechanisms, 3 million

As a result of the ever-growing drug menace, the federal government initiated a teacher-training program in the summer of 1970. Since that time state teams have conducted programs for district leaders. It is estimated that as soon as all in-service programs are conducted within each local school district, one-half of the teacher population will have been exposed to the drug education program.

While the federally initiated program has merit, it is questionable as to whether such teacher-training programs will have any noticeable effect on the increasing drug usage. It is doubtful that the training programs will stimulate incidental teaching by the classroom teacher, or pupil receptivity. Realistically, teachers will resist the added responsibility because they are too busy with their other teaching duties, or simply do not possess the necessary expertise. Pupil receptivity will not be enhanced because most present programs have been founded on a content- rather than a student-centered approach.

In her introduction, Severs presented the problem on a national level and then skillfully related it to her state and local levels.

Innovative Ideas and Exemplary Programs

Since the advent of Title III, E.S.E.A., in 1965, the terms "innovative" and "exemplary" have permeated most proposal applications in one form or another. For example, the Experimental Schools Program[12] states that "these innovations include, among others, major curriculum reforms, use of modern communications technology, differentiated staffing patterns and new modes of scheduling students' time." And the New Jersey Department of Education[13] provides mini-grants for project proposals submitted on applications entitled, "Teacher Innovation Program."

It is important that the grant applicant not only be thoroughly conversant with both terms, but also insure that his proposal is either original or an adaptation of an exemplary educational practice. The Title III Manual for

---

[11] Stanley F. Yolles, "Managing Mood Changes," *New York University Education Quarterly*, II, No. 3 (Spring, 1971), 4–5.

[12] *Announcement of New Competition for Experimental Schools* (Washington, D.C.: U.S. Department of Health, Education and Welfare, Office of Education, March 31, 1971), p. 1.

[13] *Teacher Innovation Program, N.J.D.E. 401–2* (Trenton, N.J.: Department of Education, Division of Curriculum and Instruction, February, 1971), p. 1.

Project Applicants[14] offers the following guidelines: "Projects may be developed which (1) invest a creative solution to a problem, (2) demonstrate an exemplary program which might be suitable for widespread use, (3) adapt an exemplary program to local requirements and organize its incorporation into the educational program." To clarify the confusion about the term "innovation," experts reviewing Title III proposals recommended the following definition[15]: "Educational innovation is a new or different concept, methodology, organization, or program that is systematically introduced into the classroom, school system and/or the state as a whole." It would thus seem that an innovative program need not be totally "original," but could be novel to the district into which it is being introduced. If that is the case, the proposal would probably be classified as "exemplary" because it would be an adaptation of an innovative program for the local school district. In addition, the proposal should clearly indicate how the innovative approach will be systematically incorporated in the total program.

The OFFA proposal elucidated on the innovative and exemplary aspects of the project as follows:

The program planned will be innovative in that a close working relationship with Temple University's Biokinetic Research Laboratory will assure the utilization of new research. Only those testing devices and instruments possessing high validity, reliability, and objectivity rating will be used.

The program will be exemplary in that it will afford visiting teachers and groups an opportunity to observe the latest techniques in administering fitness tests, posture screening, somatotyping, and case study procedures. This project will be an excellent in-service program for visiting teachers; the end result, a more knowledgeable teacher who will be capable of assessing the needs of each student.[16]

Severs focused on the teaching/learning process to stress the innovativeness of her proposal when she stated:

The proposed project is innovative because it is consistent with current theories related to the teaching/learning process. Students will be totally involved in the learning process; instruction will be based on "doing" rather than "receiving." On the other hand, the teacher will not be the dispenser of facts, but rather he will guide, assist, stimulate, and act as a resource person.[17]

Procedures to Be Used in Planning

Planning procedures should evidence a coordinated effort toward a common goal. The planning could demonstrate unity of purpose via a series of

---

[14] *PACE: Projects to Advance Creativity in Education: A Manual for Project Applicants, Title III Elementary and Secondary Education Act of 1965* (Washington, D.C.: U.S. Government Printing Office, n.d.), p. 1.
[15] Subcommittee on Education, *op. cit.*, p. 37.
[16] Township of Ocean, *Planning Grant, op. cit.*, pp. 7–8.
[17] Severs, *op. cit.*, p. 3.

statements, or planned student activities. An example of short, brief statements might proceed as follows:

All students will be tested to determine physical fitness or motor fitness level, and functional postural defects. Those students below predetermined fitness standards (after a six-week conditioning program and a re-test), plus students possessing physical structural limitations will take part in a case study approach designed to determine the cause or causes of their low fitness.[18]

The listing of planned student learning experiences is another approach that has merit. Severs included the following student activities:

1. Forming an anti-drug club, sponsored by the applicant (grades 6–8)
2. Discussing, designing and ordering a club emblem (status symbol)
3. Researching current literature to increase knowledge regarding drug use and abuse
4. Publishing a newsletter
5. Visiting 3rd-, 4th-, and 5th-grade classrooms of the Oakhurst, Wanamassa and Wayside [New Jersey] Elementary Schools to give presentations about the danger of drugs
6. Sponsoring field trips to private hospitals and drug treatment centers
7. Sponsoring assembly programs involving speakers and films
8. Conducting Saturday and/or after-school visits to local shopping centers to distribute drug education literature to the public
9. Involving parents and community agencies in the campaign via participation in the assembly programs and chaperoning field trips.[19]

The common theme of all proposed student experiences listed for the drug study was to maximize student involvement in the drug education program.

The Need for Financial Support for Planning

State and federal funds are usually offered to local school districts to serve as catalytic agents in the development of innovative programs rather than to support programs in perpetuity. The applicant should therefore incorporate some statement regarding the need for initial financial assistance in his proposal. The OFFA study's need was expressed as follows:

Financial support is needed to administer the tests which will be used in this project due to the added cost of selecting tests of superior scientific value. In measurement and evaluation, it is essential that qualified professional personnel, trained technicians, time and special equipment be made available. If one looks at it objec-

[18] Township of Ocean, *Planning Grant, op. cit.*, p. 8.
[19] Severs, *loc. cit.*

tively, it can be more costly if invalid devices are used for measurement due to the irreparable harm that may be incurred by students due to improper diagnosis.[20]

A List of Educational and Cultural Agencies
That Will Be Involved in Planning

Another major weakness of many proposals submitted for funding is their failure to include a plan for involving and disseminating information to agencies in a large geographic area. State and federal authorities have a vested interest in an approved proposal, and one of their prime concerns is ascertaining what target population will be affected by a funded program. The applicant should involve public and private agencies in his geographic area in his project development if he wishes to enhance the possibility of a grant approval. The Township of Ocean study[21] included four public and four private schools.

Planning Project Advisory Council

In the public schools, few teachers possess all of the qualifications necessary to guide a proposal to successful fruition, especially if it is research-oriented. Thus, to enhance success, one should form an advisory council of experts who possess a broad experiential background related to the problem being investigated. One might consider including medical personnel, county and state department officials, and representatives of institutes of higher learning. (Most federal grant proposals require the inclusion of a formal advisory council.)

Purpose of the Proposed Grant

Following the overview, the grantee should present an in-depth explanation of the purpose of his proposal. (When applying for state mini-grants, the "overview" and "purpose" of the proposal may be combined.)

Objectives to Be Achieved With the Grant

The statement of sound objectives is of paramount importance. The applicant should reflect carefully on his stated problem so that he can identify the objectives, along with their ramifications, that are an integral part of the overall problem. The importance of this phase of the proposal cannot be stressed sufficiently. One of the major deterrents to proposal

---

[20] Township of Ocean, *Planning Grant, loc. cit.*
[21] *Ibid.*

approval is the presentation of vague, ambiguous, or unattainable objectives. (At this point in the proposal, the applicant should solicit the assistance of one or more educators with expertise in the area being investigated.)

The OFFA Study[22] listed four specific objectives:

1. To assess the physical fitness status of all students in grades K–12 so that low-fitness individuals may be placed in special developmental classes
2. To screen all students to determine postural deficiencies so that students may be categorized for corrective exercises
3. To provide the following for those individuals who are sub-par physically (or who possess structural or functional limitations):
   a. Determination of nutritional status
   b. Thorough medical appraisal
   c. Psychological testing (when necesssry)
   d. Individual counseling
   e. Somatotyping to assess predictive physical capacity
4. To determine the capacity of the handicapped, postoperative and convalescent for physical activity

Severs listed two objectives, plus a rationale for each:

1. To design comprehensive drug education mini-lessons for use by the classroom teachers in grades K–8
2. To have students implement an antidrug campaign in the intermediate school, grades 6–8

The purpose of objective No. 1 is to place in the hands of the elementary teachers a complete mini-lesson on some phase of drug education. Each lesson will include: *student* behavioral objectives; *student* learning experiences; content; evaluative material written in terms of *student* behavioral changes; and *student*/teacher reference materials. (The stress of each lesson is on maximizing student involvement.) Rationale: Having comprehensive lessons available for teacher usage should enhance implementation.

The purpose of objective No. 2 is to structure a program that will attack the artificial veneer that envelopes the whole drug problem (i.e., the idea that smoking pot, etc., is the "in" thing to do). The approach will be to establish an antidrug campaign conducted by, and for, students under the supervision of a faculty advisor. Once again, the focus is being placed on maximizing student involvement as research indicates there is a definite positive correlation between the degree of student involvement and learning.[23]

General Educational and Cultural Needs of Participants

A section of the proposal should be devoted to a "needs" analysis of the subjects which are to be involved. To enhance the approval of the proposal,

---

[22] *Ibid.*, p. 9.
[23] Severs, *op. cit.*, p. 2.

the applicant should justify his request in terms of the population to be assisted. In the OFFA study,[24] the need for project approval was justified by (1) a review of the school health records of all public and private school children, grades K–12, in the district and (2) the administration of a physical fitness test battery. The results of the preliminary investigation revealed that over 25 percent of the 4,074 students manifested disabilities that necessitated scheduling in an individualized physical education program. The general classifications for disabilities were low physical fitness, postoperative, convalescent, nutritional abnormalities, physically handicapped, and postural defects.

Emphasis on Innovative and Exemplary Programming

What are the specific features that make a proposal worthy of approval? Vodola listed what he considered to be the unique aspects of his proposal as follows:

1. Innovative techniques to be used:
  a. The administration of Rogers' Physical Fitness Test Battery and the Recovery Index Test to all students, grades 9–12, to determine physical fitness
  b. The administration of the elementary school modification of the Indiana Motor Fitness Test, grades K–8, to determine motor fitness
  c. Posture screening of all students
  d. The use of case study techniques with low fitness and physically handicapped, postoperative, and convalescent individuals
  e. The use of Pryor's Width-Weight Tables, skinfold measurement, and somatotyping to determine nutritional status
  f. The use of counseling techniques to develop within each child an awareness of his physical capacities and limitations
2. Exemplary features of the program: The entire project is exemplary in that utilization of sound, valid research techniques makes it ideal for use as a model demonstration program for in-service training in measurement and evaluation. The project can be demonstrated and conducted in a manner that would make it an individual tool for in-service training for all school districts. Testing techniques and results could be made available to all interested parties through various state agencies. The dissemination of this material is particularly significant at this time because so much emphasis is being placed on identifying the physical fitness needs of *all* children by the President's Council on Physical Fitness.[25]

Description of the Project
and Information Being Sought

Many grant requests are denied because projects are not explained in detail. A good rule-of-thumb would be to assume that those who review an

[24] Township of Ocean, *Planning Grant, op. cit.*, pp. 4–5.
[25] *Ibid.*, pp. 10–11.

application have no knowledge at all of the subject and thus must be provided with a detailed, step-by-step explanation of the project and information being sought. Moreover, be sure that the testing procedures or evaluation techniques have been carefully selected so that they are reliable (or objective if two or more testers on the same items) and valid. And, most important, select those procedures or techniques that will be consistent with the stated project objectives; this approach was used in the *Optimum Fitness for All* study[26]:

1. Determination of physical fitness status: To design an activities program that will challenge each child and yet not tax him beyond his physical capacity, it is essential that a valid physical fitness test battery be administered. This will be accomplished in the following manner:

    a. Students in grades 9–12 will be administered the Rogers' Physical Fitness Test Battery to determine muscular strength and muscular endurance. The strength phase of the test is the most valid predictor of potential athletic ability; the results can therefore be used for ability grouping (thus improving learning) and for equating intramural teams. The high school students will also be administered the Recovery Index Test, a modification of the Harvard Step Test, to measure the ability of the body to adapt to and recover from strenuous exercise (cardiorespiratory endurance).

    b. Students in grades K–8 will be administered a modification of the Indiana Motor Fitness Test designed for elementary school children. (The Rogers' PFI is not recommended for use with elementary children.) The elementary battery gives an indication of the following fitness components: muscular power, agility, muscular strength, muscular endurance, cardiorespiratory endurance, speed, and body balance.

2. Determination of posture status: That good posture enhances the possibility of healthful living, makes one physically more attractive, and makes body movement more efficient is generally agreed upon by leading educators and medical authorities. The administration of the New York State Posture Rating Screening Examination, medical appraisal for validation, and prescribed exercises when necessary will ameliorate many defects and develop within all students (grades K–12) an awareness of the aforementioned values.

3. Case study procedures: Upon completion of physical fitness and posture screening, those students who do not meet predetermined fitness levels will be given a six-week conditioning program. Those who still do not measure up to minimal standards, plus convalescents, postoperatives, and the physically handicapped will enter the case study phase of the project in an attempt to determine the cause or causes, or in the case of the medically excused or physically handicapped, the extent of their limitations. Steps in the case study approach are as follows:

    a. Accumulation of the following data:

        (1) Academic status: level of scholastic work may fluctuate with physical condition.

        (2) Weight record: helpful in cases of malnutrition and glandular disorders.

        (3) Health exam: revealing the total number of defects.

---

[26] *Ibid.,* pp. 11–13.

(*4*) Medical history: revealing recent illnesses, accidents, or operations.

(*5*) Somatotyping: to determine basic body type to better interpret physical fitness scores.

(*6*) Nutritional status: the administration of Pryor's Width-Weight Test and skinfold measurements to reveal skeletal structure and percentage of body fat.

(*7*) Health habits: survey to reveal faulty health habits.

(*8*) SRA youth: survey, grades 7–12, to reveal students' feelings regarding their health and their ability to get along with others.

(*9*) Winnetka Scale for Rating Student Behavior and Activities: survey to reveal personality traits of younger children.

(*10*) School nurse's report: to reveal knowledge of a child's health problems and home environment.

(*11*) Posture rating: to assist in interpreting physical fitness scores.

b. Interview with student based on the accumulated data. The purpose is to determine the cause or causes of low fitness, or if there are none, to make the child aware of the implications of his low fitness score.

c. Referrals and other services: Mindful of the fact that physical educators are educational specialists *only*, when findings reveal medical or psychological problems, students will be referred for special examinations. Recommendations will be placed in the case study folder and will be the determining factor in designing individual programs.

d. Summary: All data will be summarized to present a total picture before a conditioning program is designed for the individual.

4. Physically handicapped and medically excused: Tensiometer testing will be used to assess the strength and fatigue limits (at the beginning of the testing program and at certain time intervals) of weakened muscles and to ascertain improvement throughout the treatment.

Personnel

Many grant applicants provide a detailed report relating all aspects of their proposals but do not carefully assess personnel needs. This lack of foresight is sometimes attributable to an endeavor to keep total costs within reasonable limits. However, on most occasions the cause is an inadequate assessment of personnel needs in light of the objectives one is attempting to achieve. The writer was guilty on both accounts when he listed the personnel needs for his fitness study.

In an effort to keep the total cost of the proposal at a minimum, personnel requests were limited to one full-time physical educator, one full-time secretary, and four part-time graduate assistants. The latter were most difficult to hire, especially since they were needed to test students during the school day. The problem was finally resolved by hiring two full-time teachers rather than one full-time and four part-time teachers.

Do not make the mistake of restricting the cost of the grant request on the assumption it will be approved more readily (unless the application stipulates specific financial limitations). Instead, relate personnel needs directly to what you are attempting to accomplish. The reviewers of grant proposals will look for *consistency* throughout the report in terms of personnel expertise and capacity to achieve the goals listed, the internal design of the study, and the validity of evaluative techniques. In the OFFA study, the author did not request sufficient personnel and as a consequence all objectives were not attained, which may be why the second phase of the grant proposal was not approved.

Facilities and Services

State and federal authorities are most concerned with the impact an educational innovation will have on a geographic area. Therefore, a proposal should specify the geographic area to be served, the facilities to be used, and other pertinent information. The OFFA study[27] provided the information listed below.

Geographic area to be served. The planning project will be conducted in the Township of Ocean School District, which has a population of 16,000. The community encompasses an area of 4 square miles and its student population of 4,074 is distributed in the following schools:

Public Schools	
Oakhurst Elementary School	587
Wanamassa Elementary School	657
Ocean Township Elementary School	925
Ocean Township High School	1430
Nonpublic schools	
Haddenwald	30
Hillel	107
Oakhurst Country Day School	58
St. Mary's	280

The other school districts in Monmouth County that will participate in the planning proposal will be encouraged to send representatives to visit the testing site so that they can use the techniques in their respective areas.

Public school facilities and services. The high school, constructed in 1965–1966, has an excellent three-section gymnasium, each section measuring 48 × 96′. It has a compact room, presently used for weight-training, which could be used to house all special apparatus and equipment. The other public schools have combination auditorium/gymnasiums.

Special equipment and apparatus for testing will be housed in the high school and transported to the various schools as necessary. The professional staff will work at the various schools on a rotational basis. All nonpublic schools have facilities for testing.

The following recreational facilities in the Township afford the opportunity of developing a diversified activity program to meet the individual needs of all students:

[27] *Ibid.,* p. 14.

1. Recreation park: (4½ acres) consisting of 4 basketball courts, 4 tennis courts, 6 handball courts, 6 shuffleboard courts, and 1 nursery playground
2. Recreation center: consists of a two-story building (30 × 60') for community activities and a basketball court which is flooded in the wintertime and used for ice-skating
3. Other outdoor areas: there are several other outdoor areas which can be used for group activities.

Materials and Supplies

State and federal agencies are reluctant to approve monies for the purchase of expensive supplies and equipment (and in most cases they will not even consider requests for building facilities). These agencies feel that most of their funds should be diverted to the provision of services and recommend renting most items. If the applicant feels items should be purchased, he must include a rationale for so doing. The OFFA study supplied the following justification for purchasing rather than renting materials:

1. Most items will be in use daily throughout the year.
2. If the proposal for the planning grant results in an operational grant for the following year or years, the equipment would be available, eliminating the need for re-renting.
3. Items requested are usually only found at research laboratories and thus cannot be borrowed.
4. No manufacturers have been located who will rent the necessary equipment.[28]

Budget

The final pages of the proposal should include a cost analysis of the total proposal. One breakdown should include expenditure accounts, line account numbers, total amount for each line account, and source of funds (federal or nonfederal). A second table should itemize the specific material needs of the project in terms of quantity, item names, descriptions, unit costs, and total cost.

Summary

In this chapter we have attempted to provide the reader with basic information necessary to apply for a state or federal grant. If the applicant uses the recommended guidelines and prepares his proposal thoroughly, he will enhance the possibility of acceptance.

In review, proposal guidelines should include:

[28] *Ibid.*, p. 15.

1. The necessary general data, with emphasis on the district's financial commitment to the program and plans for phasing out agency funding

2. An abstract of the proposal, including a statement of the problem, innovative or exemplary features, coordinated planning procedures, a rationale for the need of financial support, reference to educational/cultural agency involvement, and the names of the members of an advisory council

3. A main body of the report giving a detailed presentation of the grant request in terms of specific objectives, educational and cultural needs of the participants, innovative techniques and exemplary features of the program, and a description of the design of the project

4. Personnel needs to accomplish the task (do not forget to include clerical assistance)

5. A description of the geographic area to be served and the facilities and services that will be available

6. An itemized list of all supply and equipment needs, with a rationale, when necessary, for the purchase of expensive equipment

7. A budget section which presents a cost analysis of the total proposal

Annotated Bibliography

Announcement of a New Competition for Experimental Schools. Washington, D.C.: Office of Education, March 31, 1971. 11 pp. Describes the Experimental Schools program design for 1971 and application requirements and procedures. Requests that grants be submitted for federal aid based on creative projects which will offer significant alternatives to current educational practices. Provides general information regarding project size, eligible applicants, planning, development, and operation, target population, evaluation and documentation, and guidelines for submitting a grant request. Free upon request.

DIVISION OF RESEARCH, U.S. OFFICE OF EDUCATION. *Support for Research and Related Activities for the Education of Handicapped Children.* Washington, D.C.: Bureau of Education for the Handicapped/U.S. Office of Education, November, 1968. 24 pp. Includes guidelines for submitting grant requests under Title III, Section 302, and Title, V, Section 502, of Public Law 88–164, as amended. Provides the reader with suggestions for proposal development and detailed application procedures (regarding information which most reviewers or panels require in order to make sound judgments). Also includes an application for research support. Free upon request.

O'DONNELL, CORNELIUS R. *Project COPE: Carry Over Physical Education.* Matawan, N.J.: Matawan Regional School District, n.d. 14 pp. A pamphlet explaining a Title III project in elementary physical education. Includes a variety of pictures illustrating the teaching of various leisure time skills. Free upon request.

ROWLAND, HOWARD S., and RICHARD L. WING. *Federal Aid for Schools, 1967–1968 Guide: The Complete Handbook for the Local School District.* New York: The Macmillan Company, 1967. A basic primer for anyone interested in sources of federal aid. Recommended for comprehensive guidelines for planning, writing, and submitting a proposal.

epilogue

A virtual lack of priority exists to meet the educational needs of the handicapped. Less than half of those so afflicted are enrolled in the public schools of this "great land of plenty." Of those attending classes in our national school system, probably less than 5 percent are participating in physical education/recreation programs designed to meet their specific needs (only California and Pennsylvania have state-mandated laws).

It has been stated that the dearth of programs for the handicapped is partially attributable to the inadequate preparation of physical educators and recreation specialists. I have attempted to provide some of the information needed for program planning and implementation. However, to say that this book will have much impact on the program void is little more than wishful thinking. If the Township of Ocean School District's D&A program materials can provide teachers with some guidelines for establishing programs for the handicapped, my purpose will have been accomplished.

To insure that our "forgotten children" be afforded equal educational opportunities, I urge that the following recommendations be given careful consideration and enacted upon in each state:

1. Teacher-training institutions should revamp their curricula so that prospective teachers are prepared *realistically* to work with the handicapped. Presently, most undergraduate physical education programs offer only one course related to working with the atypical child. These institutions should provide their students with "mini-experiences," starting with the freshman year, so that they can develop teaching competencies as well as a theoretical basis for working with the handicapped. (The American Association of Health, Physical Education and Recreation has been aware of the need for the revamping of college and univer-

sity curricula, and as a result of the collected efforts of educators throughout the country has prepared curricula guidelines for teaching the handicapped.)

2. Boards of higher education, who govern the purse strings of state teacher-training institutions, should allocate the necessary finances for additional courses related to teaching the handicapped. Board decisions should be based on the assessment of teacher performance in terms of student needs rather than on any a priori basis. (the Federal government is aware of the current educational dilemma and as a consequence appropriated $300,000 for the training of physical education/ recreation personnel during the 1971 fiscal year).

3. State educational organizations should furnish the leadership necessary to insure that every child be provided with an educational program *commensurate with his needs*. They should sponsor workshops for teachers of the handicapped, conduct a campaign to make the general populace aware of the existing inadequacies and, when necessary, urge that legislation include mandated programs.

4. The teachers in the field must shoulder the major responsibility. They are the backbone of the teaching profession and as a result will be the determining factor regarding curricula change. State and federal agencies can provide the expertise, stimulate and coordinate efforts, and grant funds, but they cannot implement programs. You, the teacher, are charged with that responsibility. You must be a dedicated professional in every sense of the word if you wish to aid our handicapped children. The text has elaborated in detail what you must do to implement a program for the handicapped.

To summarize, I would say that you must: constantly seek to increase your knowledge and teaching competencies via in-service workshops; become a one-man public relations campaign to apprise parents, teachers, administrators, the board of education, and students of the values to be derived from the program; and be willing to devote countless hours, regardless of problems, until your ultimate goal has been achieved.

In spite of the problems and frustrations which confront anyone who attempts to implement a program for the handicapped, the rewards more than justify the efforts. If you have never experienced the smile on a handicapped child's face because he has achieved some insignificant task, or the gratitude of the mother, it is something to behold. May I conclude by reiterating the remark I made in the Preface, to those so dedicated (to implementing programs for the handicapped), I pledge my full cooperation and assistance.

APPENDICES

forms related to organization, administration, and implementation of a developmental and adapted physical education program for the handicapped

FIGURE A–1 Developmental and adapted physical education referral form. Courtesy of the Township of Ocean School District.

Route to: 1. Teacher
2. Principal
3. Nurse
4. D&A teacher
5. Return to principal

Dept. of Health, Physical Education & Driver Education   Date _____

Teacher making referral _____ School _____

Student's Name _____ _____ ____ Sex__ __
                       Last   First   Grade Age   M F

Suspected reason for referral (please check)
  Developmental Problem:
    Posture   _____
    *Nutritional   _____
    Low physical vitality   _____
    Motor (balance, coordination)   _____
  Adapted problem (medical)
    *Orthopedic   _____
    *Postoperative/convalescent   _____
    *Other medical   _____
  Additional remarks (please explain) _____

_____
_____
_____

*To be screened by physician

FIGURE A–1 (cont.)

Disposition of Referral

To: _____   Date _____
From: _____
Re: _____

_____
_____
_____
_____
_____

Copies for: Principal
             Teacher
             D&A teacher
             Nurse
             Learning disabilities consultant
             Director of health and physical education
             Coordinator of special services

FIGURE A–2   Letter to family physician eliciting support. Courtesy of the Township of Ocean School District.

Date _____

Physician's Address

Dear Dr. _____:

Enclosed are some materials relating to our physical education program for students with developmental or medically oriented problems. We invite you to stop in and visit with us so that you can see the program in "action."

Our staff never prescribes any activities other than for a low level of physical fitness. Either Dr. Helen Jones or Dr. John Malta, the school physicians, or the family physician involved must make the necessary diagnoses and prescriptions; our staff will comply with said instructions.

We would appreciate any suggestions or materials you may give us regarding program implementation so that we can better serve our students. I am firmly convinced our program will only be successful if we, the staff, work closely with the medical profession. Thank you for your cooperation.

Sincerely,

TMV: sd   THOMAS M. VODOLA, Ed.D.
Enclosures   Supervisor, K–12

FIGURE A–3 Developmental and adapted physical education classification approval form. Courtesy of the Township of Ocean School District.

School _____

Name _____ Date _____

Grade level _____ Age _____ Sex _____

To the physician: Please check area(s) in need of special exercises or activities; comment where necessary.

Check

_____ A. Posture _____
            _____

_____ B. Nutritional _____
            _____

_____ C. Low physical vitality _____
            _____

_____ D. Perceptual-motor (coordination) _____
            _____

_____ E. Orthopedic handicap _____
            _____

_____ F. Postoperative/convalescent _____
            _____

_____ G. Other medical _____
            _____

Additional Remarks: _____
                    _____
                    _____
                    _____

            Physician's signature _____

FIGURE A–4 Child study team classification form. Courtesy of the Township of Ocean School District.

Name _____   School _____

Birth Date _____   Grade _____

Official Classification _____

Medical inspector _____ Date _____
_____

Psychologist _____ Date _____
_____

Learning disability specialist _____ Date _____
_____

Social worker _____ Date _____
_____

Teacher _____ Date _____
_____

Nurse _____ Date _____
_____

Other _____ Date _____
_____

Principal or superintendent_____(disposition) Date _____
_____
_____

FIGURE A–5 Medical excuse form. Courtesy of the Township of Ocean School District.

Date: _____

Dear Parent:

   Recognizing the fact that students with varied physical limitations evidence different needs, the Department of Health, Safety, and Physical Education has designed a program to afford students (postoperative, convalescent, and the physically handicapped) an opportunity to participate in a modified activities program. The program is not remedial or corrective, but rather consists of a selected variety of modified games, activities, and recreational pursuits which are designed to meet the specific needs of each student. The program is determined by your family physician, or the school physician (as per your request).

   If you would like your child to be enrolled in one of the classes, please sign this form, submit to the proper medical authority, and forward to my office at your earliest convenience. Please contact me if you have any additional questions regarding the program.

Sincerely,

THOMAS M. VODOLA, Ed.D.
Supervisor

FIGURE A–5 (cont.)

To be completed by the parent:
    I would like to have my son/daughter _____ assigned to the
Adapted Physical Education Program.   (Pupil's name)

                                    _____
                                        (Parent's signature)

To be completed by the family or school physician:
Nature of the illness or physical limitation _____
_____
Approximate duration of the excusal _____
Please indicate those activities you recommend the student participate in (only
those activities you recommend will be included in the student's program):
1. Postural exercises _____
2. Limited exercises _____
3. Modified games (basketball, volleyball, soccer) _____
4. Recreational activities (table tennis, shuffleboard, bowling, quoits, archery)
5. Weight-training (modified) _____
6. Gymnastics (modified) _____
7. Rope skipping and other endurance-type activities _____
8. Other _____

                        Signed_____
                                    (Family or school physician)

FIGURE A–6 Admission/release pass. Courtesy of the Township of Ocean School District.

                                        Time: _____
                                        Date: _____

From: Dr. Vodola
To: Study Hall Supervisor
Re: Developmental & Adapted (D&A)
        Physical Education scheduling

Please add drop _____
                            (student's name)

to from the _____ study hall roster on _____ .
                period   day(s) of the week

Please initial: Time: _____
Study hall supervisor _____
Physical education teacher _____

PLEASE RETURN TO D&A TEACHER

TABLE A–1   Master Scheduling Form: Township of Ocean School District
Department of Health, Safety, and Physical Education
Developmental and Adapted Physical Education Student Classification Form

School

STUDENT NAME	DATE in	DATE out	GRADE	AGE	DAY AND PERIOD	CLASSIFICATION	CLASSIFIED BY	DISPOSITION	ADDITIONAL REMARKS

TABLE A–2 Basic Motor Skill Test

Name _____ _____ ___ ___ _____ ___

                    Last   First   Age Grade   School   Sex

Handedness: R_____ L_____   Footedness: R_____ L_____

Classroom teacher_____

Test Item	Att.	Factor Measured	Test Periods					
			1		2		3	
			P	F	P	F	P	F
1. Walk	2	Gross body coord.						
2. Creep	2	Gross body coord.						
3. Climb stairs	2	Gross body coord.						
4. Skip	2	Gross body coord.						
5. March in place	2	Gross body coord.						
Total								
6. Stand both feet (15 sec.)	3	Bal post. orient.						
7. Stand right foot (15 sec.)	3	Bal post. orient.						
8. Stand left foot (15 sec.)	3	Bal post. orient.						
9. Jump one foot leading	3	Bal post. orient.						
10. Jump both feet simult.	3	Bal post. orient.						
11. Hop both feet	3	Bal post. orient.						
12. Hop right foot	3	Bal post. orient.						
13. Hop left foot	3	Bal post. orient.						
Total								
14. Catch	3	Eye/hand coord.						
15. Ball bounce and catch	3	Eye/hand coord.						
16. Touch ball swing laterally	3	Eye/hand coord.						
17. Touch ball swing fore/aft	3	Eye/hand coord.						
18. Bat ball with hand	3	Eye/hand coord.						
19. Bat ball with bat	3	Eye/hand coord.						
Total								
20. Throw right hand	3	Eye/hand accuracy						
21. Throw left hand	3	Eye/hand accuracy						
Total								
22. Kick right foot	3	Eye/foot accuracy						
23. Kick left foot	3	Eye/foot accuracy						
Total								
Grand Total								

Date: _____

Weight: _____

Height: _____

Anecdotal Remarks	*Areas of Weakenss*	*Individually Prescribed Activities*

SOURCE: Adapted from Buttonwood Farms Basic Motor Fitness Test designed by Temple University HPER Department. Courtesy D.R. Hilsendager, H.K. Jack, and L. Mann.

TABLE A–3   Physical Fitness Test Form, K–8,
Township of Ocean School District
Department of Health, Safety and Physical Education

Name _____ _____ ____ _____ _____ ____
         Last   First   Age Grade   School   Sex

                                                                        Teacher

			Test Periods		
			1	*2*	*3*
Date					
Weight					
Height					
Test Item	*Att.*	*Factor Measured*	*Score* R. S.	*Score* R. S.	*Score* R. S.
1. Tapered balance beam	2	Gross body balance			
2. Dynamometer—push	2	Arm strength (triceps)			
3. Dynamometer—pull	2	Arm strength (biceps)			
4. Sit-ups (maximum 100)	1	Abdominal strength			
5. Standing broad jump	2	Explosive leg strength			
6. Modified Harvard Step Test	1	Cardiorespiratory endurance			
Average Standard Score					

Anecdotal Remarks	*Areas of Weakness*	*Individually Prescribed Activities*

SOURCE: Adapted from Buttonwood Farms Motor Fitness Test designed by Temple University HPER Department. Courtesy D.R. Hilsendager, H.K. Jack, and L. Mann.

TABLE A–4 Food Substitution Table

In order to reduce your daily caloric intake by *250 calories*, the department has provided the following calorie table. Simply substitute foods for other foods you normally eat until you have reduced your daily intake by *250 calories*.[a] Please be sure to keep your portions of food constant. The chart will also provide valuable assistance in the selection of balanced, nutritious meals. Good luck on your campaign to rid yourself of excess adipose tissue.

HOW TO GET RID OF THE CALORIES YOU WILL NEVER MISS

	For this	*Cal.*	*Substitute this*	*Cal.*	*Cal. saved*
Beverage	Milk (whole), 8 oz.	160	Buttermilk, skim, 8 oz.	90	70
	Prune juice, 8 oz.	200	Tomato juice, 8 oz.	45	155
	Soft drinks, 8 oz.	105	Diet soft drinks, 8 oz.	1	104
	Coffee, cream, 2 ts. sugar	95	Coffee black, sugar sub.	0	95
	Cocoa (all milk), 8 oz.	235	Cocoa, milk & water	140	95
	Choc. malted, 8 oz.	450	Lemonade (sweetened), 8 oz.	100	350
	Beer (1 bottle), 12 oz.	185	Liquor, soda, water, 8 oz.	150	35
Breakfast	Rice flakes, cup	105	Puffed rice, cup	55	50
	Eggs, scrambled, 2	220	Eggs, boiled, poached, 2	160	60
Butter	Butter on toast	170	Apple butter on toast	90	80
Cheese	Cheese, swiss, cream, 1 oz.	105	Cheese, cottage, 1 oz.	25	80
Desserts	Angel food cake, 2″	110	$\frac{1}{4}$ melon, cantaloupe	60	50
	Choc. cake, icing, 2″	445	Watermelon, $\frac{1}{2}$, 10″ diam.	60	385
	Cheese cake, 2″ piece	200	Sponge cake, 2″ piece	120	80
	Fruit cake, 2″ piece	115	Grapes, 1 cup	65	50
	Pound cake, 1 oz.	140	Plums, 2	50	90
	Iced cupcake, 1	185	Plain cupcake, 1	145	40
	Cookie, 3″ diam., 1	120	Vanilla wafer, diet., 1	25	95
	Ice cream, 4 oz.	150	Yogurt, flavored, 4 oz.	60	90
	Pie, Apple, $\frac{1}{7}$ of 9″ pie	345	Tangerine, fresh	40	305
	Pie, blueberry, 1 piece	290	Blueberries, unsw., $\frac{1}{2}$ cup	45	245
	Pie, cherry, 1 piece	355	Cherries, fresh, $\frac{1}{2}$ cup	40	315
	Pie, custard, 1 piece	280	Banana, 1	85	195
	Pie, meringue, 1 piece	305	Lemon, gelatin, $\frac{1}{2}$ cup	70	235
	Pie, peach, 1 piece	280	Peach, fresh, 1	35	245
	Pie, rhubarb, 1 piece	265	Grapefruit, $\frac{1}{2}$	55	210
	Pudding, flavored, $\frac{1}{2}$ cup	140	Pudding, diet., $\frac{1}{2}$ cup	60	80
Fish and fowl	Tuna, canned, 3 oz.	170	Crabmeat, canned, 3 oz.	85	85
	Oysters, fried, 6	250	Oysters in shell, sauce, 6	100	150
	Ocean perch, fried, 4 oz.	260	Bass, 4 oz.	105	155
	Fish sticks, 5 sticks	200	Brook trout, 4 oz.	130	70
	Lobster meat, 2 tbl., butter, 4 oz.	300	Lobster meat, 4 oz., with lemon	95	205
	Duck, roasted, 4 oz.	200	Chicken, roasted, 4 oz.	140	60

[a] Since cyclamates have been removed from the market, slight inaccuracies exist for such items as diet soft drinks.

TABLE A–4 (cont.)

	For this	Cal.	Substitute this	Cal.	Cal. saved
Meats	Loin roast, 3½ oz.	340	Pot roast, round, 3½ oz.	200	140
	Rump roast, 3½ oz.	340	Rib roast, 3½ oz.	260	80
	Swiss steak, 3½ oz.	300	Liver, fried, 3½ oz.	210	90
	Hamburger, broiled, 3 oz.	245	Hamburger, lean, 3 oz.	185	60
	Porterhouse steak, 3½ oz.	290	Club steak, 3½ oz.	190	100
	Rib lamb chop, 3 oz.	300	Lamb leg roast, 3 oz.	235	65
	Pork chop, 3 oz.	340	Veal chop, 3 oz.	185	155
	Pork roast, 3 oz.	310	Veal roast, 3 oz.	230	80
	Pork sausage, 3 oz.	405	Ham, broiled, lean, 3 oz.	200	205
Potatoes	Potatoes, fried, 1 cup	480	Potato, baked, 2½″ diam.	100	380
	Potatoes, mashed, 1 cup	240	Potato, boiled, 2½″ diam.	100	140
Salads	Chef salad, oil, 1 tbl.	160	Chef salad, diet, dress.	40	120
	Chef salad, mayonnaise, 1 tbl.	125	Chef salad, diet, dress.	40	85
	Chef salad, roquefort, Russian, French, 1 tbl.	105	Chef salad, diet, dress.	40	65
Sandwiches	Club sandwich	375	Open bacon/tomato sand.	200	175
	Peanut butter/jelly	275	Open egg salad	165	110
	Turkey with gravy	300	Open hamburger, lean, 2 oz.	200	100
Snacks	Fudge, 1 oz.	115	Vanilla wafers, diet., 2	50	65
	Peanuts, salted, 1 oz.	190	Apple, 1	70	120
	Peanuts, roasted, 1 cup	800	Grapes, 1 cup	65	735
	Potato chips, 10 med.	115	Pretzels, 10 small sticks	35	80
	Chocolate, 1 oz. bar	145	Marshmellows, 3	60	85
Soups	Creamed soup, 1 cup	135	Chicken noodle soup, 1 cup	65	70
	Bean soup, 1 cup	170	Beef noodle soup, 1 cup	70	100
	Minestrone soup, 1 cup	105	Beef bouillon, 1 cup	30	75
Vegetables	Baked beans, 1 cup	320	Green beans, 1 cup	30	290
	Lima beans, 1 cup	180	Asparagus, 1 cup	35	145
	Corn, canned, 1 cup	170	Cauliflower, 1 cup	25	145
	Peas, canned, 1 cup	165	Peas, fresh, 1 cup	115	50
	Winter squash, 1 cup	130	Summer squash, 1 cup	30	100
	Succotash, 1 cup	260	Spinach, 1 cup	40	220

Source: Courtesy of Strasenburgh Laboratories, Rochester, New York.

TABLE A–4 (cont.)

Keep a record of the calories you save during the next few weeks

Date	1	2	3	4	5	6	7	8	9	10	11	12	13	14
Total														
Date														
Total														

TABLE A–5   D&A Physical Education Prescription Form for Motor and Perceptual/Motor Skills

	Reps.										
Bilaterality											
Crawling	_____											
Skipping	_____											
Hopping	_____											
Jumping	_____											
Pushing	_____											
Pulling	_____											
Lifting	_____											
Balance, postural orientation											
Step stones	_____											
Taper balance beam	_____											
Balance beam	_____											
Figure 8	_____											
Geometric forms	_____											
Eye/hand coordination											
Bat stationary ball	_____											
Bat moving ball	_____											
Touch moving ball	_____											
Catch rebound ball	_____											
Paddleball	_____											
Tetherball	_____											
Rope skip (time:___)	_____											
Eye/hand accuracy											
Target practice												
Right hand												
Left hand												
Horseshoes	Game											
Quoits	Game											
Bean bag	Game											
Ocular pursuits											
Touch swing ball												
Right hand	_____											
Left hand	_____											
Bat swing ball												
Right side	_____											
Left side	_____											

TABLE A–5   (cont.)

	Reps.											
Catching, throws	____											
Circle catch	____											
Eye/foot accuracy												
Kick at target												
Right foot	____											
Left foot	____											
Wall volley (time:___)	____											
Kick-rebound-trap	____											
Rope skip (time:___)	____											
Perceptual/motor												
Geometric forms	____											
Pegboard figures	____											
Pegboard sheets	____											
Puzzles	____											
Body image forms	____											
Physical fitness	Number											
Curl-ups	____											
Push-ups	____											
Pull-ups	____											
Overhead ladder												
Hand-over-hand	____											
Sideways	____											
Backwards	____											
Static arm hang (sec.)	____											
Arm circles (time:_____)												
Isometric												
Arm	Reps.___ Sec.___											
Leg	Reps.___ Sec.___											
Abdomen	Reps.___ Sec.___											
Neck	Reps.___ Sec.___											

SOURCE: Courtesy of John Picarone and James Ballard, staff members, Township of Ocean School District.

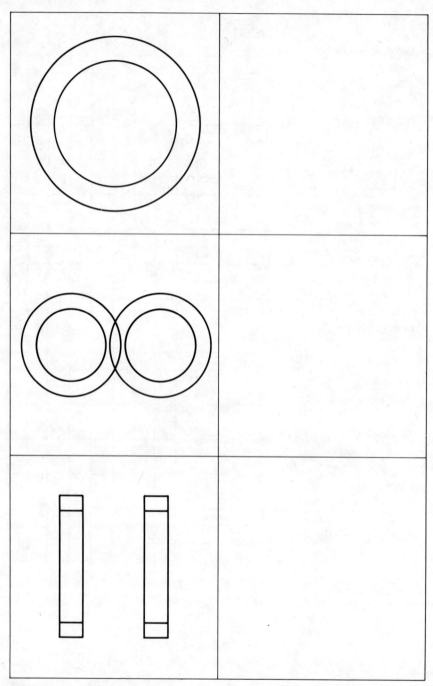

FIGURE A–7 Perceptual-motor achievement test overlay forms. Courtesy of the Township of Ocean School District.

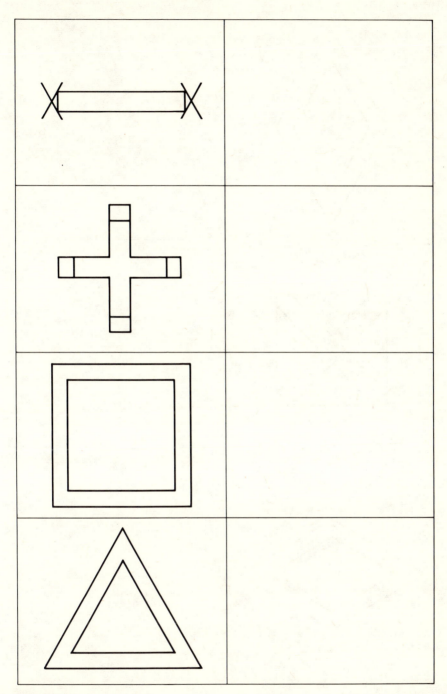

FIGURE A-7   (cont.)

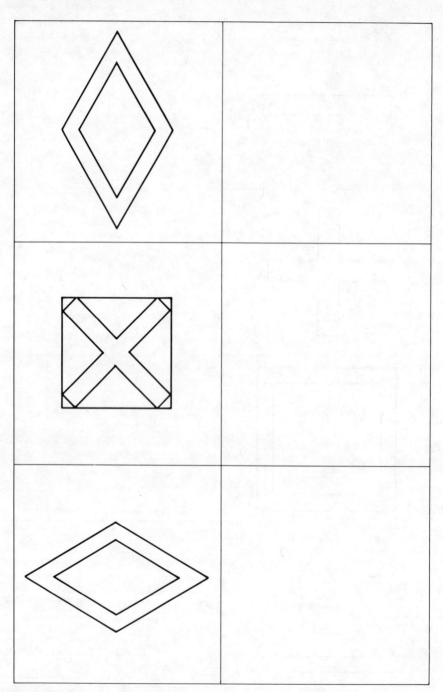

FIGURE A–7 (cont.)

Student Name

Learning experience: Have the student
complete the closure for each geometric
design and color each pair the same color.

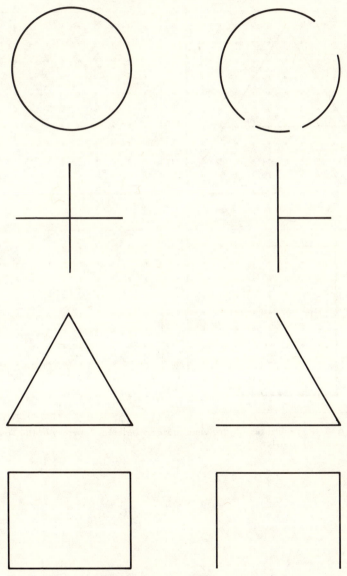

FIGURE A–8 Geometric form completion test. Courtesy of the Township of Ocean School District.

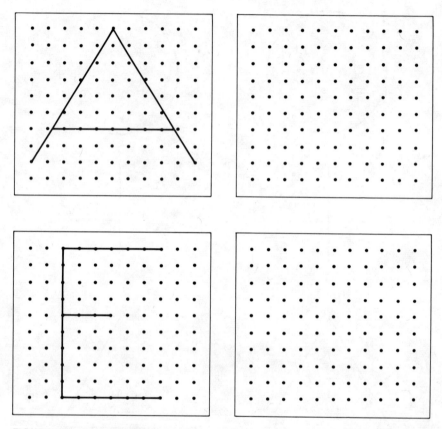

FIGURE A–9   Pegboard testing for visuomotor problems. Courtesy of the Township of Ocean School District.

APPENDIX

summer developmental and adapted physical education program

FIGURE B–1 Parental permission form, Township of Ocean School District, Oakhurst, New Jersey.

June 16, 1969

Dear Parent:

The Township of Ocean School District would like to conduct an individualized adapted physical education program for students in grades 1–8 during the summer months. The program will be designed to alleviate physical and/or socioemotional problems via varied physical activities.

Your child _____ has evidenced the following:
(student's name)

postural deficiency	_____
poor coordination	_____
orthopedic handicap	_____
medical problem	_____

The school physicians recommend this special program for your child. If you have any questions about the advisability of this program, please contact your family physician. The school doctors will welcome a call from your family physician.

If you wish to have your child registered in this program, please sign below and forward to the principal of the school he/she attends. Additional information will be forthcoming. There will not be any charge for this program.

Transportation must be provided by the parents.

HELEN JONES, M.D.   JOHN S. MALTA, D.O.

THOMAS M. VODOLA, ED. D.
Program Coordinator

_____
(Parent's signature)

A. *Preclass preparation*

  1. Compile a list of all referrals; be sure a parental consent slip is signed before a student is scheduled.

  2. Scheduling guidelines:

9:00– 9:55	5– 7 years	Try to adjust groups so that you have
10:00–10:55	8– 9 years	approximately equal numbers in each
11:00–11:55	10–11 years	class.
12:00–12:55	12 and over	

  3. Call parents and notify them as to class schedules for their child. If there is a scheduling conflict, adjust a schedule by no more than one period. Students are to dress comfortably and must wear gym shoes.

  4. Type attendance list for each class (check and record attendance daily).

  5. Prepare an individual folder for each child. On the folder tab list the student's name, instructional period (1, 2, 3, 4), classification, and home phone number.

  6. Prepare necessary forms; each folder should include:
Basic Motor Skill Test Form
Physical Fitness Test Form
Perceptual-Motor Achievement Test Form (for recording raw scores)
Perceptual-Motor Achievement Test
Parental Permission Form
Perceptual-Motor Progress Profile
Individualized Prescription Card
Asthmatic Testing Material, if applicable
Weight Control Material, if applicable
Posture Exercise Material, if applicable
Weight Training Card, if applicable
Other daily assignments (coloring, cut-outs, etc.)

B. *Individualized program*

  1. Facilities (set up each day at 8:30 A.M. and store at 1:00 P.M.)

Use diagram (Fig. B-3) as a guideline; procure necessary materials, supplies, and equipment prior to the start of the program.

Assign student leaders, when possible, to permanent stations for testing; vary their instructional stations every week (to provide them with a varied experience).

  2. Program

Pre-test all students during the first week on fitness, motor skill, and perceptual-motor batteries. Additional testing should be administered to those students who evidence posture, asthmatic, or other problems.

Weeks two through five

Students take prescribed individual program cards to designated areas and perform necessary exercises or activities; upon completion, leaders initial them. Upon completion of all tasks, individual prescription cards are returned to respective folders. (*Note:* On the Friday of the initial week, instructors are to take raw score data home, convert to norm scores, plot individual profiles, and record pertinent anecdotal remarks and then prepare an individualized prescription card for each student.) The balance of each period is devoted to individual or group activities. Incorporate such activities as tinikling, rope jumping, and movement experiences.

Week six

The week is devoted to post-testing; same procedure as week one.

Parental conferences are to be held on the Monday following the last week of the program. Interpret individual profiles and inform the parent of activities that may be practiced at home.

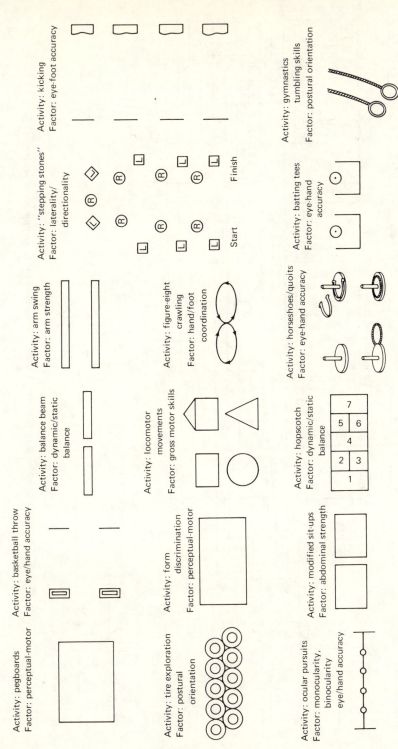

Activity: pegboards
Factor: perceptual-motor

Activity: basketball throw
Factor: eye/hand accuracy

Activity: tire exploration
Factor: postural orientation

Activity: form discrimination
Factor: perceptual-motor

Activity: ocular pursuits
Factor: monocularity, binocularity — eye/hand accuracy

Activity: balance beam
Factor: dynamic/static balance

Activity: arm swing
Factor: arm strength

Activity: locomotor movements
Factor: gross motor skills

Activity: figure-eight crawling
Factor: hand/foot coordination

Activity: modified sit-ups
Factor: abdominal strength

Activity: hopscotch
Factor: dynamic/static balance

Activity: "stepping stones"
Factor: laterality/directionality

Finish

Start

Activity: kicking
Factor: eye-foot accuracy

Activity: horseshoes/quoits
Factor: eye-hand accuracy

Activity: batting tees
Factor: eye-hand accuracy

Activity: gymnastics tumbling skills
Factor: postural orientation

FIGURE B–3 Individualizing physical education on the basis of varied developmental needs.

Department of Health, Safety, and Physical Education
Pre and Post-Test Group Mean Scores

Developmental and Adapted Program

Student's Name _____ Last _____ First _____ Age _____ Summer School _____ Classification _____ School _____

Symbols

--- 1st Test
— 2nd Test

Component Measured

Standard Score: 100 90 80 70 60 50 40 30 20 10 0

Excellent — 90, 80
Good — 70, 60
Fair — 50, 40
Poor — 30, 20
Inferior — 10, 0

Gross Coordination
Hand/Eye Coordination
Hand/Eye Accuracy
Foot/Eye Accuracy
Gross Body Balance
Arm Strength
Laterality/Directionality
Leg Strength
Abdominal Strength
Speed
Endurance
Endurance Index
Average Standard Score

Standard Score: 100 90 80 70 60 50 40 30 20 10 0

65
57

Anecdotal remarks

Post-test results reveal superior gains in motor coordination, balance, and strength development. Testing program indicated a high correlation between poor posture and weak abdominal and arm strength.

NEED

Program structure K–4 should involve a variety of physical activities that are specially planned to improve the above components. Increasing emphasis should be given to large muscle activity.

N.Y. posture screening test _____
Asthmatic (vital capacity) _____
Weight control (lbs.) _____
Orthopedic (see anecdotal remarks) _____

FIGURE B–4 Motor, perceptual-motor, physical fitness progress profile (group mean scores).

constructable items

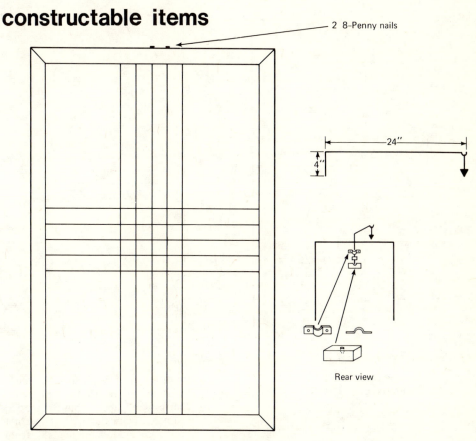

2 8-Penny nails

24"

4"

Rear view

Materials needed

Grid: one $\frac{1}{8}'' \times 4' \times 8'$ masonite
Frame: one $\frac{3}{4}'' \times 3'' \times 24'$
Rod: one $\frac{3}{8}'' \times 30''$
Clamps: two
Wooden block: one $1'' \times 4''$
Plumb bob: one
Paint: 1 quart of flat black enamel
      1 pint of fast-drying white
      lacquer
Striping tool: one
Straight edge: 8' long, 3" wide

Instructions

1. Reduce masonite to proper size.
2. Paint masonite.
3. Place frame on masonite; secure with
   $\frac{3}{4}''$ roofing nails (miter corners).
4. Draw horizontal and vertical lines.
   Start at midpoint and paint lines 2"
   apart with the striping tool. Be sure
   to secure the straight edge to the
   frame with clamps to insure straight
   lines.
5. Touch up any overrun of striping
   with black enamel border.

FIGURE C–1 Posture grid. Courtesy of the Township of Ocean School District Maintenance Department.

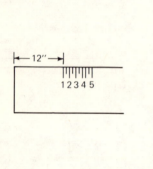

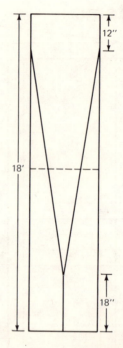

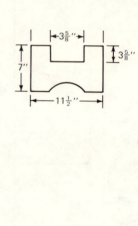

Materials needed

Beams: two 4″ × 4″ × 8′
Supports: one $1\frac{1}{2}$″ × 7″ × 4″ white pine

Instructions

1. Reduce top of beam to a 60° angle by using a body grinder (with extra-coarse sandpaper). Start tapering beam 12″ from the edge of the first beam; conclude tapering 18″ from the far edge of the second beam.
2. Measure and paint numerals on both sides of the beams in inches (from the 12″ mark to the edge of the second beam).
3. Cut out the four supports as illustrated.

FIGURE C–2 Tapered balance beam. Courtesy of the Township of Ocean School District Maintenance Department.

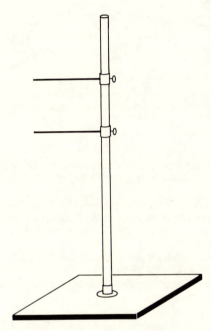

Materials needed

Upright: one $1\frac{3}{8}''$ I.D. × 5′ aluminum tubing

Adjustable sleeves: two $2\frac{1}{8}''$ I.D. × 4″ aluminum tubing

Rods: two $\frac{3}{8}''$ × $14\frac{1}{2}''$ cold rolled steel

Thumb screws: two $\frac{3}{8}''$ × 1″ steel or aluminum

Flange: one $1\frac{1}{4}''$ pipe, cast iron

Base: one $\frac{3}{4}''$ × 24″ × 24″ plyscore

Instructions

1. Attach flange to center of base.

2. Thread aluminum upright into flange.

3. Drill and tap sleeves for $\frac{3}{8}''$ thumb screws and rods. *Note:* On rod-side of sleeves, tap threads for a snug fit but do not completely penetrate the sleeve.

FIGURE C–3 Modified Howland Alignometer. Courtesy of the Township of Ocean School District Maintenance Department.

analysis of prekindergarten test results

The purpose of the prekindergarten screening test is to assess the general motor ability of the children involved so that:

1. Parents can be provided with information regarding developmental activities (games) their children could participate in to enhance their readiness for school.
2. Kindergarten teachers can be given some insight into the possible needs of their in-coming students.
3. Detailed retesting and referrals can be made for alerting the child study team or school physicians to suspected cases.
4. Summer D&A recommendations can be made for those students who evidence developmental lags.

Prekindergarten Screening Test Results—Spring 1971

	Order of frequency	Oakhurst	Wanamassa	Wayside	Total
Test Item #1: *Hopping*					
Balance on one foot	8	14	10	11	35
Shifting weight smoothly	1	31	24	15	70
Gross coordination	4	16	13	17	46
Serial order	2	19	32	17	68
Laterality	3	25	26	11	62
Concept of numbers	9	17	11	1	29
Test Item #2: *Ball bounce and catch*					
Eye/hand coordination	6	16	15	9	40
Color discrimination	15	2	10	2	14

	Order of frequency	Oakhurst	Wanamassa	Wayside	Total
Test Item #3: *Ocular pursuit*					
Tracking horizontally	17	6	2	1	9
Tracking vertically	14	7	5	3	15
Tracking diagonally	10	8	9	7	24
Tracking circle	6	18	13	9	40
Jerky pattern	11	7	11	4	22
Midline problem	13	5	8	4	17
Loses object	5	16	18	7	41
Lazy eye	18	1	—	1	2
Would not take test	12	14	5	2	21
Test Item #4: *Speech*					
Speech	16	11	4	1	12
Number of subjects tested		88	81	33	202

Analysis of the Data

The following composite results are based on the screening by Mrs. Felice Golding, Mrs. Patti Perri, Mrs. Barbara Thompson, Mr. Dennis Bender, and Dr. Vodola:

1. Of the 202 registrants, 181 were tested; 21 were not screened due to shyness, timidity, etc.
2. Of those screened, they manifested 547 possible developmental problems for an average of three errors per child.
3. Four of the five most frequent problems related to the child's general management and awareness of his body with the following percentage of errors:
   a. Shifting weight smoothly, approximately 40 percent
   b. Serial order (paterning: L, R, L), approximately 40 percent
   c. Laterality (awarencess of left, right), 34 percent
   d. Gross body coordination, 25 percent
4. The fifth most frequent problem manifested was the inability to follow a moving object without moving the head; percentage of error, 24 percent.
5. The ocular pursuit testing revealed there were a total of 170 errors in tracking for an average of almost one error per child.
6. Ocular pursuit testing revealed a consistency with developmental theorists findings: children had little difficulty tracking objects in a horizontal (9 errors) or vertical (15 errors) plane, but considerably more difficulty tracking in a diagonal (24 errors) or circular plane (41 errors).

Conclusions

1. The prekindergarten screening test provides a viable means of assessing the motor ability of children in the 4- to 5-year-old age group.
2. The greatest manifested developmental lag was evidenced in the area of general body awareness and management.
3. The preschool child needs a variety of developmental activities that enhance monocular vision, binocular vision, and eye/hand and eye/foot coordination.

Recommendations
1. Prekindergarten screening should be continued in the future with the following modifications:
   a. Modify the hopping test to hop left twice, hop right three times (the test item used was too complex for the subjects).
   b. Increase the number testers (possibly to include P.E. staff and learning disability teachers in the respective schools, in addition to both D&A teachers) for efficient and effective testing.
2. Schedule postscreening conference with all parents, children, kindergarten teachers, and the testing team in the respective schools. Plan activities in the classroom so that parents can be apprised of the types of games they could use to benefit their chldren. Also explain each child's strengths and areas wherein he or she could use developmental work. (Those students who were apprehensive and were not screened could possibly be tested during this time.)
3. Schedule those prekindergarten children who did not attend the "round-up" for testing prior to the summer vacation (testing to be done by the D&A staff).
4. The physical education curriculum for kindergarten should utilize those activities that enhance the development of general body awareness, general body management, ocular pursuits, and eye/hand and eye/foot coordination.
5. Increase the physical education offerings at the kindergarten level.

U.S. Department of Education, Office of Special Education Program, Development and Evaluation Services, Title VI: Education of the Handicapped, P.L. 91-230

Part B: Assistance to States for Education of Handicapped Children

Provides funds for the purpose of assisting the States in the initiation, expansion, and improvement of programs and projects for the education of handicapped children at the preschool, elementary school, and secondary school levels.

Part C: Centers and Services to Meet Special Needs of the Handicapped

Regional Resource Centers   Centers established or operated under this section shall (1) provide testing and educational evaluation to determine the special educational needs of handicapped children referred to such centers, (2) develop educational programs to meet those needs, and (3) assist schools and other appropriate agencies, organizations, and institutions in providing such educational programs through services such as consultation (including, in appropriate cases, consultation with parents or teachers of handicapped children at such regional centers), periodic reexamination and reevaluation of special educational programs, and other technical services.

Centers and Services for Deaf-Blind Children   The purpose of this section to provide, through a limited number of model centers for deaf-blind children, a program designed to develop and bring to bear upon such children, beginning as early as feasible in life, those specialized, intensive professional and allied services, methods, and aids that are found to be most effective to enable them to achieve their full potential for communication with, and adjustment to, the world around them, for useful and meaningful participation in society, and for self-fulfillment.

Early Education for Handicapped Children   Provides for the development and carrying out by agencies and organizations of experimental preschool and early education programs for handicapped children. Such programs shall be distributed to the greatest extent possible throughout the Nation, and shall be carried out both in urban and in rural areas. Such programs shall include activities and services designed to (1) facilitate the intellectual, emotional, physical, mental, social, and language development of such children; (2) encourage the participation of the parents of such children in the development and operation of any such program; and (3) acquaint the community to be served by any such program with the problems and potentialities of such children.

Research, Innovation, Training, and Dissemination Activities in Connection with Centers and Services for the Handicapped   Authorizes BEH to contract for (1) research to identify and meet the full range of special needs of handicapped children; (2) development or demonstration of new, or improvements in existing methods, approaches, or techniques, which would contribute to the adjustment and education of such children; (3) training (either directly or otherwise) of professional and allied personnel engaged or preparing to engage in programs specifically designed for such children, including payment of stipends for trainees and allowances for travel and other expenses for them and their dependents; and (4) dissemination of materials and information about practices found effective in working with such children.

Evaluations   Authorizes BEH to contract with independent organizations for thorough and continuing evaluation of the effectiveness of each program assisted under this law.

Part D: Training Personnel for the Education of the Handicapped

Grants to Institutions of Higher Education and Other Appropriate Institutions or Agencies   Makes grants to institutions of higher education and other appropriate nonprofit institutions or agencies to assist them:
(*1*) In providing training of professional personnel to conduct training of teachers and other specialists in fields related to the education of handicapped children;
(*2*) In providing training for personnel engaged or preparing to engage in employment as teachers of handicapped children, as supervisors of such teachers, or as speech correctionists or other special personnel providing special services for the education of such children, or engaged or preparing to engage in research in fields related to the education of such children; and
(*3*) In establishing and maintaining scholarships, with such stipends and allowances as may be determined by the Commissioner, for training personnel engaged in or preparing to engage in employment as teachers of the handicapped or as related specialists.

Grants to State Educational Agencies   Makes grants to State educational agencies to assist them in establishing and maintaining, directly or through grants to institutions of higher education, programs for training personnel engaged, or preparing to engage, in employment as teachers of handicapped children or as supervisors of such teachers.

Grants or Contracts to Improve Recruiting of Educational Personnel, and to Improve Dissemination of Information Concerning Educational Opportunities for the Handicapped   Makes grants to public or nonprofit private agencies, organizations, or institutions, or to enter into contracts with public or private agencies, organizations, or institutions, for projects for:

(*1*) encouraging students and professional personnel to work in various fields of education of handicapped children and youth through, among other ways, developing and distributing imaginative or innovative materials to assist in recruiting personnel for such careers, or publicizing existing forms of financial aid which might enable students to pursue such careers, or

(*2*) disseminating information about the programs, services, and resources for the education of handicapped children, or providing referral services to parents, teachers, and other persons especially interested in the handicapped.

Training of Physical Educators and Recreation Personnel for Handicapped Children   Makes grants to institutions of higher education to assist them in providing training for personnel engaged or preparing to engage in employment as physical educators or recreation personnel for handicapped children or as educators or supervisors of such personnel, or engaged or preparing to engage in research or teaching in fields related to the physical education or recreation of such children.

Part E: Research in the Education of the Handicapped

Research and Demonstration Projects in Education of Handicapped Children Makes grants to States, State or local educational agencies, institutions of higher education, and other public or nonprofit private educational or research agencies and organizations, and to make contracts with States, State or local educational agencies, institutions of higher education, and other public or private educational or research agencies and organizations, for research and related purposes and to conduct research, surveys, or demonstrations, relating to education of handicapped children.

Research and Demonstration Projects in Physical Education and Recreation for Handicapped Children   Makes grants to States, State or local educational agencies, institutions of higher education, and other public or nonprofit private educational or research agencies and organizations, and to make contracts with States, State or local educational agencies, institutions of higher education, and other public or private educational or research agencies and organizations, for research and related purposes relating to physical education or recreation for handicapped children, and to conduct research, surveys, or demonstrations relating to physical education or recreation for handicapped children.

Part F: Instructional Media for the Handicapped

Captioned Films and Educational Media for Handicapped Persons   Establishes a loan service of captioned films and educational media for the purpose of making such materials available in the United States for nonprofit purposes to handicapped persons, parents of handicapped persons, and other persons directly involved in activities for the advancement of the handicapped.

The law permits BEH to:

(*1*) Acquire films.

(*2*) Acquire by lease or purchased equipment.

(3) Provide for the captioning of films.

(4) Provide for the distribution of captioned films and other educational media and equipment through State schools for the handicapped.

(5) Provide for the conduct of research in the use of educational and training films and other educational media for the handicapped.

(6) Utilize the facilities and services of other governmental agencies; and

(7) Accept gifts, contributions, and voluntary and uncompensated services of individuals and organizations.

National Center on Educational Media and Materials for the Handicapped Allows for a National Center on Educational Media and Materials for the Handicapped, which will provide a comprehensive program of activities to facilitate the use of new educational technology in education programs for handicapped persons, including designing and developing, and adapting instructional materials, and such other activities.

Part G : Special Programs for Children with Specific Learning Disabilities

Research, Training, and Model Centers   Makes grants to, and contracts with, institutions of higher education, State and local educational agencies, and other public and private educational and research agencies and organizations in order to carry out a program of:

(1) Research and related purposes relating to the education of children with specific learning disabilities;

(2) Professional or advanced training for educational personnel who are teaching, or are preparing to be teachers of, children with specific learning disabilities, or such training for persons who are, or are preparing to be, supervisors and teachers of such personnel; and

(3) Establishing and operating model centers for the improvement of education of children with specific learning disabilities, which centers shall (a) provide testing and educational evaluation to identify children with learning disabilities who have been referred to such centers, (b) develop and conduct model programs designed to meet the special educational needs of such children, (c) assist appropriate educational agencies, organizations, and institutions in making such model programs available to other children with learning disabilities, and (d) disseminate new methods or techniques for overcoming learning disabilities to educational institutions, organizations, and agencies within the area served by such center and evaluate the effectiveness of the dissemination process.

index

Howe, E. C., 60
Howland, Ivalclare Sprow, 181
Howland Alignometer, 26, 181–82
Hull scale, 117–19, 127, 150, 151, 153, 154
Hyman, Dorothy, 187
Hyperactivity, 92–93, 99, 206–13
Hypnosis, 208

Identification & classification, 11–13, 31, 101, 129, 236
  for adapted phase, 79–99
  for developmental phase, 37–77
Inactivity prescription, 86 (*see also* Over-protection)
Independent study, 26
Indiana Motor Fitness Test, 259, 260
Individualized instruction, 129–30, 146–223
  adapted phase, 184–223
  defined, 129
  developmental phase, 146–82
  student attitudes toward, 129–30
Inductive teaching, 134–36, 143
Infantile paralysis, 79, 80
Intelligence quotient (I.Q.), 51–52, 212
International standard goniometer, 83
Intramural athletics, 5
Iowa Posture Test, 60–62, 65
Ishmail, A. H., 68–69, 218–19

Jack, Harold K., 12, 25, 49
Jacobson, Edmund, 209–12
Jogging, 170
Johnson, L. William, 45–46
Johnson, Robert E., 169
Joint Committee on Health Problems in Education (N.E.A. & A.M.A.), 8
Journal of Health, Physical Education & Recreation, 202
Juvenile delinquents, 97, 99

Keffer, Louis, 189
Kelley, Earl C., 6–7
Kennedy, John F., 7
Kennedy (Joseph P., Jr.) Foundation, 246
Kephart, Newell C., 12, 39, 68, 69, 96, 213
Kephart Perceptual-Motor Test Battery, 102
Kinesiology, 22
Kiphuth, Oscar W., 60
Kirk, Samuel A., 235
Kruse, R., 7

Lane, Elmer K., 77
Lange Skinfold Calipers, 57–58

Leadership, development of, 142
Learning disabilities, 6, 11, 17, 31, 68–75, 92, 184, 205, 206, 213, 236, 237
Lehtinen, Laura E., 215
Leighton, Jack R., 83–84, 172
Leighton flexometer, 83–84 (*see also* Flexometer)
Leukemia, 238
Liability problems, 4, 22, 31, 173, 185, 189–91, 223
Lifetime Sports Foundation, 167
Local control of schools, 229 (*see also* Community)
Local medical society, 16 (*see also* Physicians, family)
Local newspaper, 223 (*see also* Public relations)
Longnecker, Donald, 12
Lordosis, 174, 181–82
Lower back syndrome, 60
Lowered vitality (*see* Vitality, low)
Lyman, Howard B., 155

McAllister, F. F., 202
McCollum, Robert, 4
MacEwan, C. G., 60
McGee, Rosemary, 48, 57, 103, 111
McGynn, George J., 86
McNeil Laboratories, Inc., 195
Mager, Robert F., 38
Malpass, L. F., 9
Mandated physical education, 4, 26, 30, 32, 235, 239, 240, 265, 266
Mann, L., 12, 49
Mason, Robert D., 202
Massey, Benjamin H., 172
Mathews, Donald K., 7, 82–83, 118
Mean score, 101, 103, 105–8, 114–20, 127
Median score, 114
Medical excuses, 5–8, 18, 21, 22, 26, 27, 29, 30, 185, 203, 204
Medical society, local, 16 (*see also* Physicians, family)
Mentally handicapped children, 15, 17, 79, 92–98, 185, 189, 205–22, 231, 232, 234, 235
Mentally retarded children, 8–10, 40, 97, 202, 207, 218–22, 235, 237
Merit pay, 147, 148
Meso-endomorphy, 126 (*see also* Somatotyping)
Mesomorphy, 124, 126 (*see also* Somatotyping)
Milwaukee Brace, 179
Mini-grants, 253, 254, 257 (*see also* Funds)
Minimal brain damage, 11
Mode, 105, 114
Modeling, 124

Rehabilitative exercises, 190–98 (*see also* Remedial physical education)
Relevancy, 147–48
Remedial physical education, 22–23, 198 (*see also* Rehabilitative exercises)
Resource person, teacher as, 136–37, 143
Ringleheim, Daniel, 239
Roach, Eugene G., 69
Rogers, Frederick Rand, 51
Rogers, Marion, 181
Rogers PFI Test, 38, 51–55, 77, 162, 259, 260 (*see also* Physical fitness index; Physical Fitness Test Battery)
Rote learning, 69
Royal National Institute for the Blind, 188
Running, 29–30
Ryan, Allan J., 56

Scheduling, 16, 18, 26–31, 146, 186, 190, 223
 inflexible, 5
 modular, 147
School doctors (*see* Physicians, school)
School newspaper, 14
School nurse, 5, 6, 14, 16–18, 20, 21, 24, 26, 27, 30–32, 89, 173, 184, 231, 232
School psychologist, 17, 75, 79, 97, 98, 156, 184, 205, 236
Scoliosis, 5, 30, 31, 172–73, 175, 177–80, 237
Scott, M. Gladys, 60–61
Self-evaluation, 142
Severs, Evelyn, 253–56, 258
Shaw, S., 7
Shay, Clayton T., 82–83
Sheldon, W. H., 124–26
Sheldon's somatotypes, 39, 124–25
Shriver, Eunice Kennedy, 8
Siegel, Irwin M., 186
Sigma scale, 117–19, 127
Skinfold calipers, 38, 57–58
Skinfold measurements, 57–58, 167, 182, 259, 261
Slow learners (*see* Learning disabilities)
Smith, G. Milton, 103
Snellen Eye Chart, 57
Social workers, 17, 236
Socioemotional problems, 6, 9–12, 15, 17, 40, 79, 95, 97–99, 185, 189, 205–22, 231, 232, 235, 237
 as source of weight problems, 56, 59
Somatotyping, 13, 38, 39, 49, 123–27, 259, 261
Spastic conditions, 80, 83
Special Education, 99, 239
Special services, 3, 11, 26, 236
Special services team, 6, 14, 16–18, 21, 31

Speech impediments, 17, 80, 81, 186, 189
Spirometer, 38, 87
Square roots, 109, 111
Staley Sports Field Kit, 188
Standard deviation scores, 101, 103, 107–11, 115, 116, 118–20, 127
Standard scores, 101, 116–18, 143, 149–55, 233
 time prescriptions and, 150–55, 182
Stanine scores, 155–56, 182
Statistics, use in student assessment, 101–27
Steele, Nancy L., 198–99
Stein, Julian U., 9, 92, 246
Stein, T. A., 9
Steinhaus, Arthur H., 208
Step interval method, 105–10, 112–15, 119, 127
Stevens, S. S., 125–26
Stigmatization of handicapped children, 5, 12, 32 (*see also* Peer group)
Stone, Thomas E., 97, 98
Strauss, Alfred A., 215
Strauss-Lehtinen Visuo-Motor Perception Test, 215
Strength Decrement Index (SDI), 82–83, 99
Structure & Measurement of Physical Fitness, The (Fleishman), 47–48
Student-oriented philosophy, 13, 31, 80, 131–34, 138, 143, 147
Study halls, 24, 26–28
Subject-centered philosophy (content-centered philosophy), 13, 31, 132, 133, 147
Subjective evaluation, 102, 156
Success, as student's motivation, 6, 95, 125, 126, 198
Symmetrigraf, 63

T-scale, 117–19, 127, 139, 153
Taba Curriculum Development Project, 134–36
Taxonomy of Educational Objectives (Bloom), 141
Teacher-centered philosophy, 132, 133, 142–43, 147
Teacher Innovation Program (N.J.), 254
Teacher-pupil interaction, 129–43
 pupil's role in, 140–43
 teacher's role in, 130–40, 143
Teachers:
 as resource persons, 136–37, 143
 training of, 5, 11, 12, 208, 230, 249, 265–66
Teaching Physical Education: From Command to Discovery (Mosston), 96
Teaching Strategies for Developing Children's Thinking (Earl), 136

Temple University, 40, 52, 167
  Biokinetic Research Laboratory, 255
Tensiometer, 52, 261
Terman I.Q. Formula, 51–52
"Transfer of learning," 220
Trevena, Thomas M., 187
Tuberculosis, 80, 238
Tucker, W. B., 125–26
Turner, Edward T., 130

Ungraded schools, 147
United States Health Survey, 86
Universal Goniometer, 84–85
University of San Francisco, 86
Ury, Claude M., 80

Varieties of Human Physique (Sheldon, Stevens & Tucker), 125–26
Vergason, Glenn R., 136, 146
Visual Achievement Forms, 69
Visually-impaired students, 9, 80, 81, 156, 186–89, 237 (*see also* Blind students)
Visuo-motor exercises, 95
Visuo-Motor Perception Test, 215
Vitality, low, 5–6, 13, 20, 39, 47, 60, 92, 120, 182, 186, 206, 238, 247
  testing for, 157–66
Vocational Education Amendments (1968), 242, 252
Vodola, Thomas M., 4, 8, 11, 20, 38, 69,

Vodola, Thomas M. (*cont.*)
  80, 91, 92, 129–30, 147, 150, 152, 157, 203, 213, 219, 232, 237, 250, 259
Voucher plan, 147, 149

Wallen, Norman E., 134, 135
Watkins, Arthur L., 82
Wear, C. L., 129–30
Wear Attitude Inventory, 129–30, 153
Weight control programs, 14, 29, 30, 39, 56, 58–59, 126, 153, 170–71, 182 (*see also* Nutritional problems)
Weight problems (*see* Nutritional problems)
Wells, Katherine F., 182
Welsh, James, 149
Wetzel Grid, 57
White, Paul Dudley, 203
White House Conference on Children (1970), 240, 246
Wickens, Stuart, 60
Widness, Joanne, 52, 53
Wilgoose, Carl E., 126
Williams, F. Neil, 187
Winnetka Scale for Rating Student Behavior & Activities, 261
Wyden, Peter, 56

Yolles, Stanley F., 254
You Must Relax (Jacobson), 209